COI

STORIES AND RECIPES

DANIEL PATTERSON

COI

STORIES AND RECIPES

DANIEL PATTERSON

Photographs by Maren Caruso

Φ

FOREWORD
by Harold McGee

I'm lucky enough to live in San Francisco, a good city for eating, and Daniel Patterson's restaurant Coi is a favorite of mine. It's on an unlikely stretch of Broadway as it slopes down to the bay, with office buildings and parking lots below, the glare and racket of adult clubs just uphill. Coi is a quieter den of pleasure. The name is an old French word that rhymes with *moi* and means tranquil. It suits the place, the comfortable earth-toned rooms, the subdued atmospheric music, the polished but unobtrusive service, the simple handmade tableware.

And the place suits Daniel's food, which I first enjoyed a couple of years before Coi's opening in 2006. It's not obviously luxurious, or elaborate, or experimental. It focuses tightly on primary ingredients from our region, and it highlights their qualities with exacting technique and seasoning, and with thought-provoking swerves from the expected. Daniel is constantly looking beyond what he already knows to find fresh facets of deliciousness and meaning. So his dishes reward attentive savoring. They also simply reward! It was at Coi that my teenage daughter, warily taking on her first tasting menu, discovered to her happy surprise and my happy chagrin that she could actually love salmon.

Daniel is one of the most articulate cooks I know, and a gifted writer. He's often stirred up the food world through the printed word: championing the use of essential oils in cooking, decrying the use of synthetic truffle oil in the best restaurants, pointing out San Francisco's culinary conservatism, sharing the ease and advantages of making butter in-house, or the unlikely excellence of poached scrambled eggs. Daniel is the only writer with whom I've shared a byline, for an article about terroir, and it was his experience and directness that gave the piece life.

So it's wonderful to have this book from Coi, for all the usual pleasures of a chef's book, but above all, for Daniel's accounts of the experience behind each dish, the mix of insight and inspiration, of missteps and rethinking and refining. Daniel isn't at all reluctant to analyze his own efforts, to acknowledge failure and celebrate accomplishment. The result is this handsome record of a fine restaurant's dishes, and the absorbing self-portrait of an exceptional cook.

FOREWORD
by Peter Meehan

Sometimes, when I'm talking to a person not given to spending grand-ish sums on dinner, or to somebody who might be more conversant in obscure vinyl releases on Ecstatic Peace than the topics I write about in *Lucky Peach*, it can be hard to explain why a particular restaurant *matters*. Why I feel a connection to it, or feel that its food is "cool" in the way that other methods of expression are, and so much more naturally.

Coi is one of these places, these cases. Not so much in that it is capital-I important as it is a trip that's worth taking, and one you wanna take again as soon as it's gone, like Highway 1 running through the redwoods. Of course it's expensive and refined and pretty and professional and I imagine the bilious billionaires who keep the world of fine dining spinning on their golden fingers feel perfectly catered to when they're there. But it's not for them, and it's not exactly for me, eating there in my hoodie and Vans, either.

It's Daniel's place, and, on some level, it's there for him. It's one of a handful (maybe a couple handfuls, let's be generous!) of restaurants around that's a truly personal space. It is where Patterson does his thing. Where he distills the landscape that surrounds him and the choppy wake of the stories of his life into Things That Can Be Eaten. The filmstrip images of Jackson Pollock spilling and splattering paint or Pablo Picasso drawing with light come to mind—not to draw an underbaked comparison between Chef and Artist, but because the magic of those blips of sound and vision are the feeling that we are witnessing something being made, of creativity in action, kinetic and alive. A vital transference of ideas and energy into something we can, on some level, digest. The best meals at Coi capture some of that energy.

This is no small feat. It's easy enough to impersonate what's come before in the kitchen and easier still, in this Instagrammed era, to impersonate what else is going on right now. Daniel's cooking has always run contrary to those impulses: he cooks what he knows, what he feels, what his imagination commands him to. When that kind of cooking works, that's the thing. That's the experience. In the realm of star-spangled dining, I'd trade you a million penguins and their bottles of Dom Pérignon for one plate of honest food. (And I'd parenthetically assert that it's much harder to create that honest feeling while up on the high-wire of high-end cooking than it is down here, lower to the ground, where we all usually eat.)

All of that is a long ramble to say this: I couldn't be more excited to have this book to spend time with. It offers everybody who hasn't had the chance to meet Daniel—with his hidden poetic tendencies and inky black humor and ability to actually string sentences together into stories that take us places—to see what goes on back there in his head, and how that tangled mess of Boston back story and pink-orange melting California sunsets gets smelted into some of the best fancy food in the U.S.A. To Daniel: Kudos on putting this beauty together.

Everybody else: remove the cloche, inhale deeply, and dig in.

01

CALI-
FORNIA

I began working in kitchens in Massachusetts when I was fourteen, sweeping floors and washing dishes. Eventually I graduated to prep cook and then line cook. After high school I attended college for a year, but found that I felt far more comfortable in the kitchen than I did in the classroom. I dropped out and moved to San Francisco, for no particular reason. It was 1989.

I arrived in the early fall to find rolling, dust-brown hills scattered among towns and highways, and later watched the winter rains turn them glowing, verdant green. I saw the endless dreary suburban sprawl of the cities east of San Francisco, the worn, ghost-ridden haunts of North Beach and the cold, unsettled sea that roiled under a sky that was vast and wide. I never expected to stay, but I found it hard to leave this place, with its strange, mysterious beauty.

A month after I arrived I found a job in downtown San Francisco as a cook in a mid-priced bistro. There I met my first wife, Elisabeth. She was also from the East Coast, and we shared a similar attitude about the natives. We enjoyed the California sunshine, but not so much the culture. "The weather's great," we would tell inquiring friends from back home, leaving the rest of the story implied. I struggled to acclimate to the languorous way people talked and moved here, the relaxed approach to life.

In 1991 we moved to Sonoma and worked in a few places in the wine country. Three years later we opened a tiny restaurant called Babette's, which we started with credit cards and little else. Sonoma wasn't much of a food town then, but it was an agrarian paradise, far from the pressures of the city. The social isolation, proximity to farms and the freedom to experiment as chef of my own kitchen allowed me to begin to develop my cooking voice. I learned about the life cycle of plants and their seasons. I discovered wild ingredients. I visited dairies, farms and ranches, and formed friendships that I have to this day.

After five years we lost our lease and moved to San Francisco, where we opened Elisabeth Daniel in 2000. It didn't last long. The aggregated stress of living and working together had taken its toll, and we dissolved our marriage, and the business, a few years later. I tried to be an employee at a new restaurant, but that didn't work out so well either. By the summer of 2005, I was adrift.

After sixteen years in the area, California still seemed strange to me. I had few friends and little connection to the community. The time I'd spent here had softened some of my sharp East Coast edges, but not enough to feel like I really belonged. That changed when I started dating Alexandra. We'd met through mutual friends when I opened Babette's, and she even worked there while on a break from graduate school. When both of our marriages ended we reconnected, fell in love, and we've been together ever since.

She introduced me to a California that I never knew. Her family has lived here for five generations on her mother's side. She grew up in rural Northern California, Chico and environs. On our way to meet her family for the first time we drove by barns and grain silos and cows, through a part of the state where orchards still outnumber people. In Greenville, where her mother lived the last years of her life,

I found mile after mile of untouched forest, with rivers slicing through valleys and mountains etching the sky.

Alexandra's mother was an archaeologist. She specialized in Native American culture, and one of her jobs was to examine new building sites for signs of burial grounds or historically significant areas. She knew everything about the Maidu tribe of the Sierra Nevada mountains and foothills, including what they ate and how they lived. Alexandra knew much of that as well. When we visited we'd take long walks, and they would point out plants that were part of the traditional diet, things like acorns and wild grasses and herbs that I'd never considered edible.

We saw her sporadically for the first few years Alexandra and I were together until 2005, when a cancer that her mother had already beaten back once returned. That year we traveled to see her as often as we could. It was late spring when Alexandra called to tell me that her mother was very sick, and that I should drive up the next day. By the time I reached her mother's house it was early afternoon. She had passed away at dawn.

Nothing I had experienced before prepared me for what it felt like when I arrived. The force of Alexandra's grief took my breath away. I held her while she cried, but I had no idea what to say to comfort her. So I did the only thing I know how to do. I cooked.

There is only one grocery store in Greenville. I found some pork shoulder, carrots, onions, fennel and wine. That night I made a passable stew, a salad of hearts of romaine, bread, not much in the way of dessert. We toasted and ate and drank until everyone finally staggered off to bed, exhausted.

We stayed for four days. There was a ceremony to plan, people to notify. Through it all I cooked constantly, for everyone in the house and those who stopped by, all day and into the night. I felt Alexandra's mother's presence as I rifled through her pots and pans, searched her pantry for salt and spices and the olive oil we'd given her the year before. As family and friends gathered around the little kitchen I remembered, after so many years of producing fancy restaurant food, what it meant to cook for someone. It was then that I began to think about the restaurant that would become Coi.

Later that fall we returned to scatter her mother's ashes. The site that her mother had chosen was a stone outcropping on a ridge high above a valley, with spiral petroglyphs depicting the universe. A stream flowed through a channel cut into the rock, and next to the stream was a round mortar-like depression, worn smooth from thousands of years of pounding acorns into mash. Far below a covey of quail scattered across the scrub, and I suddenly felt in that place the presence of those who'd lived there. If there is personal memory and shared cultural memory, why not a memory of a place, the shared experience of those who have hunted, lived, and gathered there sunk down into the physical contours of the rock, into the land and trees and plants and running water? Perhaps, I thought as I looked out across the valley, in my cooking I could summon something of the place where I live through what time has left behind.

I started to look more deeply at California's history, at its landscape and its culture. There was so much that I wanted to know. I wanted to embrace the people who grew up here, incorporating their ingredients as well as their culture. The menu that I planned for Coi evolved into a cuisine based on carrots and pork, but also Douglas fir and wild sage, on wheatgrass, avocado and sprouts, reflecting the natural setting but also the tastes of the current inhabitants.

I modeled Coi after Babette's, but scaled even smaller—I had no great confidence in the number of people who would be interested in our food on any given night. I wanted the warmth and emotion of home cooking, combined with the sophistication and intellectual qualities of modern restaurant food. Inspired by Alexandra's vaguely hippie Nor-Cal aesthetic, we designed an intimate, organic-looking space. We served the food on handmade pottery. We offered only a tasting menu of ambitious, highly personal food, at a time when fine dining was in retreat. We did not fit neatly into any traditional haute cuisine categories. Yet, somehow, we thrived. The food and the restaurant have improved over time, and we've never lost our focus on the joy of cooking for others. Now, all these years later, this strange, mysterious place called California has become my home.

This is not a cookbook. This is the story of Coi, written through the food. It's a little bit my story as well.

I hope that you like it.

Daniel

2006

02

THE COI

KITCHEN

This may not be a cookbook in the traditional sense, but it is very much a book about cooking.

Every image of a dish is accompanied by a short essay. Sometimes it's about how the dish was created, but more often it uses the ideas behind the food as a jumping off point to talk about themes like belonging, identity and culture; connection to nature; inspiration; creativity; emotion and memory. The accompanying images of places, people and ingredients tell the story in their own way.

And then there are the recipes, which follow the essays. As I sat down to write them, I realized how poorly our dishes have been documented at the restaurant. I think of recipes as more of an oral history than a factual accounting of a process, so ours tend to have gaping holes. In truth, recipes in our kitchen are usually comprised of only a few ratios. I don't use them myself and, although I have many cookbooks at home, I rarely read the recipes. I look at the pictures and read the text. As reading material, recipes bore me.

I also realized that we don't use highly detailed recipes because I want my cooks to understand what they're doing, not just blindly follow instructions. Our food demands thinking cooks, not robots. Reflexive adherence to a recipe can sometimes distract a cook from analyzing the food that's actually in front of them and using their intuition to make the best choices possible. A recipe cannot capture the moments of magic that make food transformative.

The recipes that I wrote for this book—and which my cooks checked for accuracy—are my best attempt to give you the information you'll need to recreate the dishes, if you so choose. They're not exhaustive. I wanted them to be fun to read, so I delved deeply into some aspects of the processes and not others. I wandered off on tangents as they presented themselves. I tried to find moments of interest and say why I think they matter. There's no way that I could explain everything about every dish, but I hope that I was able to capture at least some of the reasons why I cook the way that I do.

This is food that we have served in our restaurant, but you don't need to be a professional cook to follow along. The Internet will have answers to any questions you might have about terms or ingredients. Sometimes I identify specific sources for ingredients, but that is more for the purpose of furthering the story than it is to suggest a place to purchase them. Almost everything in the recipes can be ordered online.

This was not designed to be an everyday cookbook. Most recipes, in their entirety, would be too labor-intensive or troublesome to make outside of a professional kitchen, the required equipment and ingredients too hard to find or too expensive. Even I don't cook like this on my days off! But there are many sub-recipes and techniques that could fit well in a home kitchen.

At Coi, we like to dismantle and reassemble techniques, trying to find the best way to express what we think is important about our ingredients, and to say something about how we feel about the world. Along the way, we occasionally—and accidentally—stumble onto something interesting or different. I try to make explicit how we turn ideas into realized dishes. You may or may not ever cook anything in this book, but my hope is that, even if you only read it, you might learn something.

DELICIOUSNESS

Deliciousness is the beginning, the middle, and the end of every conversation we have in our kitchen. Everything we do, from sourcing to handling to presenting ingredients, is for the purpose of making delicious food. Given the level of the restaurant I also feel an obligation to make the food interesting, thought-provoking and memorable. But never at the expense of deliciousness.

Deliciousness is subjective. I once visited a little village on the Peruvian Amazon with chef Pedro Schiaffino, who explained how the indigenous tribes lightly salt their fish after they catch them and let them hang outside for a few days until they are half-dried, half-fermented. "Disgusting," he told me. But it obviously means something else to the people who live there. Deliciousness is closely linked to culture, memory and experience, and everyone perceives it differently.

This is a book about what we think is delicious, and what we do to achieve it. My ideas about deliciousness involve food that follows these principles: fresh and light; concentrated, balanced flavors; plants more than animals; and, in a metaphysical sense, food with energy and life.

HERE, NOW

We work with what we have, when we have it. Every dish is tuned to exact ingredients—*these* carrots, *these* beets, *this* duck. We try and find perfect moments, when the ingredients are at peak flavor. Even though many of these recipes could be made throughout the year, in our kitchen they each belong to a specific moment in time.

That rigor, that sensitivity to subtle variations from day to day, means that we pay attention to when the season begins to drift, when a new field is being harvested, when there is more or less heat or water. This is what drives our menu. Beyond that, we think about the feeling of the season, our mood, and how we can capture those things on the plate. Even if I could get amazing tomatoes in January, I wouldn't use them. It wouldn't feel right. In mid-winter I don't crave the bright sunshine of summer, distilled through the most iconic of savory fruits.

Each season brings new discoveries, either a fresh look at familiar ingredients or new ingredients that we've never used before. But you will find some repetition in the recipes. Wild fennel, lemon, potatoes, carrots, beets. These are our flavors, this is what we use. I would rather explore deeply than broadly.

We cook a lot with plants, especially vegetables. The range of flavor in plants far exceeds that offered by animals. They are also among the best products we have. California vegetables are densely sweet and concentrated, and they require salt and acidity for balance. The flavors of wild plants, on the other hand, are varied, evocative, often bitter or sour, and we often use them for contrast and depth.

We select everything ourselves, at farmers' markets, farms and in the wild. We are constantly exploring new areas and ingredients, constantly trying new things. We check everything before we buy it, even when it's from the same farm we bought from two days before, to be used for the same dish. We don't trust anything unless we taste it.

If you live outside the Bay Area, you will have many of these ingredients, but they won't have the same flavors. Use what you can get. Modify the recipe to fit your mood and the season. Make a dish with pine shoots instead of redwood shoots, if that's what you have. If you can't find kohlrabi, cook celery root instead. How you're inspired by the underlying idea of a dish is more important than copying by rote.

SEASONING

I may not be the best-trained cook from a technical standpoint, but I'm really good at seasoning food. I know this doesn't sound like much, but it is the foundation of all of my cooking.

When I say "seasoning," I don't just mean adding salt. Seasoning also means managing acidity, which not only plays against oil and fat but against sweetness and rich, concentrated flavors. Seasoning means using bitterness to create balance. In our case, the way we season imbues the elegant language of haute cuisine with a guttural, peasant inflection. Ours is a kind of cooking that seldom relies on fats, as in traditional butter and cream sauces, to fix flavors. It's an ephemeral cuisine that is held in place by the seasoning, a kind of internal harmony that animates dishes, making them glow from within. The kind of seasoning that makes them better than they have any right to be.

What I've learned is this: Salt pulls up acidity, pushes down sweet and bitter. Acidity pushes down salt, sweet and bitter. Bitter balances sweet. And sweet softens salt and acid, mutes bitter. That's most of what I know about cooking.

When you're in the kitchen tasting, think about the aftertaste. If it seems to fade, to just drop away on the finish, that usually means that there's not enough salt. If the acid is low, that also points to lack of salt. The salt will both pull up the acid and give the flavor length. If the salt is a tiny bit high, a few drops of lemon juice can bring it down. If the acidity is high, it could need a little more sweetness. A few grains of salt here or a drop of vinegar there, those are the kinds of little adjustments that make good food great.

In a simple dish like the Carrots Roasted in Coffee Beans (see page 70), the carrots should be sweet and earthy. The sauce should be sweet and sour. They need to have a similar level of sweetness as common ground. Think about it like a bunch of people in a room. If they have nothing in common and no way to relate to each other they'd mostly stand around awkwardly and stare at the walls. Ingredients also need to have something in common in order to get along on the plate. One way that we use seasoning is to create and solidify those relationships.

Throughout the book I talk a lot about balance. Balance describes the relationship between ingredients and seasoning. There are generally two ways I think about it. One is a balanced dish, which may have many individually balanced components, like the Beets (see page 238). Balance can also be found through two or more elements that individually are out of balance (too acidic, too rich), but together create a dish that is in balance, like Fried Egg (Not Fried), (see page 180).

The balance of the seasoning in a sauce or vinaigrette is important, but so is the ratio of sauce to ingredient. Not enough dressing and the ingredient will be bland. Too much and the ingredient will lose its identity. Above all else, a cook's job is to respect the identity of the products.

There is one thing I don't mention in the recipes, something so primary and essential that I assume it: Taste everything, constantly. Taste ingredients, taste components and especially taste everything together to understand how they affect each other. If you don't know how the components of a dish interact then you don't know enough to plate the dish. Tasting is how you build up your database of sensory memories.

The way I season food is idiosyncratic and hard to replicate, even in my own kitchen. It evolved unthinkingly, instinctually, over many years. The dishes in this book are built around that way of seasoning food, which in turn evolved out of my palate, my ingredients and my place. The dishes are not very technically complex. I would say that a good home cook could make almost any recipe in this book. But the precise recreation of the seasoning is much harder to achieve. In the end, cooking is a craft passed from person to person, and no amount of written words can explain exactly how food should taste. You should practice and make your own opinions about what's right for you.

TEXTURE

After seasoning, texture is the most important element of our cooking. Texture is the delivery mechanism for flavor. A thin broth disappears quickly, while a viscous gel lingers on the tongue. Mastery of texture is about controlling how flavors are revealed. (There are, of course, dishes of texture without flavor. Those foods are not interesting to me.)

Texture helps define the identity of a component and solidifies its role in relation to the rest of the dish. Consider a potato purée. For a steamed piece of sole you might want a thin, almost sauce-like purée, barely thicker than a butter sauce, to complement the delicacy of the main ingredient. For the dandelion-potato purée (see page 224), the texture should be a bit thicker, but still loose enough to melt into the broth. The potato-pine needle purée (see page 102), on the other hand, needs to be an equal partner to the grilled matsutake, so we make it thick and aerated, both lingering and evanescent.

I love all textures: soft, firm, crunchy, gooey, brittle, and everything in between. The snap of a twig, the soft mush of a jellyfish, the froth of sea, the scratch of curling bark and the scrape of a pebbly beach: Like flavor, texture starts in nature and is endlessly evocative. Texture has plenty to say.

PROCESS

We make everything every day. We do not hold any preparation from one day to the next, unless it improves, like cured, preserved or fermented foods. When there is a very time-sensitive preparation, like juicing sorrel (which turns brown quickly), we do it just before serving. We cut herbs only when we need them. One of the reasons that we have so many people in the kitchen is not because the processes are complicated, but because they're precise. It is possible to cook high-level food by preparing the components ahead of time and then assembling them to order, but that's not what we do. I feel like that practice enervates the flavors, making them less savory and delicious. We do a lot of cooking during dinner service. It's harder to execute the dishes with perfect consistency, but the effort shows in the immediacy of flavor.

Many of the essays in the book talk about the process of evolving dishes. What it boils down to is this: We work really hard and we try lots of things. Many of them don't work. Even though I've been cooking for a while, at Coi it took years to evolve our style. When we opened I cooked much more spontaneously, which led to some successes, myriad disasters, a lot of frustration and a rule: nothing goes on the menu until we've tried it and, as much as possible, perfected it. Just because two components are amazing, doesn't mean that combining them will work. I have learned this lesson over and over, usually right before service begins, at which point I spend the rest of the night miserable because I know we are producing less than our best. We take chances. We expect failures. We just try not to serve those failures to anyone but ourselves.

You, on the other hand, are presumably not charging for your efforts. Critics are not going to show up at your house to judge you. You can—and should—take chances as often as possible. Try new things. Make terrible mistakes, technical errors so bad that your spouse reminds you about it for years. That's how you learn and grow. Since you're not going to be able to make the dishes taste the way they do in the restaurant, make them taste right for you. If you think it needs more salt, less acid, more fat, go ahead and add it. Do you want it more or less cooked? No problem. Have a sense of humor and an adventurous spirit: Cooking should be fun.

EQUIPMENT

Circulator

A circulator is a machine that heats water very precisely at low temperatures. It is essential for consistency with low-temperature cooking.

Combi Oven

The combination oven can steam and bake at the same time, and both variables—heat and moisture—are controllable. We use it for many things, including drying, low-temperature cooking and baking tuiles—it's very accurate. Dehydrators and circulators can do most of the things that a combi can do.

Cryovac

A Cryovac machine creates a vacuum in a sealed chamber. We use it to seal ingredients in a bag, like the onions in Spot Prawn (see page 62). We also use it to draw flavored liquid into a solid object, like the watermelon in Melon and Cucumber (see page 142). That process is called compression. There are home versions of these machines, but they cannot compress and infuse the same way. We use a commercial machine.

High-Speed Blender

This is a blender that turns faster than a typical home blender, and it purées more effectively, especially when blending gels. When a recipe says, "blend," it refers to a high-speed blender unless otherwise specified.

Pacojet

You will probably not have a Pacojet at home, although a home version has been rumored for years. It works by lowering a strong blade spinning incredibly fast into a beaker full of frozen material. Basically you pour your ingredient into the beaker, freeze it, and spin it down. It creates incredibly creamy ice creams and sorbets, and has a range of other uses, like infused oils and savory purées. The best temperature to freeze the beakers at is -4°F (-20°C).

Plancha

A plancha is similar to what they call a flat-top or griddle in the United States. Planchas are made out of thick pieces of metal, and they can get very, very hot. For a preparation like abalone cooked on the plancha in Monterey Bay Abalone (see page 72), it allows the fish to brown quickly without overcooking.

Scale

It's the twenty-first century. You should use a digital scale when you need to measure a weight.

Scissors

We use scissors for many tasks. I think that they are one of the most underrated pieces of kitchen equipment. They are especially good for cutting herbs. If you had a magic wand, you could shrink herbs into tiny versions of themselves, without cutting them at all. Herbs are plant leaves, and like the rest of the plant they hold a matrix of cells, which in turn hold water and chlorophyll and essential oils and all the other stuff that make the plant taste like what it is. Every time you cut a leaf it damages those cell walls, which leak a little bit of life. If you pile up a bunch of herbs on a cutting board and chop away, your board will turn green, and you'll lose a lot of flavor to the board. Since you're not going to eat your cutting board, this seems to me like a waste. Using scissors to snip bits of herbs as you need them will keep the herbs as fresh as possible and damage them very little.

Silpat

These are silicone based non-stick pan liners, which are more effective than parchment paper for many applications.

Siphon

A siphon is also known as a whipped cream dispenser. We don't put cream in it very often, though. We use it mostly to aerate all kinds of mousses, purées and meringues. You can carbonate by charging them with CO_2 (carbon dioxide), but the recipes in this book all call for NO_2, (nitrous oxide). The same stuff we called whip-its as kids. Or some people did. Add the chargers one at a time, shaking after each addition. The gas is a preservative, so siphons should be charged when filled, and they can sit for hours without any ill effects.

Strainers

In this book we use two kinds of strainers. Chinois are fine mesh sieves. Strainers are coarse mesh sieves.

Thermomix

This is a blender that has the ability to heat and purée at the same time. It is invaluable for certain techniques, like the Chilled English Pea Soup (see page 94) and the potato-pine needle purée (see page 102). They are very expensive, but great for home cooking as well as restaurant cooking—in fact, they are common in home kitchens in Europe.

Vegetable Juicer

The recipes call for two kinds of juice, citrus and vegetable/herb. Citrus juices can be squeezed by hand, but for vegetable juice you will need a vegetable juicer.

INGREDIENTS

Abalone

Not too long after Manresa opened in Los Gatos, California, I had a pretty fantastic meal there. So many of the dishes were memorable, but one in particular spoke to me. It was a dish of abalone and pig's feet, with plenty of butter and lemon. It was my first introduction to abalone.

Abalone are slow-growing mollusks (technically, marine snails—the ones we use are two to three years old), and prodigious kelp grazers. In the wild, they can live a hundred years or more. Wild Californian abalone are endangered, and they've been banned from commercial use for many years.

After I opened Coi, I called Manresa's chef, David Kinch, to get the source for the abalone he used and to find out how to prepare them. He introduced me to Trevor Fay and Art Seavey at Monterey Abalone Company, whose abalone, raised under an old pier in Monterey, are what I consider a great modern luxury ingredient: Meticulously cared for, fabulously expensive, environmentally sound and delicious. The relationship that I started with Trevor and Art has continued for seven years, and we have had abalone on the menu almost the entire time.

Abalone is one of the most difficult marine products to handle well, easy to undercook or overcook, with a tendency towards toughness. I have used Japanese and Australian abalone while cooking abroad, both of which I found far easier to work with and more tender. But we have a few ways of handling Californian abalone that are consistently successful.

If you order abalone, they will come live. To clean them, use a spoon to separate the meat from the shell, scraping along the shell at the bottom to loosen the foot. There is a sack of guts and whatnot attached. Discard it (at least for these recipes). Trim the hard bit on the end, then pack them in between moist towels in a refrigerator for three to four days, until the muscle has relaxed. Before cooking, trim the frilly edges, which are tough, and pound the abalone gently on both sides, until tender and the foot no longer juts out of the body. In these recipes we either sauté them whole, or thinly slice and sear them quickly on a plancha. In either case they cook very quickly. If you're thinking of trying abalone for the first time and aren't sure what direction to go in, I can only tell you that far more people find the texture of the whole abalone preparation challenging. The thinly sliced version is a crowd pleaser.

Essential oils

Essential oils are a very traditional product that have been used in cooking since before Roman times. They are the most concentrated expression of a plant's aromatics. They are made by cold-press, steam-distillation or solvent methods. Used properly they add intensity, a complexity that can't be achieved any other way. They appear here and there throughout the book, not as the backbone of a dish, but as a supporting element to an ingredient—lime essential oil to boost the aromatics of lime juice, for example.

Essential oils are very strong, and must be handled carefully. We store ours in small glass jars with dropper tops. Dispense them a drop at a time, tasting after each addition, to understand their strength. Try not to spill them—they're hard to clean up, and they'll hang around your kitchen for a while. Don't drink them, as they're very strong. All the oils that we use are OK to eat . . . but, like most things, only in moderation.

And please, don't use synthetic oils. They don't taste or smell good. Because they're fake.

Fresh Seaweeds

When we first started working with fresh seaweeds we cooked and cut them, and then added salt, just like we would with any plant. But something quite different happened—they got slimier and slimier and slimier, until they vaguely resembled monster ooze from a cheap '50s horror movie.

Many of the seaweeds that we work with are called carrageenophytes. In other words, they contain carrageenan, often used in cooking as a thickening agent. In some recipes, like the seaweed sauce (see page 228), we use the natural thickening quality of the seaweed to give texture to the sauce. But that quality doesn't always make for good eating.

Salt draws out the thickening agents in the seaweed, so we learned to salt just before serving. But the seaweeds still seemed pretty slimy. Then one day in 2007 a cook remembered that his father's boat would be rinsed with fresh water during the off-season, which would neutralize the sliminess of the seaweed and allow the hull to be cleaned. So after we cooked and cut the seaweed, we soaked it in fresh water, changing it a few times, and then rinsing it at the end. You'll know by feel and taste when the seaweeds are clean.

To understand when to cook fresh seaweeds and for how long, taste them raw. If they're tough, then cook them until they're tender but not mushy. If the seaweeds are tender and delicious, serve them raw. The plants will vary quite a bit throughout the year. Cut the seaweed into whatever shape seems right to you, based on texture and flavor.

Oils

For vegetable oil, we use soy oil. It's a flavorless oil that we use for cooking, frying and some sauces.

We use pure olive oil, from the second pressing of the olives, for cooking and infused oils, and to create texture in soups, sauces and purées. Use a neutral, clean-tasting oil. I've used the same pure oil for nineteen years, Mission Trail from Nick Sciabica & Sons in Modesto, one of the oldest producers in California.

For finishing dishes, sauces and dressings, we use extra virgin olive oil (don't bother cooking with these oils, heat ruins them). We use about five different kinds, all from California. They change from year to year, depending on many factors, so we try them each year, and use what we think is the right flavor profile for each dish. Sometimes we want a medium flavor profile, like Sciabica's Sevillano Fall Harvest, which has notes of banana and fresh pepper. Sometimes we look for a more delicate and nuanced oil, like Sylverleaf Estate. Other times a dish calls for a more powerful flavor, like the freshly cut grass and artichoke aromas of the oils from McEvoy Ranch.

Regardless, the oils that we use are all harvested in the fall, which gives them the fruity flavor profile called for in many of the recipes. I like Italian-style oils, harvested early, with a fresh, green taste.

Salt and Seawater

We use only sea salt. A lot of people will tell you that it doesn't matter. I think it does. For normal seasoning we use fine sea salt. For finishing, we use several different kinds, from flaky and sweet (Murray River pink salt) to flaky and aggressive (Maldon salt) to small and aggressive (fleur de sel) to small-to-large and minerally (sel gris). The main thing is consistency. Find a salt you like and tailor your seasoning to how strong it is. (I've been known to travel with my own salt. Weirdly obsessive, I know, but it makes a difference.)

We use seawater in several recipes. We get ours from fishermen who go well off the coast in search of fish. Depending on where you live, the water by the shore will probably not be very clean, and should not be considered a cooking ingredient.

Sprouts

We use a lot of different kinds of sprouts in our cooking. There are seeds sprouted in water and then grown in a jar. We call them "bottom sprouts" because the roots appear to grow downward from the seed. These are sturdier, with crunchy roots. "Top sprouts" are grown in soil, with green shoots reaching upward from the seed. We grow both kinds at the restaurant.

Sugars

We use unrefined cane sugar. It has a little bit of molasses in it, so it's a tan color instead of pure white. The recipes call for a few other kinds of sugar as well. Trimoline and glucose are inverted sugars, less prone to crystallization and with a lower freezing point. Isomalt is a type of sugar alcohol that is less prone to crystallization, and far less sweet than sugar. Dextrose, also called glucose, is a simple sugar.

Vinegars

One of our favorite specialty fruit farms is DeSantis in Fresno. Rosa and Matteo DeSantis emigrated from Italy thirty years ago, starting a farm where they grow many of the fruits that they grew up with, like mandarins, blood oranges and figs. They also grow grapes. A few years ago, when our then chef de cuisine Evan Rich showed up at their stand at the market, Rosa brought out a little bottle of vinegar. She was planning on making some wine with their grapes that year, left the juice in a barrel somewhere and forgot about it, and returned months later to find that it had turned to vinegar. And what a vinegar it was! Oxidized, like sherry vinegar, and a pale rose color, neither white nor red. We bought everything she had, and then used the mother to start making our own. We call it Rosa's vinegar. You can substitute a light sherry vinegar.

We also make our own red wine vinegar, which we barrel age for a year in oak. We got the starter from Camino restaurant in Oakland. Thanks Russ!

TECHNIQUE

Cleanliness and Order

Every day, around 5:30 p.m., we receive a pile of clean, moist (not wet, not dry) serviettes, cloth napkins with which to clean plates before we put food on them or to clean up any drips after. Too wet and they leave moisture on the plate. Too dry and all they do is smear the thing you want to remove. They need to be folded just so and rolled, not too tight, not too loose. They need to be perfect.

A few months ago, we got our pile of wiping napkins and distributed them around the kitchen. There was a funny silence, and then the kitchen erupted.

"What the fuck is this?"

"Who rolled these?"

And the entire kitchen, in unison, started rerolling their napkins, grumbling under their breath. In that moment, I was proud. The staff understood one basic thing: details matter.

Perfect food is born of perfect order. There are many delicious things in the world that arise out of chaos; none of them are in this book. When it comes to cleanliness, give special consideration to anything that comes in contact with the food. Smell all pots, pans, containers and strainers to ensure that no traces of soap or whatever it was last used for remain. If there is water in a pot or a bowl, wipe it out with a paper towel, not the rag with which you wipe down counters or dry your hands.

The cutting board is where most of the contamination issues occur. Your cutting board should be pristine at all times. After cutting onions, garlic, herbs—anything, really—wash your board with soap and water. If you cut an onion and then a carrot without washing the board in between, then the carrot will taste like onion, and you will not have respected its nature. The job of a cook is to make ingredients better, not worse, and not cleaning your cutting surface will mindlessly make one ingredient taste like another. This is especially a problem in a cuisine based on purity and intensity of flavor. Use something stronger like a light bleach solution whenever necessary, and always when you cut animals. The same goes for your knives.

Treat your hands as you would your other equipment—they are, in fact, the most sensitive piece of equipment you own. What they tell you—about the texture and doneness of a cut of meat, the toughness of a plant or the thinness of a crust—is something no machine can relay with the same accuracy. Your hands also pass on unwanted flavors as easily as your cutting board, so wash them often, especially when working with very aromatic ingredients. Consider wearing gloves when handling onions, garlic or proteins.

Work in the most orderly fashion you can. Try not to have several projects spread out across the kitchen at once; it makes the different processes harder to control. When trimming and cleaning, don't just plop your ingredients on a counter, but put them in containers, one for dirty and one for clean. These are the kinds of things that don't matter much in home cooking, but they are extremely important in executing these recipes.

Cooking Vegetables

To cook vegetables in salted water, taste the water and, if you have time, cook one vegetable first to check the seasoning. Lightly simmer, don't boil. Except for a few leafy greens in a noted few circumstances, don't cool anything by plunging it into ice water. Cool by spreading out on a plate or a sheet tray. Yes, do this even with asparagus, which will stay vibrant green, contrary to popular belief.

When heat is applied to a vegetable, its cells suddenly expand. In green vegetables, the gases trapped between those cells escape, allowing the vibrant color of chlorophyll to shine through. The starch molecules in the cells of starchy vegetables absorb water and swell, morphing from chalky to tender. The cell walls collapse, and a sudden plunge into ice water causes those distressed cells to absorb the cold water, leading to slimy vegetables. When allowed to cool at room temperature, the residual heat on the outside of the vegetable evaporates the excess water, and they cool down drier and not slimy.

Ice baths also change the seasoning. When you work hard to make something as delicious as possible, when sometimes the success of an entire dish rests on a vegetable being perfectly cooked and seasoned, why soak it in water? Water doesn't taste like anything. It will only degrade the flavor.

Typically we like vegetables either raw or cooked, and not in that twilight zone called "al dente," as though vegetables should be cooked the way Italians cook pasta. Cooking to tenderness but not mushiness brings out fullness of flavor and sweetness. Half-cooked vegetables are a lot like half-cooked meat—of limited usefulness, an exception rather than a rule.

When I was a young cook, chefs would say, when describing vegetable cooking water, "It should taste like the ocean." I didn't realize that they meant, literally, the ocean. Our dish of tofu coagulated in seawater (see page 244) led to experiments with cooking vegetables in seawater, which we discovered had the perfect salt level. You can mimic seawater by dissolving 3.5% salt in water, but the sea itself has lots more going on than just salt, like flavorful minerals. Now we cook many of our vegetables in seawater. We're a coastal restaurant, so it makes perfect sense.

Wild Plants

During the first winter of Babette's, a farmer came in the back door of the kitchen with a garbage bag full of a kind of lettuce I'd never seen before. It had round leaves and protruding stems, like little green spaceships. Miner's lettuce, he called it, a wild plant named after the miners during the Gold Rush, who ate it during the winter to ward off scurvy. The next day, as I left my house in the hills above Sonoma, there it was, growing everywhere. Miner's lettuce was my introduction to wild plants.

Much of our food is made with wild plants. California's history is written in these flavors, and yet we know so little about them. For years, I have worked with botanists and herbalists to learn as much as I can about the edible plants that grow in our area. Our cooking wouldn't be the same without these ingredients.

But this book is about cooking, not foraging. I do not suggest where or how to gather non-cultivated ingredients. Foraging is dangerous (not to mention technically illegal in many places) and should only be undertaken with proper training. Many edible and poisonous plants closely resemble each other, and many have to be prepared in order to render them edible. Foraging must also be done with sensitivity to the environment. Harvesting wild plants in tune with nature means knowing when and how much of a plant to take, and how to encourage regrowth.

I hope that this book will inspire cooks to look at nature the way we do, as a resource to be protected and nurtured. Through our cooking at Coi we are creating taste memories of sour grass, angelica root and wild sage, using these flavors to establish an emotional connection to the place where we live. Perhaps, in some small way, it can inspire conservation in a time of endless growth.

Thickening Liquids

Part of our approach to texture and flavor is to carefully control the texture of liquids, whether in a sauce, a broth or a dressing. The thickness affects how the flavors are perceived, and the way that the liquid interacts with the other components. For example, the taste of a thickened sauce will not only have more length, because it lingers on the tongue, but it will cling more closely to whatever it is coating.

We use several kinds of gelling agents in the recipes, and they all have different properties and hydrate in different ways. There's a ton of other extracts and derivatives out there (like carrageenan and kuzu root) that we don't use in these recipes.

For gels, the amount of thickening agent is often expressed as a percentage of the total weight of the liquid to be thickened. For example, "Set with 2% gelatin" means that, if the liquid weighs one hundred grams, you should use two grams of gelatin.

We use guar gum, a thickener derived from the seed of a tree, commonly used to improve the texture of an ice cream. We use a special kind of pectin to set a gel. But those are one-offs. The ones we mostly use are:

Gelatin

This is the simplest, most traditional gelling agent. It is derived from animals. All you have to do is soak the gelatin in cold water for five minutes until it softens, drain the excess water, and then melt in a hot liquid. It takes hours to set up, and it must be refrigerated. It is a long-strand, soft gel, with a gentle, unctuous texture. The recipes all call for leaf gelatin. The measurement refers to dry gelatin—soak it just before using.

Agar

Agar agar (which I call agar for brevity) is a seaweed derivative. It is vegetarian. It must be boiled hard in order to hydrate. It is stable up to 185°F (85°C), but it is not as strong as gellan. It sets as soon as it cools into a short-strand, brittle gel, with a hard, almost crunchy texture.

Gellan

Gellan gum is fermented from sugars. It is vegetarian. It must be boiled hard in order to hydrate. It is stable up to about 175°F (80°C) and it is perfect for high-heat gels. There are two kinds, low-acyl (F), which is agar-like, and high-acyl (LT), which is gelatin-like. They are used in only a few recipes.

Fluid gels

Both agar and gellan can be set into hard gels, which are puréed in a blender to create a shiny, viscous liquid. These are called fluid gels. We use them to thicken broths, and to create sauces and dressings.

Xanthan

Xanthan gum is produced by fermenting sugars. It is a fine powder that is used for thickening liquids. It can be hydrated by boiling, or by blending cold. We use it to thicken without cooking, which keeps the flavor fresher. Sauces like wheatgrass (see page 242) would not be possible without xanthan. If you've ever tasted hot sauce then you've most likely eaten xanthan.

The Ice Bath

One of the first things that a new cook at Coi learns is that we take ice baths really, really seriously. Ours is a cuisine of intent, where nothing is left to chance or inattention. If we want something to cool slowly, we let it sit at room temperature. But for many things, we want it cooled *fast*. In a perfect world we would have a special cooling machine called a blast chiller, but the building that houses our restaurant doesn't have enough electricity to add any more equipment. So we use ice baths.

Take a large bowl and fill it with ice. Next—and here's the important part—add water, enough to create, well, a bath. The water should be up to the surface of the ice, not below it. Water conducts temperature far more efficiently than air. Put a smaller bowl inside the larger one. Add the liquid you wish to cool into the top bowl. Stir until cooled, to bring down the temperature as quickly as possible. Don't overagitate, which will create air bubbles.

Measurements

Sometimes our measurements have to be very precise. Where they are important I provide them mostly in metric units, which is what we use in our kitchen.

Other times there are no measurements at all. This seems inconsistent, but it's not. Cooking is a craft, not a manufacturing process. There are some things that can't be measured, decisions that rely on the experience and intuition of the cook. The amount of liquid in a soup is the culinary equivalent of a term of art: in theory it's useful, but in reality it's impossible to measure precise starch, sugar, moisture and fiber characteristics in each vegetable. You can only achieve the taste and texture you want by paying attention and tweaking, adding a little water here or stock there. Or, if the soup seems like it has a lot of liquid, hold some back. You can always thin it out, but thickening is much more difficult.

If you do not see a measurement for a seasoning like lemon juice, rice wine vinegar or salt, assume that it is to taste.

Certain recipes (like a gel) can and should be measured, as accurately as possible. Use a gram scale. For any powdery substances, use a gram scale that measures to the tenth. They're easy to find online, and most head shops carry them. We call them drug scales.

Smoking

There are many awesome smoking setups in the world. We don't own any of them. We use a smoking branch of whatever tree we think has the best flavor. We burn it over an open burner until it's smoldering, and then rest it on aluminum foil in a deep metal pan. (When you start the branch, burn and cool a few times to break it in, and then discard it as it gets down to a charcoal-like nub.) We put whatever we're smoking on the other side of the pan, and wrap the whole thing in plastic wrap. You can recreate this at home pretty easily.

Yields

The ratios in the Weights and Measures section (see page 286) are based on the ones that we use in the restaurant. That does not mean that they are infallible, or that they will work for you. I tried to reduce the yields where I could, but really they're all over the place. You might only need a spoonful of a purée, but the blender won't work without enough material in it, so you'll end up with way more than you need. Other times, as for sauces, there needs to be enough liquid to have the cooking time to properly develop flavor and texture. The way I split the difference is to give approximate yields and then let you know what you'll probably end up with too much of.

Stocks

I don't look back very often, and I have a bad habit of not documenting what I make. I have no idea how many dishes I've created over the years, but I'm sure I've forgotten most of them. It's always a surprise to find out that a particular one made an impression on a diner or a cook, and they can describe it in exquisite detail years later, even as I strain to remember what was in it. I made a decision early on in my career to always move forward, and even when I bring back an old dish, I rarely recreate it in the original form.

So I was a bit taken aback when I realized that I've used the same basic stocks, mostly unchanged, since 1993. We make all kinds of very specific sauces and stocks, many of which you'll find throughout the book, like the charred onion broth (see page 224). But the following ones are the foundation of many of the dishes.

AP (all-purpose) stock

In the early '90s there was a craze (since died down, thank god) to make animal jus from dark chicken stock. In order to get the right texture, chefs would reduce and reduce and reduce, until the flavor was bitter and impacted. I didn't like those anachronistic stick-to-the-lips veal-based sauces that these chefs were rebelling against either, but there had to be a better way. So I split the difference. Half duck bones (deeper-flavored and more giving than chicken) and half veal bones, with a few pig's feet thrown in for body. It's neutral in flavor, and it can go in any direction. Most of the animal sauces in our cooking are based on this stock.

Roast the veal bones and duck bones, separately, in roasting pans. Brown deeply, stirring occasionally. When they're done, deglaze with water and scrape up the fond, the stuff at the bottom of the roasting pan. If it's delicious, then put it in the stockpot. If it tastes burnt, then discard it—at least you've cleaned the pan.

Add the bones, fond (if usable) and pig's foot to the pot. Start the onions with a little pure olive oil—no salt!—in a heavy, covered pot. We use enameled cast iron. Sweat until tender over low-medium heat. The pot should be in between tall and wide, so that the liquid that comes out of the onions as they cook does not burn off right away. When you take off the lid, the onions should be swimming in their own juices. Add the carrots and cook over medium heat, stirring often, until the liquid reduces and caramelizes. The point here is that you want to release the juices containing sugars from the vegetables, and then burn off the liquid and caramelize those sugars. This will give the vegetables a deep, rich flavor. Don't just brown the vegetables and then throw in some water to standardize the color, which will give you something that looks similar, but is nowhere near as tasty. When the vegetables are mahogany brown and sweet, add them to the stockpot.

Add the water and bring to a boil, skimming as it comes up. Throw in a bunch of ice, bring to a boil again and skim. Turn down to a low simmer for at least 12 to 15, and preferably 24 hours. There should be bubbling action on one side of the pot, but not the other. Before straining, throw more ice in and bring it up to a boil again, and skim.

When it's done, carefully scoop out everything except the bottom 4 inches (10 cm) of the contents of the pot. Do NOT simply dump out the stock into another container. Doing it this way will mix the murk on the bottom with the clear elixir on top that you worked so hard to create. Strain the stock through a fine mesh sieve. Cool in a very cold ice bath, letting the fat rise to the surface and harden. If you're not using it immediately, then the fat cap will protect the stock. Once the fat cap is broken, the stock should be vacuum sealed. It freezes very well.

Now, that pot that still has bones and a bit of murky stock in it? Add more water and boil away for 4 to 5 hours. It's called a remi. It's perfect for a stock for braising, or French onion soup, or whatever.

Vegetable stock

Maybe we should call this our AP stock, because this is by far the most used stock in this book, and the base of much of what we do in the restaurant. It's sweet and concentrated, without excess water. It's reasonably neutral, with all of the elements merging into one taste. It's used as a background flavor, an enriching component.

Many years ago, there was a chef who worked at a now-defunct restaurant. A review mentioned that he charred his onions before putting them in his chicken stock. I thought that was brilliant. This was the early '90s, and although I'd learned the pleasure to be found in things burned in a cast iron pan with no fat, the way they do in Mexico, this was new to me.

The charred onions are a crucial element of this stock, and they are the main reason why it will act a bit differently than most vegetable stocks. They lend a smoky, bitter element that balances the sweetness and turns the stock from saccharine to complex.

To char the onions, cut them in half and blacken on a plancha, a flat-top (cook them on aluminum foil so they don't stick to the surface), or a gas burner. By char, I mean blacken the cut side, but not completely, about half to two-thirds of the surface.

The vegetables should be cut in relatively large pieces so they don't break down too much, and so that they release their flavor slowly and completely. Combine all of the ingredients in a stockpot and simmer until the flavor is sweet and concentrated, about 3 hours. If it's too dilute, none of the recipes that use it will work, because they rely on the sweetness of the stock to balance the acidity. If it's too concentrated, the flavor can get overcooked and tired.

Standard mushroom stock

The base of this stock is shiitake, to which we add whatever wild mushroom scraps we have around, and always some dried porcini. During the winter season, when wild mushrooms are plentiful, we order too many mushrooms so that we can build a supply of dried mushrooms that we use throughout the summer.

Combine all the ingredients and simmer gently, covered, for 2 hours, until the flavor is clear but not overly concentrated. Strain through cheesecloth set into a strainer and cool in an ice bath.

03

OUR

MENU

I have always cooked tasting menus. I love the way they flow, the elegance of form, the element of surprise. Within haute cuisine, they allow for the highest level of expression. They are all that I know as a professional cook, and all that I care about.

When we opened Coi, there were no other restaurants in San Francisco that offered only highly personal tasting menus, nor was there much of an indication that there was any demand for one. I thought that the business would have a better chance of success if I opened with a shorter, less ambitious format. Our first menu was a four-course fixed-price affair with three choices in each course.

It didn't last long. Guests wanted and expected a tasting menu, and I missed the challenge and excitement of creating them. After about a month I added an eleven-course tasting menu to go alongside the four-course menu. A few months later I dropped the four-course menu entirely. It wasn't how I like to cook, and I figured that there's not much point in killing yourself for something you don't love. For the next two years we served a daily changing eleven-course menu, with vegetarian choices for the few protein based dishes. Then one day, I realized that there were sixteen possible permutations of that one menu, but only one was, to me, the best. Why not just choose the best dishes based on the best ingredients that day? Now we serve one menu of eleven to thirteen courses every night.

It seems like it should be easy to prepare only one menu, but it's not. If all we do is offer a collection of tasty dishes, then we've failed. The menu should be a story and each course a chapter, one building on the next, the transitions fluid, graceful, surprising. The dishes should of course be delicious. They also should express new ideas, techniques and ways of looking at the world. I want diners to leave inspired, excited, changed in some small way. The menu should have a context: A place, a time, a culture. And, above all, it should have a voice worth listening to.

This was our menu on September 14, 2012, at the peak of summer. The products at this time of year are sweet, richly flavored, full of captured sunshine. It is a happy time, and a feeling of plenty fills the markets, a moment of optimism and playfulness just before the light changes and cools into the sharp, narrow rays of fall.

We started planning this menu at the beginning of August. Menu development for us is a little like a chess game—if we're not three steps ahead of the season then we're behind. Dishes need to be developed and tried. They need to be adjusted to accommodate the other dishes around them. Allowance must be made for failure, and we have to keep a close eye on our products.

Our dishes start with ingredients. Always. Technique is what we use to bring out the best in those ingredients, to put them in a context that gives them life, energy, meaning. A stretch that's too hot or too cool, and we might find too much sugar in the plants, or not enough; if the ripeness of a fruit declines, or the flavor changes, the product becomes unusable, and the dish is lost. There are dozens of micro-seasons that happen throughout the year, and we've learned, by carefully paying attention, what to expect. But there are always surprises. So we buy everything we need at farmers' markets and a few things farm direct. We grow the products that we need young and super fresh, like sprouts, herbs and flowers, and pick wild ingredients every morning. For meat, fish and dairy we rely on close relationships with our suppliers that we have developed over many years. We control the quality of what we use as closely as possible.

Our menu changes radically throughout the year in all sorts of ways. Sometimes we serve a longer menu of smaller, lighter courses, and other times fewer, more substantial dishes. The winter brings richer flavors, with more dairy; in the summer, we use mostly olive oil. In the spring you will find something green on almost every course; in the fall the colors are jewel-toned and deep. We might have three courses with protein, or five, or two. The only constant is that we're always trying something new, which means changing the structure as well as the content.

You will notice some themes in this menu. Three items are grilled over charcoal, evoking the summer barbeque, but also grounding and giving an earthy soulfulness to flavors so light as to float off the plate. There are fewer wild ingredients, as the fresh greens and herbs have mostly burned up in the summer's dry heat. And the dishes are simple, often using only a few ingredients. Not easy to produce—in fact in some ways harder, because there is nothing to hide behind. Dishes with an open, wide-eyed quality, almost child-like in spirit, the way I remember the summers of my youth, the forms uncomplicated but powerfully evocative, the flavors clear, penetrating and strong.

MENU
December 11 – December 15, 2012
FROZEN MANDARIN SOUR
kumquat, meringue scented with angostura bitters
OYSTERS UNDER GLASS
shigoku oysters, yuzu, rau ram
BEET AND GOAT CHEESE TART (BROKEN, INVERTED)
rye, dill
DUNGENESS CRAB / BEEF TENDON SOUP
asian pear, finger lime, cilantro
NEW OLIVE OIL
brassica, charred onion broth
YOUNG CARROTS ROASTED IN HAY
radish, pecorino
MONTEREY BAY ABALONE
grains, fresh seaweeds, raw turnip
GRASS-FED VEAL
chicories, caper berry, seville orange
TOMME DOLCE
fruit and vegetable leathers, apple
FROZEN LIME MARSHMALLOW
coal toasted meringue
WINTER FRUIT SALAD
cedro, absinthe
GOOSEBERRY BABA
honeycomb, shiso, white chocolate
MENU
$165
WINE PAIRING
$65 (7 wines)
$105 (12 wines)
18% SERVICE CHARGE SHARED BY THE ENTIRE STAFF
MENU
September 18 – September 22, 2012
February, 1994
s on celery root pancakes with
and champagne beurre blanc
8.00
sturgeon with multic
a and curried crè
7.00
rabbit en ge
Week of February 19
s and tomatoes
white truff
An eggshell
Sautée

CALIFORNIA BOWL

TOMATO
olive oil, basil

MUSK MELON
nasturtium, buttermilk

SPOT PRAWN
new onion, sorrel

CHILLED SPICED RATATOUILLE SOUP
nepitella, cilantro

POPCORN GRITS

PIG HEAD
fresh pole and shelling beans, charred okra, wild sage

CARROTS ROASTED IN COFFEE BEANS
mandarin, roman mint

MONTEREY BAY ABALONE
nettle-dandelion salsa verde, spicy breadcrumbs, wild fennel flowers

POACHED AND GRILLED LAMB
chard leaves and stems, garum, rosemary

FRESH MIXED MILK CHEESE
fig steeped in beet juice, burnt fig leaf oil

LIME MARSHMALLOW
coal-toasted meringue

STRAWBERRIES AND CREAM
tiny herbs

PASSION FRUIT BABA
white chocolate, honeycomb, shiso

CANDIED RASPBERRIES

CALIFORNIA BOWL

When the term "California Cuisine" was coined over thirty years ago, it promised to usher in a brave new era, one in which the constricting shackles of conventional cooking would be thrown off in favor of a style as wide open and vast as the Western horizon. (Smoked salmon pizza! Grilled fish with fruit salsa! Beet and goat cheese salad!) The food was light and brightly flavored, energetically mixing together disparate cultural traditions. Its effect rippled across the country, but nowhere was it felt more strongly than in Northern California, where it came to represent a simple, rustic way of cooking.

I never intended for Coi to be a destination restaurant. From the beginning I set out to cook food that Californians would enjoy. I brought the connection to nature, to the plants that they grew up with, into our kitchen. I used only local vegetables, fish and meat, in many cases the same ones that they could find at nearby markets. I incorporated familiar culinary tropes.

My attempts at calling our food "Californian," however, met with some resistance. I remember answering fact-checking questions for our first review while waiting in line for coffee at the farmers' market in 2006. "Really," the young woman asking the questions practically snorted, "Californian? How about I call it Modern French." She may have been right. I love my adopted home, but I definitely still have an outsider's sense of humor.

This dish is a playful take on cliché California hippie food ingredients—brown rice, sprouts and avocado. The cracker started as a garnish for a dish that I made in 2007. Basically, brown rice is overcooked, blended and then dried into a crisp. We brought the idea back in 2010, at first served in sheets studded with bits of seaweed and chile flakes, and then with a dipping sauce. Eventually our pastry chef, Matt Tinder, figured out that, dipped in insanely hot oil, the crackers puffed and blistered like chicharrón.

We want the first food that we serve to be a welcome, not a challenge. So the chips and dip have remained constant, something to snack on at the beginning of the meal that doesn't require deep contemplation. We serve them with a seasonal purée: tofu-wheatgrass, kale-fromage blanc, or, as in this recipe, avocado-lime. We add sprouts to the finished dish, to have something fresh. And because, well, this is California.

Cook the rice, water and salt in a heavy pot, covered, until it's completely overcooked, and all of the liquid is absorbed. Blend in a Thermomix until it's smooth and spreadable. Spread in thin layers on two baking trays lined with Silpats. Dehydrate at 127°F (53°C) overnight. In the morning the layers should be completely dry and peel away easily from the Silpat.

Fry in 550°F (290°C) soy oil. (We heat the oil until it is practically smoking and our thermometer needle is all the way on the right, past all of the numbers). Break the dried rice into pieces and place carefully into the oil. Fry them one piece at a time. They should blister and puff within a few seconds. Flip, wait a few seconds and then remove onto a sheet tray lined with paper towels. Sprinkle with piment d'Espelette (a sweet, slightly spicy dried pepper, originally from the Basque region of France, now grown here), or other mildly spicy, flavorful dried chile. Hold warm.

For the dip, cut the avocados in half and remove the pit. Sprinkle the cut sides with salt and sear on a hot plancha with a little pure olive oil until lightly browned. Scoop out the flesh and blend in a mixer until smooth. Season with lime juice and salt.

To serve, pile a few crackers in a bowl. Add a spoonful of avocado purée next to them, and sprinkle a few different kinds of sprouts on top of the crackers.

TOMATO
olive oil, basil

I knew from the beginning that I wanted to define the restaurant on my own terms, however unresolved those might have been. In the past my restaurants had employed all of the touchstones of fine dining—the delicate French china, the formal service—to indicate that it was a Serious Restaurant. I didn't feel that way when I opened Coi. I wanted an over-achieving neighborhood restaurant, not a temple of haute cuisine. We designed a warm, comfortable space, with soft lighting, bare wood tables, fuzzy pillows on the banquettes and lots of handmade touches, like mohair cocktail napkins that Alexandra made. In the end, the décor bore a striking resemblance to our home.

I didn't have much money, so I found a location in a less expensive, not so nice part of town. Instead of fancy china we used handmade pottery, which at that time was associated with a rustic style of cooking. We offered casual, friendly service and played lively music. It kind of worked, kind of not. By scrambling so many of the traditional symbols of fine dining, often we just confused people.

Our cooking, on the other hand, has always been ambitious, even if we tried to hide the effort—I wanted the presentations, like the restaurant itself, to be understated. I think of the first dish as a way to reset diners' expectations and prepare them for the rest of the meal. It is always based on humble ingredients in an unexpected form, with a finely tuned balance of salt and acidity. It has to deliver something new, even to the most sophisticated guest. It is the hardest dish to create, and the one that changes the least.

This dish is unusually simple for a Coi first course, but perfect for this menu. It speaks loudly of pleasure, and whispers of surprise. We use Early Girl tomatoes from Dirty Girl Produce, which runs a forty-acre organic farm in Santa Cruz. By mid-September their tomatoes are at peak flavor, at the height of sweetness and concentration.

We turn their flesh into a clear gel and combine that with the natural gel/seed sac (the most flavorful part). Underneath we put diced tomatoes seasoned with raw tomato juice, salt, pepper. Basil pesto sits on the bottom of the bowl. It's all of the flavors of summer that you'd expect . . . but wait a minute. What's this sorbet? It's super creamy, almost gelato-like, but umami-rich, not sweet. It tastes in fact a little like Parmesan. It is actually green olive oil, tomato water and bread. Everything you'd expect out of a summer starter, in a form that you wouldn't, which you can ponder—or just enjoy.

The day before, make the sorbet. Pulse whole, cored tomatoes with coarse sea salt. Put into a covered container and leave it in the refrigerator for a few hours. Strain through cheesecloth and then through a coffee filter. We use a Chemex. It takes a while, so leave the pot in the refrigerator while it's dripping through, and when it's done, put it in a tightly covered container. When it comes to tomato water, heat and air are not your friends.

Soak the pain de mie* in the tomato water until soggy, then blend with olive oil and xanthan. (Add a little xanthan at a time, just enough to create a strong emulsion. Pay attention as it's blending, and stop before it gets snotty. No one likes that texture.) Season with salt, but not too much because it creeps upwards as it sits. Freeze in a Pacojet beaker. If you have leftover tomato water, use it in a soup, or drink it or something. It won't be good the next day. You can also freeze it into ice cubes for a Bloody Mary.

The next day make another recipe of tomato water. Peel the 4 remaining tomatoes by scoring the bottom with a tiny "x," plunging them into boiling water for 5 seconds, and then removing them to a sheet tray lined with parchment paper. I know, everything you've read tells you to cool them in ice water. Don't do it.

Slip off the tomato skins and remove and reserve the seed sacs for the gel. Dice the flesh into pieces of about ½ inch (1 cm) for the salad. No need to make them perfectly square, or exactly the same. Save the excess juice for dressing the salad.

For the gel, weigh the tomato water and set it with 2% gelatin, and cool in an ice bath. When it's half-set, stir in the reserved seed sacs and transfer to a covered container. Refrigerate for at least 3 hours.

Grind the pine nuts in a food processor, and pass them through a medium sieve. Start the pesto by mashing together half of the basil and a large pinch of salt in the frozen mortar. (The pestle gets cold—it's no crime to hold it with a towel.) When the purée is fine add enough pure olive oil to make a smooth paste. Transfer to a bowl set into another bowl filled with ice water, and press plastic wrap over the top so that no air gets at it. Repeat. Put all the basil purée back into the mortar and stir in the pine nut purée, lemon juice and more oil. Season with salt. It should be bright and a little lemony, with the pine nut on the low side, just enough to add richness and to make a creamy emulsion. If you're not planning on making the dish immediately then vacuum seal the pesto in a plastic pastry bag and refrigerate. Only open the bag when you need it, otherwise the oxygen will turn the pesto brown.

To serve, spin the sorbet. Put a quarter-size round of pesto on the bottom of a cold bowl, and a scoop of sorbet on top. (Note: If you spin the sorbet in advance, put it in the refrigerator, then monitor softness, adjusting by moving back and forth between freezer and fridge. If it gets too hard or too soft it's unusable. The texture is best right after it's spun.) Season the tomato pieces with tomato juice, salt and a little pepper, and form a ring around the sorbet. Spoon some pieces of gel on the tomato. Garnish with 3 tiny basil leaves (opal is pretty) on top and, if you can find them, 3 basil flowers.

*If you want to go no-gluten, you can make the sorbet without bread. Mix 2 parts olive oil to 1 part tomato water, blend with enough xanthan to make a good emulsion and season with salt. Spin to order, as it hardens fast. It's more elegant and texturally voluptuous than the bread-based version, and it has all kinds of savory uses.

60

MUSK MELON
nasturtium, buttermilk

Restaurants were once places where cooks could hide from the world. The kitchens where I began my career were filled with every manner of social misfit, and from the beginning I felt right at home. Those were the days when no diner ever, ever asked to see the cook.

Times have changed. In this strange, new world where people are interested in chefs, I get invited occasionally to stand in front of a large group of strangers in faraway places and tell them what I think about food. The prospect of stumbling awkwardly through a presentation that I put together on the plane ride over is not the reason that I accept invitations to travel abroad. I do it to see friends from around the world, a community at least as strong as the one where I live. And I do it to learn.

I love seeing what people in other places eat, how they think about food and what it says about who they are. It reminds me of how much there is to discover. Usually I'm inspired in a general sort of way, but sometimes an idea or a flavor that I come across lingers in my memory, eventually becoming a new dish. In this case, tacos.

I grew up eating bastardized Russian-American Jewish food. In restaurants I learned to cook French food, and eventually Mediterranean and Asian influences crept in. Lately, though, I've become increasingly interested in the countries to the south. After all, California was once part of Mexico and now we share a continent—why do I know so little about our neighbors?

There is a vibrant, emerging food scene in Mexico, and I've travelled there a few times, most recently for a food conference in Mexico City put on by chef Enrique Olvera. At Daniel Ovadia's Paxia I had tacos with fried worms and huitlacoche. At Enrique's place, Pujol, I had tacos with ant eggs. It was all delicious, and inspiring to see chefs there re-examine their own traditions, from street food to haute cuisine. I guess the form just kind of stuck.

At Coi, we use a lot of nasturtiums, but before this dish never the leaves in whole form. I don't know why, but I was thinking about musk melons and their gamey, complex aromatics while I was picking nasturtiums in my garden at home one day. The smell of the flowers in the warm morning sun triggered an idea: maybe the peppery, sweet leaves would be a good match for the melon. I wanted something early on in the menu that was eaten by hand, something a little playful. A good menu has passion and intensity, but also playfulness and humor. What if I made tacos?

When I thought of the form, the rest fell in place. A chunk of melon grilled and then doused in lime and coarse salt, wrapped in a nasturtium leaf and then eaten by hand, folded up like a soft taco. The spiciness of the nasturtium took the place of the chile. On the side, a shot of cold melon-buttermilk cordial, reminiscent of horchata, to wash it down.

It was fantastic. As I ate it for the first time and felt the smooth nasturtium against the warm melon and the energy of the lime, salt and grill, I thought that maybe leaving the kitchen every once in a while isn't such a bad idea after all.

Choose really fragrant, ripe musk melons. I like green-fleshed Ha'Ogen, a Hungarian melon that gets its commercial name from the kibbutz in Israel that grew it commercially in the '60s, and orange-fleshed Charentais, a type of French melon that's been grown for almost 100 years. Cut them into 1-inch (2.5-cm) wedges, discard the seeds, cut away the peel and the pale layer next to the peel, and portion into ¾-inch (scant 2-cm) chunks. Keep the look organic and not too square.

To make the cordial, take the scraps of the green melon only and purée with fresh buttermilk (we use the cultured buttermilk that we produce when we make butter). Season with enough salt to sharpen the tang of the buttermilk and temper the sweetness. Keep it very cold.

Pick nasturtium leaves about 2½ to 3 inches (6 to 7 cm) in diameter. Or use bigger ones, and cut them down with scissors—just make sure they're tender and not too peppery.

To serve, grill the melon over very hot charcoal, turning often, just until the interior is warm. Don't let the outside get overcooked or mushy. Transfer to a plate, douse with lime juice and sprinkle generously with coarse sea salt (we use Murray River here). Place two nasturtium leaves on a plate, and one piece of grilled melon on each one. Wrap the melon in the nasturtium leaves and eat them with your hands, like a taco. And then drink a shot of ice-cold melon-buttermilk cordial.

SPOT PRAWN
new onion, sorrel

West Coast waters aren't as bountiful as they once were. Through pollution, overfishing and general resource mismanagement, the fin fish supply has been reduced to a handful of varieties, sporadically available. Worse, the fish are often handled poorly after they're caught. It's not possible in our area to buy fish killed with the technique that the Japanese call ikejime, where the fish is bled out, making the flesh firmer and tastier. I looked.

The fish are often packed and transported in less than ideal conditions, and show up damaged, soft or worse. When I put a fin fish on the menu, even if it's in season, I can be sure that at least one day a week the quality will be too poor to serve. There are many environmental reasons not to eat fin fish, but inconsistent quality is why we don't use it on our menu very often, and why you will not find any recipes for fin fish in this book.

I am well aware of the irony of a coastal restaurant that does not serve fish. We find other ways to incorporate oceanic flavors, like seawater, coastal plants and shellfish. The shellfish in our area can be astonishingly good. We source from as far north as Washington state and as far south as Santa Barbara, where the best spot prawns are found. The spot prawns that we use during the summer are spectacular, the meat sweet and firm. We buy them live every day.

Because the second course in this menu is unusually small, I wanted to add another small dish, something warm and comforting. Here we kill, brine, and quickly sear a spot prawn, then serve it with a clarified butter made from the shells and freshly juiced sorrel. As a third component, we cook new onions at a low temperature so they remain crunchy even when fully cooked, and then grill them next to the prawn.

As the natural world around us evolves, cuisine will change as well. Some ingredients will fade, while others will improve. The nearby oceans might not support the diversity of life that they once did, but the quality of what we do get is superb. This dish relies entirely on the purity of a pristinely fresh prawn, perfectly cooked.

Kill the prawns by dropping into boiling water for 3 seconds, and then transfer them immediately into ice water. Peel, saving the heads and shells, and de-vein. Soak the tails in seawater for 3 minutes. Refrigerate, but not forever–it's best to kill the prawns as close to cooking as possible. We do it a few hours before serving, so we have time to use the shells.

Clean the shells by rinsing them with water, until they are clean of guts, roe and so on. Drain. Sear them in a thick layer of hot butter until they turn red, then remove and pulse them in a food processor. Weigh the shells and return them to the pot with an equal amount of butter. Simmer for a few hours at a low burble, until you have made clarified, intensely flavored prawn butter. Strain through cheesecloth.

Vacuum a spoonful of the prawn butter with the new onions and a little salt in a bag, and steam at 170°F (75°C) until they are cooked but still crunchy, about 45 minutes to an hour.

To serve, juice the sorrel and season with salt. Spear the prawn with a thin metal skewer through the length of the tail, and lightly season with salt. Sear it on the plancha, on all sides, until the outside is golden-red but the inside is still translucent. Brown a few pieces of cooked onion next to the prawn, and remove them both to drain. We use a small tray lined with paper towels.

Place the prawn in the center of the bowl, with the most beautiful side facing up. Scatter a few pieces of onion around, spoon a generous amount of warm prawn butter over everything, and dot with a large spoonful of sorrel juice here and there.

CHILLED SPICED RATATOUILLE SOUP
nepitella, cilantro

I made this soup for the first time in 2005, as part of a dinner I cooked at home for Rajat Parr. It was summer, when the new restaurant was strictly theoretical. I didn't know that it would be the first Coi dish that I created.

Raj is one of the greatest sommeliers in the country. Originally from India, he has spent much of his adult life trekking through French terroir, learning what makes wine so delicious. The soup is a playful nod to both his homeland and his vocation, Provence by way of Calcutta.

It's actually three chilled soups that are combined in the bowl. Yellow squash with turmeric and lime, roasted eggplant with cumin and coriander, and tomato-pepper. Over the years, I've served each one independently: Squash soup with nasturtiums and vadouvan (a fermented Indian spice blend); eggplant and piquillo pepper soups, both with the same garnish—tomato water gel, a salad of fresh pole and shelling beans, nepitella (a wild Italian herb that tastes like a cross between oregano and mint) and preserved lemon.

On that night, and soon after opening, I served them all together, with ratatouille proper in the center. I forgot all about it until Andrew Miller, my chef de cuisine, reminded me of the dish in 2012.

"You know, I came in right after you opened," he told me soon after he started. I tensed up a bit. At that point we hadn't exactly hit our stride. "There was this soup I really loved, it was like three soups . . . "

"Ratatouille."

"Yes. Why don't we do that one again?"

So we did. We usually have a soup on the menu, usually around the fourth course, and in the summer usually chilled. It's a moment of comfort and recognizable form, a kind of island in the middle of a swiftly flowing river. This fit all the parameters.

Trying it again for the first time was both a shock and eerily familiar, like running into a friend from high school years later, and your friend is just the same but you've changed. As I ate I remembered cooking the dish in my tiny galley kitchen at my apartment, carefully blending soup after soup, trying to understand how they would relate to each other. Later Raj came with his girlfriend and the four of us sat and ate and drank champagne and talked into the night, I remember that as well.

"By the way," I asked Andrew, "How was the rest of the meal?"

He paused a moment too long. "It was good."

A few things about the soups. They change as they cool and sit. A lot. So season them, put them in the refrigerator for an hour or two, and then re-season them. Salt and acid drop out, sweetness fades, all kinds of untoward things happen. You may need to add sugar, if the vegetables are not sweet enough, or if the vegetable stock isn't concentrated enough. Sacrilege, I know, to bolster vegetable sugars with cane sugar. But if you're looking for fullness of flavor, a sweet/sour balance, the perfect level of salt and to highlight the vegetables as the stars, sometimes only a pinch or two of sugar will get you there.

For the squash soup, cook the cut squash, vegetable stock, water, saffron, turmeric, chile, salt and pure olive oil at a brisk simmer, covered, until baby-food tender. Blend, pass through a chinois, and cool quickly in an ice bath. When it's cold, season with salt and lime.

For the eggplant soup, grill the eggplant in a cast iron pan, or on a grill or a plancha, until well blackened. Bake in the oven at 350°F (175°C) until tender. Cool and scoop out the flesh. Simmer with vegetable stock, olive oil and spices. Blend, pass through a chinois into an ice bath and cool. Season with lemon juice and an oxidized vinegar, like sherry vinegar. We use Rosa's. There should be much more lemon than vinegar, which can give the soup a harsh flavor if you add too much.

For the tomato-pepper soup, use sweet red tomatoes, like Early Girls, and ripe piquillo peppers. Cook the tomato, pepper (no seeds) and the vegetable stock at a brisk simmer for 10 to 15 minutes, until the pepper has softened. Purée, pass through a chinois into an ice bath, and cool. Add the tomato and pepper juices, and season with salt. If the soup seems too sweet, add a little lime juice.

All of the soups should have the same thickness, so that they creep instead of run across the bottom of the bowl when poured.

For the ratatouille, mince the onions and cut the vegetables in ¼-inch (5-mm) dice. Squash and eggplant: cut so that one side of the dice has the skin. Pepper and tomato: peel and seed first. Cook the vegetables separately in pure olive oil—enough to coat but don't drown them—over high heat, stirring constantly. They're small, they'll go fast. Start with the squash, then the eggplant, then the pepper, using the same pan the entire time, not cleaning it in between. Season with salt as they cook. As each vegetable is done, spread out on a plate to cool. After the peppers are cooked, turn the heat down to low and add the onion and cook until tender and sweet. Add the tomato, stir to combine, and cook 30 seconds more. Pull the pan off the heat for a minute and then add to the rest of the vegetables. Allow them to cool in the refrigerator for 15 minutes, then combine and season with salt, a little black pepper, minced cilantro stems and minced nepitella. Refrigerate.

To serve, ladle 30 g of each of the squash and eggplant soups simultaneously on each side of a soup bowl so that they meet in the middle, '80s style. Spoon a heaping tablespoon of ratatouille in the center, and drizzle a little fruity olive oil around. Garnish with cilantro sprouts or small cilantro leaves, and nepitella flowers. Pour 20 g of the tomato-pepper soup into one spot in the squash soup. To eat, put your spoon in the red dot, stir once around and have at.

Note: If you want to make a straight piquillo pepper soup, combine raw pepper and charred pepper with the vegetable stock. Cook at a brisk simmer for 15 minutes, until the peppers are just tender. Blend, strain and cool. Add the fresh pepper juice, and season with salt.

POPCORN GRITS

When I was young I wanted to be a writer or a poet when I grew up. (Instead, I ended up as a cook. The *other* high-paying profession.) I loved the delirious brilliance of Rimbaud and the gentle wit of e.e. cummings, but my hero was William Carlos Williams. He was a doctor who ran a practice for most of his life, raised a family, and in the interstices between everything else, changed American poetry. While T.S. Eliot and Ezra Pound grounded their work in references to European culture, Williams tried to write in an American vernacular, as he understood it. He pulled universal, meaningful experiences from the banality of everyday life. I loved his direct, expressive language, clear and engaging, with never a wasted word.

I named my second restaurant, Plum, after one of his poems, "This is Just to Say." That was in 2010, when I had started thinking a lot about what it means to be an American cook making American food. When we built the bar next door in 2011, Scott Kester, our restaurant designer, proposed that we paper every square inch of the walls with pages of books, kind of an ironic reference to the cheesy newspaper wall coverings found in chain bars. Great, I said, how about American poetry? And so we did. Over 12,000 pages, applied one by one. Applied mostly by me. "I want it to look like a crazy person did it," Scott had told me. I didn't realize that I would be the crazy person.

I still had my day job, which still involved figuring out what to put on the menu. The morel season was just starting, and at the farmers' market I found tiny, first-of-the-season new potatoes from Full Belly, one of my favorite farms. As I was picking through them for the littlest ones I noticed the bags of popcorn beside them. Of course, I thought. Popcorn. How perfect.

I had never cooked with popcorn, but as I looked into its history I found that it made a lot of sense. Corn is one of the oldest and most important cultivated foods in the Americas. For thousands of years Northern California was inhabited by nomadic tribes, who lived off the land. Those Native Americans ate popcorn.

I made a popcorn sauce through successive infusions of popped popcorn in water and butter. This made a nice bouillon, but it needed more body to stand up to the intensity of the butter-roasted morels I wanted to pair them with. I pushed the corn through a coarse mesh strainer, and then puréed it with the bouillon. A short rest in the refrigerator allowed the starches to bind together and the sauce to thicken. The creamy, custardy texture was just right with morels, new potatoes steamed and warmed in butter, and basil sprouts. A little buttered popcorn brought additional flavor and texture. The dish was complete (see Morels Roasted in Butter, page 222).

The real moment of discovery occurred when I re-examined the cooked popcorn I'd passed through the sieve before blending it. It had the exact same texture as grits. I added a little of the bouillon and heated it, and there it was: popcorn grits. They're buttery, slightly sweet, and capture the ephemeral aroma of freshly popped popcorn. It's almost too simple to be called a dish, but it's fun and surprising and breaks up the flow of complex flavors around it in a really nice way.

In modern culture, popcorn is a deeply embedded pop-culture touchstone. Grits are one of the few important regional American dishes. It seems impossible that such a simple cross-pollination has never been done in the same way—grits made from corn that's popped instead of ground. But there does not seem to be any record, which is one of the charms of the dish, the element of surprise. Two extremely common foods, both part of our shared heritage, combined to become something new. Something we could maybe call American food.

It's amazing to me how many well-traveled, well-trained cooks have no idea how to pop popcorn. Give them a bag of gellan and they'll spew out ratios. Give them a bag of popcorn and they'll look confused.

So here's what I've learned: Start with good popcorn. Get an heirloom variety if you can. They taste better, even if sometimes they don't pop as uniformly. Red, purple, black, yellow, it doesn't matter, although I'm partial to yellow for this dish. Also popcorn doesn't fry open, it steams, so there has to be enough moisture in the popcorn to work. No stale corn.

Popcorn requires a lot of heat and a lot of oil. In a large pot (the one I use at the restaurant can pop an entire recipe of popcorn at a time), heat a generous amount of vegetable or corn oil to smoking. Add a thin but solid layer of kernels, cover, and shake the pot a few times until you hear the corn starting to pop. Lower the heat to medium-high, shaking often so there are no hot spots, and listen—it's the only way to know when to pull the popcorn. When the popping slows to a trickle, remove the pot from the heat and let it stand one minute. Uncover and pour the popcorn into a bowl, watching for any burnt pieces on the bottom, which should be discarded. If the corn tastes burnt, the grits will taste burnt.

Bring the water, butter and some salt to a simmer. Throw in a big handful of popped kernels, simmer for 30 seconds to a minute, until the corn has softened, and strain through a fine mesh sieve. Transfer the liquid that strains through back to the pot, and bring to a simmer. Add more popcorn. Repeat until all the corn is gone. Add water as necessary, although you shouldn't need to add too much.

Press the softened kernels through a medium strainer basket, discarding the hulls and seeds that cannot be pushed through. Transfer the strained corn, which will look like stiff grits, into a pot. Add the reserved cooking liquid, which should be slightly thickened from the corn starch, and should taste like popcorn (on its own, this makes a nice sauce for steamed fish). Add butter and more water as necessary to make a grits-like texture—we find that slightly on the thicker side is better. It should taste like a cross between grits and a movie theater. Serve with a bowl of buttered popcorn on the side. (You don't need a recipe for that, do you? Good.)

68

PIG HEAD
fresh pole and shelling beans, charred okra, wild sage

This started as a suckling pig head dish in 2007. Another chef, at a large restaurant in town, was using a ton of suckling pigs, but not the heads. So the vendor asked me if I could use them. The heads were terrific, and I made an entire dish around them: torchon glazed with its consommé, fried ear, pickled tongue and a sauce I called "brainaise." I took the brain out of the skull after simmering it in water for the stock, and blended a little bit—just enough to bring out a complex, gamy quality, not enough to be gross—into a mayonnaise sharpened with a generous amount of vinegar.

I wanted to recreate it for this book, but I kept putting it off, until I finally realized that I didn't feel the same way about the dish any more. It was fine then, but it's not where my cooking is now. For one thing, I didn't think the world needed yet another deconstructed animal dish (Beef three ways! Lamb duo!). Also the sauce had started appearing on other menus, so it was time to move on.

There are so many different ingredients in California, especially during the summer, that it's not possible to use them all at one time. Because of the nature of our menu and the focus of our dishes, every season we leave many products untouched. Each year I try to pick out a few things that I've never worked with before, so that our knowledge is always expanding.

This was the summer of okra for me. I remember walking though the market and seeing beautiful red and green okra at one vendor's stall, upside down and standing at attention in their little green cartons, and all of a sudden I felt in a visceral way that I had to cook with them. At another stand there were several varieties of fresh pole and shelling beans, chives and Padrón peppers. And that was how the dish was born.

It's a brightly flavored, generous dish. There are overtones of the South, a whisper of succotash, with tiny, aromatic leaves of wild sage adding savory punctuation. It's not a dish that says, look at how many cool things I can do with a pig head. It says, in a quiet way, I put a few things on the plate that I think taste good together.

Remove the skin, fat and flesh of a mature pig head, leaving it intact. Salt generously on both sides, and roll tightly in plastic to form a log with no air holes. Seal in a vacuum bag and cook in a circulator for 12 hours at 150°F (65°C), until tender. Cool by plunging into an ice bath for at least 20 minutes. Refrigerate for at least a day, and then shave tissue-thin slices just before serving.

Wrap the sad, denuded head in cheesecloth, blanch once in boiling water for 20 seconds, and then cook in simmering water, just enough to cover, with a charred onion and a chopped carrot, for 3 to 4 hours. When the stock is flavorful, strain.

For the bean purée cook fresh cranberry beans in the pork stock–start with about twice as much pork stock as beans by volume. Add salt and cook until the beans are very tender. If there is a surplus of pork stock left when the beans are cooked, reduce a bit–but watch for saltiness. Blend with fruity olive oil and just a little lemon juice. It should be a fairly thick purée.

Sauté the Padróns in a generous amount of pure olive oil and salt over high heat for a few minutes, until just softened. Cool, remove the stem but leave with seeds intact, and finely chop. Mix with equal parts smoked oil* and good, fruity olive oil, and balance with champagne vinegar. It should be bracingly acidic. Season with salt, it will need a lot.

To serve: Cook a few kinds of shelling beans in salted water until tender, and then cool down in their cooking liquid. "Tender" means creamy and delicious, keeping in mind that they will firm up a bit as they cool. Please don't undercook the beans. So yucky.

Cook yellow wax and haricots verts separately in their own pots of well-salted water until just tender, then cool on a sheet tray lined with parchment. Dice in even ¼-inch (5-mm) pieces.

Season the okra with pure olive oil and salt over very high heat, leaving it raw in the center. Slice ⅛-inch (2-mm) thick. Fry tiny leaves of wild sage in vegetable oil over medium-high heat (about 350°F [180°C]) until crisp, drain on paper, and season with salt. (We use a kind of wild sage that has fruity, eucalyptus-like notes.)

Spread a spoonful of the Padrón vinaigrette in the center of a shallow bowl, and dot with 3 small piles of cranberry bean purée, about a scant teaspoon each. Cover with 2 slices of the pig head, filling the bottom of the plate and sprinkle with coarse salt.

Make a salad of the diced yellow wax beans and haricot verts, some julienned raw romano beans, minced chives, and the various cooked shelling beans. Season the salad with red wine vinegar, fruity olive oil, salt and black pepper. The salad should have the sharp taste of vinegar, yet not so much that it drowns out the beans. Scatter everything across the top of the pig, add 5 slices of charred okra, and 7 to 8 pieces of wild sage.

*Smoked oil is a kitchen staple, and so easy to make. Put pure olive oil in an uncovered bowl. Smoke in a smoker. That's it. It has many, many uses.

70

CARROTS ROASTED IN COFFEE BEANS
mandarin, roman mint

Coi is part of a well-established tradition of restaurants that serve expensive tasting menus. We are mindful of that history, but there are some aspects of an haute cuisine dining experience that feel more symbolic than heartfelt, like building the menu around a procession of luxury ingredients. Products like truffles and caviar are expensive, but they aren't hard to find or challenging to prepare. They don't carry any particular emotional value for me, just the wan connotation of a bygone era when waiters wore white gloves. Nothing wrong with that, it's just not how I cook.

I find it much more challenging—and rewarding—to construct an extraordinary dish out of ordinary ingredients. Making something commonplace seem special requires hard work, imagination and discipline. Failure is always close by, and under the best of circumstances there will be those that complain about being served carrots rather than truffles.

The farmers' markets and the different farms that we work with directly bring us flavors from diverse ecosystems and soil types, which allow us greater range of expression than if we used products from only one area or farm. This way of sourcing ingredients provides both challenges and inspiration. Sometimes the products I expect aren't there, and we have to change the menu. Other times, as in this dish, something new arrives when I wasn't expecting it, and I build a dish around it. I like to be surprised sometimes, to be forced by circumstance to improvise. Some of my best ideas happen under pressure, when I'm forced to cook spontaneously.

You don't expect to find mandarins in the middle of the summer, but there is one grower who is farther south, and his seasons start and end later than anyone else we work with. This dish started with a need for a vegetable dish between the pig head and the abalone, and a new crop of screamingly good mandarins.

The carrots roasted in coffee beans were already part of our repertoire (see page 194), and it seemed like it would be a brilliant pairing. Carrot and mandarin are classic, and so we thought of combining their juices in a broth, with a few drops of rice wine vinegar and some salt to sharpen the flavors. The coffee would add earthiness and substance to the sweetness of the carrots. For the garnish, roman mint that I grow at home. Roman mint has tiny leaves and flowers with explosive flavor, a little wild and perfect to finish the dish.

I remember taking Alexandra to a grand old Parisian hotel restaurant a few years back. There was an acre of space around each table, and waiters in suits danced a kind of ballet. There were rivers of cream and mountains of butter and truffles, and by the end we wanted nothing more than the strongest digestif we could get our hands on. We had a better, fresher, more exciting dinner at L'Astrance the night before, but I was glad that we went, for the same reason that we saw the gold dome and majestic lawns of Les Invalides. Tradition has its place.

Clean the carrots well, but leave the skin on. Use big or small carrots, of any color, just use ones that are sweet. Toss them with a little pure olive oil and salt, and place them on a bed of dark roasted coffee beans in a covered container. Cook in a 350°F (180°C) oven, shaking the pan occasionally, until the carrots are very tender. Don't undercook the carrots, as their sweetness will not be fully revealed. Remove to a plate or baking sheet and let cool. Cut as you like.

To serve, slice small rounds of young carrots, or the tips of a larger one—not too finely or you will lose the texture—and season with rice wine vinegar and salt, kind of a quick pickle. You will need three slices per dish.

Warm the cooked carrots in a low oven, covered, until just warm. Combine the carrot juice and mandarin juice. Season with rice wine vinegar and salt until the juice is on the sweeter side, with gentle yet persistent acidity. You might need to add more carrot or more mandarin juice, depending on the taste. Heat until just warm, check seasoning again and spoon some broth in a bowl. Drizzle in half a spoonful of fruity olive oil, and arrange the carrots in the bowl. Top with slices of the pickled carrot, and leaves and flowers of roman mint.

MONTEREY BAY ABALONE

nettle-dandelion salsa verde, spicy breadcrumbs, wild fennel flowers

The emotion of home cooking is something that I hope is always in our food at the restaurant. Cooking for family and friends is one of the most primal ways to show caring and love. But I also learn things cooking at home—when I'm relaxed, not trying too hard, working with whatever ingredients are at hand in limited time and space—that inform our cooking at the restaurant.

This dish started with something I made for Alexandra for Valentine's Day several years ago, when it happened to fall on a Monday and I could actually be there to celebrate. I steamed sweet, aromatic bintje potatoes, and then peeled and sliced them. We had a bunch of dandelion greens in the refrigerator, so for the sauce I made a kind of salsa verde by blanching and chopping the greens, and seasoning them with shallot, caper, lemon juice and olive oil. The greens swelled as they absorbed the liquid. Their form gave body to the sauce, the bitterness mingling with the acid and salt to create a new, vibrant flavor. I garnished the dish with a few herbs and flowers from our garden. It was the first time I made a sauce like that, but not the last.

We don't have a fish course exactly, because we normally don't serve fish. Abalone is usually our fish course, and it sits a course or two before the meat, in a nod both to tradition and the shape of the menu. This is a fresh, summery abalone dish with a salsa verde of dandelion and nettles. The nettles soften the bitterness of the dandelion greens, and add a nutty, earthy note. The abalone is thinly sliced and cooked very quickly—about twenty seconds—on the plancha. The intense heat gives the abalone a smoky char that heightens its flavor, and the fast cook keeps it tender. We toss it with lemon juice and top with a spicy breadcrumb-almond mixture, lemon zest and wild fennel flowers.

Wild fennel is one of our most important native plants, no less special for being common. We use it throughout its life cycle, from tiny sprouts to green buds and mature yellow flowers, and we even dry it for the winter. You can make this dish almost year-round with dried fennel flowers, but we only serve it in late summer, when we can get them fresh.

For the salsa verde, cure the minced shallots in champagne vinegar and salt for 20 minutes. Blanch the dandelion greens and nettles in different pots of salted water. Use the entire leaf and stem of the dandelion greens, and only the leaves and very small stems of the nettles. They should be tender but not slimy—you're not making a purée. Rinse in cold water over a strainer to cool. Squeeze out all of the water and chop, keeping the dandelions and nettles separate. In a mixing bowl, combine the cured shallots, lemon juice, fruity olive oil and minced caper berries. Add the greens and season with salt. The greens will absorb a LOT of oil. If the dandelions are very bitter, use less; if they're meek, use more. If you make it ahead then store it in the refrigerator. Re-check the seasoning before serving, it will change a lot.

Toast crustless levain bread at 300°F (150°C), until hardened. At the same time that the bread is cooking, toast the almonds to golden brown. Cool and chop finely. Grind the bread in a food processor to make crumbs. Transfer to a bowl and add the chopped almonds, a little red Padrón chile powder, enough fruity olive oil to make it nice to eat, and salt.

To serve, toss the abalone with enough pure olive oil to coat, and spread out on a small tray. Season with salt and a little pepper. Sear on a hot plancha for about 20 seconds, tossing often, and then remove to a bowl. It should be tender, with a charred flavor from the grill.

Toss the abalone in lemon juice. Spoon a circle of the salsa verde in the center of a bowl (extra points if the inside of the bowl looks kinda like the inside of an abalone shell), and mound the abalone on top. Sprinkle with breadcrumbs, zest a little lemon on top, and with scissors cut the wild fennel flowers and scatter over everything.

POACHED AND GRILLED LAMB
chard leaves and stems, garum, rosemary

We don't cook a lot of meat. This will be clear as you flip through the book. Each night we offer only a few dishes that involve protein, and only one or two of those proteins are meat. But even though the dishes on our menu are mostly made from plants, we always serve a proper meat course.

This dish started with chard stems. Star Route Farms had begun harvesting beautiful gold chard, and it reminded me of Provence, where they often use the stems. I have no idea how the garum (a traditional fermented anchovy sauce from Italy) came into play, but it made sense: lamb, chard, anchovy, olive oil, typical summer flavors of Southeast France, where the Italian influence is strong.

A lot of young cooks today spurn sauces as old-fashioned or uncool, which is too bad; sauce is the backbone of a dish. It's the glue that connects disparate components, or amplifies focused flavors. It could be a solid sauce, like a gel. It could be a vegetable juice or vinaigrette. Or, as in this dish, it could be a sauce that looks familiar but tastes totally new. The sauce is a meat jus that is rethought from the bottom up, carefully constructed in theory and difficult to make in practice, and which shows the skill and intuition of the cook. A sauce on which the success of the entire dish rests.

We use golden chard stems, and cook them with garum, vegetable stock and olive oil. The resulting liquid—vegetal, sweet and slightly funky—is combined with a well-made natural jus. Half and half. Then we do what you're never supposed to do: Boil the shit out of it. The reduction concentrates the flavors, intensifies the sweetness and creates a temporary emulsion, the olive oil leaking out in discrete droplets around the edges. We add champagne vinegar during the reduction to balance the richness of the jus and the sweetness of the vegetable stock. In the end it looks and feels light, but tastes intensely savory.

This is an easy to understand dish that you think you've seen a million times: lamb, natural sauce, a few greens. The grill adds complex aromatics to the lamb, which jump off the plate, the smell of lightly charred meat mingling with fermented aromas of garum and vinegar simmered into the lamb juices, a sensation at once familiar and strange.

Even though I don't cook (or eat) much of it, I have strong feelings about meat cookery. For meat that's cooked to temperature (as opposed to braised or confit) like this lamb, I like to cook it once, without cooling, as you would with sous vide. I think the taste is fresher and the meat is juicier. Often times, like here, we cook in two stages, first at low temperature and then finishing on a hot grill. This allows us to control doneness, and also the internal temperature, which should be high enough to activate the juices. Meat that's overly rested is boring to eat, like some abstraction of perfection. I like a sheen of moisture and fat shimmering across the top of the meat, the juices bursting when chewed.

Trim the lamb, but leave plenty of fat. Don't like fat? Choose another animal. Lamb without fat is no fun. At Coi we French (remove the fat and clean the bone) only about 1 inch (2 cm) at the top of the bone. It's a nod to tradition, and to show that we know how to do it, but we want to leave the best, most fatty part of the rack attached to the loin, because it tastes great.

Brown the scraps of bones and meat deeply. The intensity will be tempered by the other ingredients in the sauce. Add the onion and the carrot and cook, stirring occasionally, for 10 minutes, until the vegetables are softened and a little browned. Add the white wine and be sure to scrape up the fond, the bits of meat that cling to the bottom of the pan. It's the good stuff. When the wine has reduced almost to nothing, add the AP stock and simmer until flavorful, but don't skim. Strain through a chinois and reduce in a pot that's taller than it is wide—you want as little surface area as possible. Reduce, skimming, until it achieves sauce consistency, just thick enough to cling to the meat. Don't season it.

Cut the leaves off the chard stems, and trim the leaves into 1 to 2-inch (2.5 to 5-cm) pieces. Peel the stems. Combine the vegetable stock, pure olive oil and garum, season with salt, and vacuum in a bag with the chard stems. Steam at 185°F (85°C), until the stems are tender, about 45 minutes. Cool and slice into ½-inch (1-cm) pieces. Reserve in the cooking liquid.

To serve, blend the rosemary and pure olive oil, reserving a piece of rosemary for the sauce. Put the oil in a metal container and warm to 150°F (65°C) by setting the container inside a water bath controlled by a circulator. Put a mesh rack at the bottom. Salt the rack of lamb and let it stand 20 minutes at room temperature to melt the salt, before dropping it into the oil. Cook to a uniform pink inside, 30 to 45 minutes. Remove the lamb and grill over charcoal to brown the outside; to raise the internal temperature to make it juicy; and to give the fat and meat a whiff of smoke.

While the lamb is grilling, simmer the chard leaves with the cooked stems, salt and a little water and fruity olive oil, covered, until tender. Drain on a paper towel and then arrange on one side of the plate.

Make the sauce by combining equal parts lamb jus and chard cooking liquid, and reduce at a rapid boil. This will temporarily emulsify most (but not all) of the oil into the sauce. Reduce it until the flavor is concentrated, adding the reserved piece of rosemary towards the end. Season with champagne vinegar and more garum if necessary. It should be light and flavorful, sweet and sour, complex from the fermented fish. When it's right the parts meld into an indivisible whole—it's hard to explain, but there's an "aha" moment where it suddenly becomes a great sauce. This is a difficult sauce to make perfectly, and it has to be done in the moment, because it will change quickly. Ladle a spoonful over the chard to dress it, and 2 more next to it for the lamb. Slice the lamb into chops, and lay them in their sauce, not touching the chard.

FRESH MIXED MILK CHEESE
fig steeped in beet juice, burnt fig leaf oil

A few years back, New York chef David Chang made a comment in an onstage interview (which was taken out of context and blown out of proportion) that all chefs in San Francisco know how to do is to put figs on a plate. Naturally every chef in the Bay Area got a little bent out of shape.

The reaction was more revealing than the comment itself, which was pretty accurate. At that time, the local food culture skewed more towards rustic peasant food than refined cuisine, not only in chefs' cooking styles but in diners' tastes. At Coi we struggled for years to fill our restaurant, because we were perceived as different, weird. What Dave said in jest from afar, I felt acutely up close.

This dish started as a bit of a joke about the whole thing. I poached the figs in reduced, sweetened beet juice, and paired them with fresh cheese. It turned out to be an inspired combination, the beet lending the fig an earthy gravitas.

I used the poaching liquid from the figs, balanced with a little lemon juice and rice wine vinegar, for the sauce. I added oil infused with fig leaves that had been barely touched with a blowtorch to deepen the flavor. Fig leaves taste uncannily like coconut, and the oil combined with the fig-beet liquid to create a surprisingly exciting, exotic-tasting sauce.

The cheese is a mixture of three kinds of fresh cheese, made with goat's, cow's and sheep's milk. For the dish to work, each of the cheeses needs to be made precisely and with the best ingredients. When it's executed properly it becomes, as if by magic, far better than the sum of its individual parts. The different milks deliver a lovely balance of sweetness and gentle lactic acidity, and it's even better the next day.

Things have changed quite a bit in San Francisco, which now supports what seems to be the highest per capita number of ambitious, tasting menu-only restaurants in the country. My thoughts about the dish have changed as well—it's actually a pretty honest expression of the kind of food that I like. It's a perfect late summer cheese course, sweet and light and fun.

The cheese itself came from trying to use a few odds and ends of different products we had in the restaurant, and a little bit of inspiration. For a long time I only made it myself, because I enjoyed it, and because I wanted to learn about the different ways that it changed every day, depending on proportions. The ratio I found to be perfect is in the recipe, but this cheese is designed to accommodate whatever you have around. Any ratio works, it's more a question of what flavor you prefer.

To make the cow's milk cheese, bring the milk and cream to 180°F (82°C), and then add the distilled vinegar, a spoonful at a time, until it breaks into curds and whey. Ladle into a colander lined with two layers of cheesecloth to drain. Add the sheep's milk fromage blanc and fresh goat cheese and let them all drain together. When the cheese is moist but not wet, transfer to a bowl. Stir to combine and season with salt. Refrigerate. It gets better as it sits, up to a day.

The figs should be densely sweet, not at all watery. Missions and unusual strains are best. (Knoll Farms, from whom we've bought our figs for years, have several oddball strains of fig, often only a tree or 2 of each, growing on their 18 acres in Brentwood. I love the Melissa variety, which they named after a woman in an Allman Brothers' song who was as sweet, presumably, as a fig.) I'm less enthusiastic about Turkey figs, and definitely not Adriatic. In all cases, if you find a tiny drop of syrup at the bottom of the fig, it means that the fig is very ripe.

If the figs are soft, cut them in half and lay them out in a lipped metal pan just big enough to hold them. Reduce the beet juice by half, and add sugar if necessary—it should be sweet. Season the liquid with salt and rice wine vinegar to balance the sweetness, and then pour the warm liquid over the figs. If the figs are a little sturdier, then gently poach them whole in a pot in the reduced and seasoned beet juice until they're tender. In either case let them cool at room temperature in the juice. Once cooled, remove 125 g of juice (about 8 spoonfuls, plus a little for tasting) and season with lemon juice, rice wine vinegar and more salt to make a sauce. The earthiness of the beet should recede, and the sauce should glow as though lit from within.

For the fig leaf oil, put the fig leaves in a metal bowl and burn a few spots with a torch. Don't go crazy—it's just to give a little complexity, not to reduce the leaves to ashes. Blend the leaves with pure olive oil on high for a minute, then transfer to a container and refrigerate for a few hours. Strain through cheesecloth.

To serve, scoop a spoonful of cheese on one half of a shallow bowl. On the other side, drizzle a spoonful of seasoned fig cooking liquid and a scant spoonful of fig leaf oil. Place half of a fig on top of the sauce, and season it with a little flaky salt on top.

LIME MARSHMALLOW
coal-toasted meringue

So many tasting menus end in a whimper, the energy of the savory menu petering out into sweet, vapid surrender. Or worse, a succession of dishes that try so hard to be creative that they lose all sense of pleasure. That is the deadliest sin, because a dessert has no reason to exist but for pleasure.

This falls at that important moment in the menu when savory transitions to sweet. The interplay between the two throughout the menu is constant, so it's not a complete about-face. But, perhaps because the menu is so nuanced, we want that moment to be demarcated clearly, defiantly, to say that it's time to pay attention: we're about to accelerate again.

This is a fierce dish. At the bottom is a marshmallow, but frozen and mixed with an insane amount of lime juice. The acidity is electric, almost punishing. It's a complete inversion of the saccharine pillows that the name conjures up.

But from looking at the top of the dish, it does look something like a marshmallow—one that's been toasted over an open fire. On top of the lime marshmallow is a lime meringue, which we brand with a piece of charcoal.

All food is about memory. But some dishes tap a fat vein of cultural commonality pulsing under the surface, releasing shared experiences full of emotion. This is one of them. It's a childhood memory dish for grown-up palates, turning a youthful, innocent form into a train wreck of sweet, sour and burnt.

It's also my very favorite dessert we've ever served at Coi.

To make the marshmallow, start by making the ginger syrup. Heat the sugar and water until the solids are dissolved, and cool. Add the ginger essential oil.

For the marshmallow, put the ginger syrup and the bloomed gelatin in a mixer fitted with a whisk. Make the warm syrup by combining the trimoline, water and sugar and heat to 233°F (112°C). Add to the mixer while mixing at medium speed, and then increase speed to high and mix until it's completely cool. Spread it out on a sheet pan lined with a Silpat for at least 3 hours, until it's set.

Blend the marshmallow, sugar, lime juice and a pinch of salt. Freeze in a Pacojet beaker overnight. Spin it at least an hour before serving, so that it has time to set up. (The frozen lime marshmallow was inspired by a similar technique that Laurent Gras and pastry chef Shawn Gawle developed at L20.)

Combine the egg whites, citric acid and sugar, and heat over simmering water until the temperature reaches 113°F (45°C). Transfer it to a mixer, and start by whipping on slow speed, gradually increasing over time, until it cools and develops into thick ribbons. Season with a few drops of lime essential oil and salt. Transfer to a plastic pastry bag.

To serve, take a frozen bowl out of the freezer and scoop a large spoonful of the marshmallow into it. Cover completely with the meringue, adding a little more on top than the sides—the charcoal will push it down.

Now the fun part. You have your charcoal red-hot and glowing all angry-like, yes? We use high quality Japanese charcoal that is thin and cylindrical. Pick up the charcoal with your tweezers. (Small tweezers are great for control, but dangerous, and inevitably you—by which I mean me—will forget what you were holding seconds after returning the charcoal to the fireplace and touch the ends, burning your fingers, stupidly and repeatedly. You may want to use tongs.) Blow on the piece of charcoal away from the food, making it even hotter and removing any ash. If the charcoal is not screaming hot then it will stick to the meringue. Press it into the meringue, starting on one side and then rolling it slowly to the other, smoke rising off of the meringue the entire time, keeping it pressed in for a few seconds to get a deeply brown color. Zest a little lime on top.

STRAWBERRIES AND CREAM
tiny herbs

Simple is not a simple word. In the context of food, too often it is used to mean facile, uninteresting, plain. In fact, it is nothing of the sort. Simple is hard to understand and hard to execute. When the elements of a dish are stripped down to their bare essence, when there is nothing to hide behind and nothing extraneous, that is, in a way, a simple construct. But it is hardly simplistic.

I use the word a lot, always as a compliment, as something to which to aspire. I think our dishes are simple, in that the forms are easy to understand. It's cooking that reaches out an open palm to be grasped, that offers the promise of accessibility. In language terms, we don't use big words when small ones will suffice. We try to communicate something true, in the most immediate, powerful way possible.

But surface understandability does not mean that there is not a wealth of meaning underneath. We try to create dishes that can be enjoyed only for what they present on the surface, yet also reward closer examination.

Sometimes, though, we really just make simple, delicious food, with no deeper meaning. I think a long menu requires moments of unthinking, sybaritic pleasure. The tomato, which began the dinner, was one such moment. This dish is another.

Simple does not mean easy. Like the tomato dish, this is a technically precise, time-intensive process. Perfect raw strawberries are compressed and then glazed in a pectin-based gel of seasoned strawberry juice. Some of that strawberry juice is made into a sauce. A few little herbs are added for interest. On the side, fresh cream ice cream with no egg, that tastes like sweet cream and nothing else. Strawberries and cream. Simple.

To make the ice cream, heat the milk to 130°F (55°C) with all other ingredients except the cream. Off the heat, mix in the cream. Blend with a hand blender, and freeze in a Pacojet beaker overnight. Spin just before serving.

For the strawberry liquid, combine the strawberries and sugar in a covered mixing bowl and hold over 98°F (37°C) water for 4 hours. Strain the resulting juice through a chinois, pressing the strawberries to extract all of their liquid. Discard the strawberries, which have given everything.

For the compression liquid, combine the strawberry liquid and Meyer lemon juice, and season with salt—not to make it salty, just to bring up the flavor. Compress the strawberries once at 100% power with the compression liquid. After the compression, remove the strawberries and then strain the liquid. Season the liquid with fruity olive oil, Meyer lemon juice and salt. This is your sauce.

To glaze the compressed strawberries, mix the sugar and pectin and dissolve in the water and remaining strawberry juice. Heat to 130°F (55°C). When fully dissolved, bring to a boil and transfer to another container. Keep the temperature around 120°F (50°C), and dip the compressed strawberries in the pectin gel twice, allowing the glaze on the berries to set between each dip (about 60 seconds). While you are glazing the strawberries hold them on a wire mesh rack, to allow the extra glaze to drip through. When the glaze is set transfer to a sheet tray lined with parchment paper and hold at room temperature.

To serve, put a few bowls in the freezer for the ice cream. Place 3 glazed strawberries in the center of the plate and sauce around them with a spoonful of the reserved sauce. Add a few herbs on top of the strawberries, whatever is sweet, floral and aromatic, nothing bitter. Serve with a scoop of fresh cream ice cream in frozen bowls on the side.

Note: You may not need to compress the strawberries, depending on their quality. This spring we put the dish on the menu, without the ice cream, as a transition course after the meat. The early season strawberries were intensely flavored, with both high sugar and high acidity, and needed nothing in the way of seasoning. So we glazed them raw.

PASSION FRUIT BABA
white chocolate, honeycomb, shiso

White chocolate is a terribly misunderstood ingredient. It's often criticized for being boring, but it was never meant to stand on its own, the way dark chocolate does. White chocolate is cocoa butter without the cocoa powder, and therefore not really a chocolate at all. Its lack of a strong point of view makes it perfect as a sidekick, an assistant, something that can hang back, away from the spotlight, keeping things tight while the ingredients around it shine.

In this dish, white chocolate holds the center of a dynamic relationship between passion fruit and shiso. The dish is based on a baba, a traditional French cake soaked with rum. Matt grew up eating passion fruit in Hawaii, so when he found a local farmer selling it, he had to put it on the menu. In this version, he replaced the rum with passion fruit juice, which turns the cake from boozy to floral. The white chocolate is cooked into a kind of frosting, dotted with pieces of honeycomb, and covered with a crisp, lacy piece of baked pain de mie brushed with melted beeswax. Bread on bread.

The edges of a shiso leaf always remind me of its taste, jagged and angular. We make a purée of shiso and water, so strong that it seems like too much, softened with a bit of sweetness and sharpened with a little salt. It needs the intensity to punch through the passion fruit, its minty/cumin notes lifting the dish. The other sauce is passion fruit juice, thickened to amplify its effect (the thicker a sauce, the longer it stays on the tongue and the greater the impact), but otherwise unadulterated, sour and punchy to offset the sweetness of the cake.

When it comes to fruit in California, every year is different. Some years the winters are too warm, the stone fruit trees don't get enough cold time, and the quality suffers. Other times there's a late storm when the trees are flowering and the crop is damaged. Even the quality of the berries go up and down. It's one reason that our desserts change radically from year to year.

There is one constant though: Summer in California means desserts with bright, buoyant flavors based on ripe fruit and herbs. We save dark chocolate for winter, when the markets are bare and the nights are long. In September we have passion fruit dancing with shiso, and tying them together is the white chocolate.

For the baba, mix the water and yeast to make a smooth purée. Mix the flour with the other dry ingredients. In a mixing bowl set with a paddle, combine the yeast paste and eggs, then whisk in the dry ingredients, then the butter. Mix for 5 minutes on low until well incorporated. Cover with plastic, and leave to rise for 1 hour at room temperature. Brush a pullman mold well with melted butter. Place the dough in the mold. Leave to rise for 1 hour at room temperature, or until doubled in size. Bake at 400°F (200°C) for 15 minutes, then turn the oven down to 350°F (180°C) for another 15 minutes. (We use the Combi, which changes temperature very quickly. A normal oven won't be as responsive.) Check doneness by inserting a toothpick. If it comes out clean then it's done. If not then give it a few more minutes.

While the baba is cooking, make the syrup. Bring the water, sugar and dextrose to a boil to dissolve, cool and then add the passion fruit juice. When the baba comes out of the oven, let it stand 15 minutes, and then unmold. Cut the baba into 1½-inch (4-cm) slabs while it's warm, and put the slices side by side on a lipped metal sheet tray. Pour the syrup over the baba and refrigerate. Turn every few hours. The cake can stay in the syrup for up to 48 hours.

For the frosting, combine the milk, cream, Ultra-Tex and egg yolks in a mixing bowl. Place the bowl over a pot of simmering water and whisk until it becomes custardy. Add the white chocolate and stir until melted. Cool.

Thinly slice the pain de mie and bake at 300°F (150°C) until browned and crisp. Grate some beeswax on top, and put back in the oven one minute to melt. Hold at room temperature.

For the shiso sauce, make a syrup by boiling the water and dextrose, and allow it to cool. Blend the shiso leaves with ice and the syrup until the mixture is bright green. Strain through a chinois and blend with a few drops of vegetable oil and xanthan. Season to taste with salt.

Season the passion fruit juice with a tiny bit of salt, and blend with xanthan to thicken.

To serve, drain the cake and cut a 2-inch (5-cm) square piece. Spread white chocolate frosting on top, and dot with a few small pieces of honeycomb. Spoon the shiso and passion fruit sauces into a bowl, and place the cake on top. Break a piece of toasted bread into a shape about the same size as the cake, and place on top of the cake.

CANDIED RASPBERRIES

The first time I dined at a Michelin-starred restaurant I was fourteen. I was living with my family in the southwest part of France, in a little town on the coast called St-Jean-de-Luz. One day we took a drive inland through Basque country, to a restaurant perched on the edge of a hill. We sat on a patio overlooking a lush valley, and from a menu unlike anything I had ever seen I ordered turbot with beurre blanc. I'd eaten plenty of fish by that point, but this was a revelation. The flesh was flavorful, perfectly cooked and moist. The sauce had a texture just thick enough to cling to the fish, the flavor bright but balanced. It was the first time that I understood that food could be extraordinary, that a restaurant could create a memory that could last forever.

I've eaten in a lot of nice restaurants since then. I've had three-course menus and a fifty-course menu, and everything in between. I have noticed little correlation between the length of the menu and the success of the meal, but I've seen a lot of connection between a great meal and its appropriate form, the kind of synergy that requires self-knowledge and honesty on the part of the chef. You can't cook someone else's food any more than you can sing in their voice, and part of a cooking style is the way that the dishes are presented.

The length of a menu directly impacts the composition of the dishes. I like to cook two or three component dishes, tight and focused bursts of ideas and flavor. Those only work as part of a series. The format allows me the freedom not to worry about piling a lot of food on each plate just to satiate hunger.

Our menu is a little on the shorter side by today's standards, but we're in a city, not a country idyll, and the three hours that the meal encompasses already strains the attention span of many locals. A longer menu would only alienate them further.

We're not a flashy restaurant. We don't have a lot of bells and whistles, just good ingredients and sensitive cooking. A modestly sized menu suits us. Eleven or so courses allows me enough time to create a progression that weaves a spell over the table, the ebb and flow of dishes creating a kind of story with a beginning, a middle and an end.

This is the end. It's a time that traditionally the chef at a fancy restaurant digs deep into his bag of tricks to produce a flourish of pastries and candies, called mignardises, to finish the meal. We don't do that. Really, who has room after a long menu for a procession of sweets? An array of ornate delicacies can distract from each other and from what came before, which should be strong enough to stand on its own merits without any last minute lobbying.

We also don't believe in shelf-stable food. A magazine once asked us to mail them a selection of mignardises for a tasting in New York for an article, which made me laugh—every one that we create is highly perishable by design. Mignardises are traditionally storage items like dipped chocolates, which can be made ahead in big batches and doled out over time. Ours, like a crisp honey-almond candy served straight from the freezer, fall apart minutes after being served. The rest of the meal represents a precise moment in time, so I don't know why the last bite wouldn't as well.

This version is the result of an expensive and intensely labor-intensive process that captures the essence of summer. Perfect raspberries are carefully selected and preserved under a thin, crunchy shell of sugar. They don't look impressive but they taste great, which suits us just fine.

The hardest part of making these raspberries is choosing the right ones. They have to be firm, although not hard or under-ripe. There cannot be any broken cells, or the raspberry will weep juice and the shell will sog. We usually yield less than 50% under the best of circumstances. (In my ideal world there would be no berry baskets, where the bottom layer, by the time I buy them, has been so mangled that they are only good for sauce. All berries would be laid side by side on a paper towel in a container that was undisturbed on the journey from farm to restaurant. I mean, a guy can dream, can't he?)

Place the egg whites and gelatin in a metal bowl set over a pot of simmering water, and heat to 120°F (50°C). When the gelatin has melted, stir and remove from the heat. Using a pastry brush, carefully cover each raspberry with a thin layer of egg white. Roll the raspberry around on a piece of parchment to remove the excess. Let the raspberries stand until the gelatin has half-set and they are a little tacky. Roll them in sugar. Transfer to a wire mesh rack, and let them stand for at least 20 minutes. Roll them again in sugar and hold on the rack at cool room temperature. They'll last a few hours, if you can wait that long.

04

A SELECTION

OF RECIPES

2006

PINK GRAPEFRUIT
ginger, tarragon, cognac, black pepper

In 2001 a friend introduced me to a natural perfumer named Mandy Aftel. Mandy was looking for a chef to collaborate with her on a book about the relationship between taste and smell. She brought oils with her, essences of plants, which were far more intense and expressive than anything I'd worked with. Although they'd been around for thousands of years, there was no modern context, no guide for how to use them in food and drinks. So we wrote one together, a weird and wonderful book called *Aroma* that combined perfume and food recipes. It sold about eight copies.

The most important thing I learned from working with Mandy was not the use of essential oils in food, but the relationship between taste, smell, emotion and memory, all of which are locked together in our limbic system, our prehistoric brain. Our sense of smell is the only sense that goes directly to our nervous system, unmediated by our cerebral cortex. It's the reason that what we eat and smell leaves us with such strong, enduring memories. Every time I cook now I try to use that relationship to make the experience more meaningful and the food more connective.

This dish came out of my collaboration with Mandy. It's from an early menu, when I was still finding my way. Knowing how conservative the customer base was in our area, we had opened with simpler, more mainstream dishes, which met with mixed reviews. It seemed like people wanted, or expected, a more creative style of cuisine. This was the first dish where we started to push boundaries.

The concept is simple. There is a bowl of pink grapefruit salad with tarragon and cognac; pink grapefruit sorbet; and a pink grapefruit mousse flavored with ginger and black pepper essential oils on top. By itself it's delicious, and hits all of the sweet/sour/salt/bitter notes that would flow through the rest of the meal. It was a good first course.

What made it a great one is that Mandy formulated a perfume with the same flavors, diluted in oil, and we served a drop on the plate next to the bowl, for the diners to rub on their wrists and smell. Because most of what we taste is what we smell, the diners' perception of the taste of the dish changed after smelling the perfume. If aroma is largely about memory, the experience of smelling perfume while eating food was certainly memorable for many people. Some of them freaked out (mostly guys). Others giggled, which was fine—it was supposed to be not only provocative, but fun. Writers wrote about it. Eventually I got bored and took the dish off the menu.

Seven years later, creativity has become an important part of our cooking. That's what people come for—not just delicious food, but also a sense of discovery. When this dish came to feel like a relic, a talisman of a bygone era, I retired it. Then one day in 2012, Matt decided to revive it as a dessert. It enjoyed a second life at the end of the menu, lightly reworked, although even he came to agree that its original form was pretty good.

The day before, make the sorbet by combining all of the ingredients, and seasoning with salt and lemon juice to diminish the sweetness—it should capture the sharpness of the grapefruit. Freeze in a Pacojet beaker overnight and spin 30 minutes before serving.

To make the foam, heat 50 g of grapefruit juice with sugar and honey. Whisk until the sugar and honey are dissolved, and then stir in the gelatin. Combine the grapefruit-gelatin mixture with the rest of the grapefruit juice and the other remaining ingredients in a bowl set into an ice bath. Add the grapefruit, ginger and black pepper essential oils one drop at a time, tasting with each addition; the strength of each will vary. Season with salt—it's meant to be savory, so it takes quite a bit of salt, and it might need extra lemon juice as well, depending on the sweetness of the grapefruit. When set, transfer to a siphon and charge twice. Refrigerate for at least 2 hours.

For the grapefruit salad, cut the grapefruits into supremes, and cut the supremes into small pieces. Season with chopped tarragon, cognac, a touch of simple syrup, salt and black pepper. It should be sweet, sour and savory, with pronounced licorice notes from the tarragon and a bit of burn from the cognac and pepper. This can be made up to 30 minutes in advance.

For the Coi perfume, combine all the ingredients with the fractionated coconut oil (a kind of neutral oil used in perfume making). The recipe will be close, but since the oils are living ingredients, you'll probably need to tweak it a bit. Try it on your skin to make sure that it's right.

To serve, place a spoonful of grapefruit salad in the bottom of a bowl with a little bit of its liquid. Place a small ball of grapefruit sorbet on top of the salad. Barely but completely cover the sorbet with enough pink grapefruit foam so that it looks like a pink blob from the top. The discovery of what lies underneath is part of the fun of the dish. Serve on a plate with a dot of Coi perfume on the side. Tell people to rub it on their wrists, and watch them make funny faces.

NOW
FULLY
LET US
AND

CHILLED ENGLISH PEA SOUP
our buttermilk, meyer lemon, nasturtium

I met Diane Goodman the year that we opened Babette's. She was a farm consultant and advocate, a lover of growing things and the people who grew them. She spoke in quick, explosive bursts, punctuating her sentences with vigorous hand gestures, expounding passionately on cooking and vegetables and dirt and farms and the life force of plants. She was, in many ways, a kindred spirit.

Walking a field with her was a joy. I loved the moments of discovery, when we found a row of flowering herbs that had been forgotten, or a ripe, fragrant heirloom tomato, the taste of which the farmer had developed over many years of seed saving. I remember one time making a lunch—just a big salad, really—from what was growing around us, and sitting with her and the farmer, who was a friend to us both, in the middle of his field in the late September sun, eating and talking. It was a moment of perfect happiness.

Through the first few years at Babette's we spoke often. She taught me about how things grew, and why there were flavor and intensity variations in the same plants from different farms. She taught me about water, seeds and soil, and how growing was a process, kind of like cooking, dependent on the skill of the farmer to coax the best qualities out of each plant. When we tasted together Diane helped me learn to trust my instincts, to analyze what was actually in front of me, unmediated by expectation.

We fell out of touch for a few years after I moved back to the city, and then, soon after I opened Coi, I saw her again at the farmers' market. The farmers' market changed everything for me, and it came to dictate how we cook. It reconnected me to the immediacy of the seasons, to those moments when the ingredients were at their most vibrant. Through Diane I met her daughter, Allyson, and Allyson's husband, Laurence. They had opened their restaurant, Nopa, a week after we opened ours. A year later Ally became pregnant, a few months before Alexandra. There were dinners and baby showers and apprehensive phone calls; we shared information about farms and deliveries and diapers.

Diane did much of their restaurant's market purchasing. She knew everyone and, it seemed at times, everything. She pushed, prodded, debated each item, each farm, each product. Were the seascapes or chandlers better today? Had I seen the baby radishes at Marin Roots? Why weren't we using the blood oranges at Paradez? She charmed all the farmers and, whenever I would leave something untasted, she would scold me. She was constitutionally unable to compromise.

She passed away a few years ago, but I still feel her nearby, when I'm walking a farm or sorting through figs in the back of a farmer's truck, in those moments of intense energy when I find an ingredient that crackles with life.

To make this soup you will need peas so fresh and sweet that you could mistake them for candy. And a Thermomix. Without both, this recipe is not for you.

We have made this soup every year since we opened. It is an incredible technique that was, to be honest, dumb luck. And by dumb, I mean me. It took me four years to figure out why it was so good.

Part of the answer is the peas. We only make this soup in the spring, when they're at their best. That's obvious. What's not obvious is the role that the Thermomix plays. It allows me to cook and then blend the soup as part of one continuous activity. But the real trick is that it blends the peas incompletely—it does not break down the outer hull of the pea, which is captured by the chinois when the soup is passed through it. In essence, it peels the peas, keeping only the sweetest part. No other machine will do that.

We've done this soup many ways, but this is my favorite. Some tiny raw peas tossed with ripe, end-of-season Meyer lemon. The sweet, gently cultured buttermilk from making Our Butter (see page 98). Petals of spicy, aromatic nasturtium. Simple, clean and bright.

For the buttermilk mousse, warm the crème fraîche and melt in the gelatin. Combine with the buttermilk and pass through a fine mesh strainer. Season with salt (just enough to bring out the flavor, not so much that the sweetness is diminished), and transfer it to a siphon. Charge it twice. Refrigerate for at least 3 hours.

For the garnish, slice the Meyer lemon thinly, then simmer them in water for 5 seconds. Taste one, and if it's still bitter, cook them again. Repeat as necessary (usually 2 to 3 times is sufficient, otherwise the texture will be compromised, and you don't want to cook out the lemon flavor). Cool, then mince and season with salt, sugar and fresh Meyer lemon juice. It should taste brightly sweet and sour, like a fresh preserve.

For the soup, shell the peas by pressing your thumb and forefinger gently into the seam of the pea pod, which will pop the pod open without damaging what's inside. Pick through the peas, reserving the tiniest ones for garnish.

To make the pea shell infusion, bring the pea shells and water to a strong simmer, and then strain through a chinois.

Put some serving bowls in the refrigerator to chill, then get your ice bath ready: a large metal bowl set into a larger metal bowl filled with ice water, a chinois, a 30-g ladle, a rubber spatula. Bring half vegetable stock and half pea shell infusion to a boil with a little salt, and transfer 300 g to the Thermomix. Heat on speed 1 and temperature 212°F (100°C) until boiling, and then, while the blade is still moving, add enough peas that the blade cannot turn them. Raise the speed to 2 to 2.25, at which point the peas should spin around as if in a whirlpool. Cook briefly, until the peas just turn the corner from raw to barely cooked. Turn up the speed to the highest setting and blend for 1 minute, until the soup is a smooth, bright green purée. Pass through the chinois into the metal bowl, pushing the soup through vigorously with the ladle. When the soup is completely strained, stir constantly until it's cool. Season and refrigerate. Repeat as necessary, combining each batch as they cool. Refrigerate at least an hour, and then season with salt and thin with water as necessary. It should be thick-ish and creamy, but still on the light side. (This soup won't keep, by the way. There's no fat to fix the flavor. Use it the day you make it.)

To serve, toss a spoonful of the small garnish peas with Meyer lemon preserve and put in the bottom of a chilled bowl. Distribute some buttermilk mousse on top, and then scatter nasturtium petals. Pour the soup in front of whoever is eating it. It's prettier that way. And the mousse will drift upward like a floating island.

(I can't give you an exact ratio of peas to liquid because the starch content of peas varies wildly. The tiny, sweet first picking of a field has very little starch, and requires use of less liquid. The big, starchy peas picked at the end of a field's life require more liquid. Also, depending on the sweetness of the vegetable stock and the sweetness of the peas, you may want to adjust the ratio of vegetable stock to pea shell infusion.)

2007

OUR BUTTER

Twelve years ago Soyoung Scanlan showed up at Elisabeth Daniel with a selection of extraordinary cheeses to taste. We became friends, and since then she has been one of our closest and most important collaborators.

A biochemist by schooling, Soyoung moved from Korea to Boston to pursue a doctorate in the sciences. She discovered her passion for cheese while on vacation in France and Italy. After a few years on the East Coast she moved to California with her husband, studied dairy science, and eventually opened her own dairy in the late '90s. Her first production facility was the old space of Laura Chenel, godmother of the artisanal cheese industry and the first American to make French-style goat cheese. Now Soyoung makes cheese out of a tiny building on a farm in Petaluma. Given that she didn't grow up eating it, she might be the most unlikely cheese maker in the country. She is almost certainly the best.

Soyoung is one of the reasons that our food tastes the way that it does. Partly it's her products. The fresh goat cheese—an iconic staple of local cooking—is better than anything I've tried in this country, its flavor pure and round instead of piercingly acidic. The aged cheeses are even better, with marked delicacy and depth. She handles the milk sensitively and makes everything by hand, which allows her to achieve an unusually fine crust. Sometimes she fine-tunes her cheeses—a little richer or more acidic—according to what we need for each dish. Other times she invents something entirely new. Like us, she is both guided by tradition and restlessly searching for something better. Her passion for excellence inspires everyone in the kitchen.

At the end of our first year, Soyoung gave me a small piece of butter that she had made. It was extraordinary. It was also not available for purchase: Her entire production of extra cream went to make butter for The French Laundry. It was Thomas Keller who asked Soyoung to make butter in the first place. So I went to visit her at the dairy, and she showed me how to make butter. The next week, we started making our own.

It was an important development for the kitchen. This sounds silly, even sentimental, but butter-making caused me to start looking at other ingredients and processes that we took for granted, like baking our own bread and making our own vinegars. At first we made sweet butter, until a well-known butter producer visited the restaurant. She sniffed at our butter, calling it too simple. She was right, which we discovered after she was kind enough to send us some of her culture. We began to culture our butter, and also used the starter to make crème fraîche. Eventually we learned to age the butter, a process that Brett Cooper helped to develop.

We've improved our butter-making a little bit every year. I think our butter now is better than what is commercially available in our area. We control the process carefully to get exactly the taste and texture that we like. More than the butter itself, there's something else that is important about the process, a feeling that is hard to explain, that has to do with mastery of a craft, and something more.

When I wrote about our butter-making in 2007, it struck a chord with many people around the country. Readers wrote letters to the paper reminiscing about sitting on the porch at dusk, shaking a jar of cream to make butter. In a way, it evoked memories of a bygone era, one in which we felt more connected to our food, and perhaps to each other. Chefs around the country started to make their own butter as well, and now it's not so uncommon to find housemade butter in a nice restaurant.

A restaurant is not the work of one person. No matter how personal the vision, it is the result of the hard work of many people. Coi has been informed and improved not only by employees, but by friends and family and producers, and I see their influence every day.

Acquire starter culture or active, cultured buttermilk. Two nights before you make the butter, stir 50 g of culture into each liter of cream, cover, and leave at room temperature for 24 hours. The next day, refrigerate the cultured cream for at least a day, and up to 5 days. (It depends on the culture–if you make it often you'll get to know how long it takes for the flavor to develop. It should be pleasantly sour, but not cheesy.)

When the cream is ready, remove it from the refrigerator and transfer to the bowl of an electric mixer fitted with a whisk. Tightly cover the top of the bowl with plastic wrap (trust me) and start the mixer on medium speed. The cream will go through the whipped stage, thicken further and then change color from off-white to pale yellow; this will take at least 15 minutes. When it starts to look pebbly, it's almost done. After another minute the butter will separate, causing the liquid to splash violently against the plastic wrap (aren't you glad it's there?). At this point stop the mixer.

Set a strainer over a bowl. Pour the contents of the mixer into the strainer and let the buttermilk drain through. Strain the buttermilk again, this time through a fine-mesh sieve set over a small bowl; set aside for other purposes. You can hold it for up to a week, and use it to culture more butter, or for making crème fraîche. Once you get into a cycle, you'll always have some cultured cream to work with. If you're not using it right away, freeze it. The culture will die, but it will remain tasty for cooking purposes.

Put the butter back into the mixer, and use a paddle, on very slow speed, to force out more buttermilk. Drain. Repeat. We've learned that good butter-making is about controlling temperature. We use a machine to force out much of the buttermilk and aggregate the fats, because hands will warm up the butter. The less you touch it, the better. (You're wearing gloves, by the way, right?) Transfer the butter to a sheet tray and form it into a rough block. Dunk it in ice water, to wash the buttermilk off the outside, and to cool it down. Wrap the butter in cheesecloth and use it to press the rest of the buttermilk out. The texture should be dense and creamy, with an almost waxy look. Fold in sel gris or another coarse salt. At this point we wrap the butter in cheesecloth, put it in a shallow-lipped container, and vacuum it once on high. If there is still a little buttermilk it will come out around the edges, and we blot it with paper towels. Typically, though, it's completely dry, which is what we want. Buttermilk left in the butter is what causes off-flavors during the secondary aging process.

Pack the butter into a clean container and set in a cool, dark place (we use our wine room), for a few days, or until the taste has fully developed. Wrap and refrigerate.

102

PAN-GRILLED MATSUTAKE
potato-pine needle puree, wood sorrel

This combination was something of a breakthrough, in a small way. For over a year I'd been exploring the ecosystem around my house, the coastal greens, spring flowers and winter herbs. Then one day I took a long look at the pine trees across the street.

It was matsutake season. I'd never cooked with matsutake before, and in fact I had to ask a friend how they were traditionally prepared. I decided on a simple, direct approach—grill in a pan with a little salt, until they're barely juicy but still maintain their firm texture. But I needed something to go with them. I looked at the pine trees, thinking of the way that pine smelled and the mushrooms tasted. It made sense but the pine needed a medium, and the dish needed something creamy—maybe a potato purée, lightened in a siphon. And then I remembered that Mandy had some pretty spectacular pine needle absolute.

The dish came together quickly. I made the purée with waxy potatoes, which improved the flavor over russets, and made the texture just a little denser. A drop or two of the pine needle essence in the potato while blended gave it a resiny, green, woodsy feel, totally transformative. As a garnish I dehydrated the pine needles and ground them with the barest suggestion of pine needle essence, salt, and a pinch of citric acid, to accentuate the natural sourness of the pine.

The dish was just the matsutake, perfectly cooked and seasoned, and the purée, a little pine needle powder on the side. We did the same dish three seasons in a row, but in the back of my mind I wondered if there wasn't one more element that could elevate the combination. In 2010 I found it: Shaved raw matsutake and wood sorrel, sprinkled on top of the purée, adding one more element of natural acidity, another forest note.

This was one of the first dishes that felt like it grew organically out of the natural elements around me. The matsutake and pine seemed to belong together. Which, of course, they did. After I'd put the dish on the menu I learned that matsutake are also called pine mushrooms, because they often grow under pine trees. The Japanese grill them over charcoal scented with pine needles. What I thought was a creative discovery was in fact a cultural standard that's existed for at least hundreds of years, as several friends were happy to tell me. I'm such an idiot sometimes.

It was also a step forward in our constant pruning of non-essential elements from the dish, a minimalism that requires perfection in its ingredients and its cooking, as well as concept and balance—although there still needs to be sensuousness, an element of pleasure, in even the most stripped down of dishes. Perhaps my favorite compliment about this dish came from a Spanish chef a few years ago. At the end of the meal he stopped by the kitchen to say hello. "Man," he said, "it takes a lot of *cojones* to put only mushroom and potato on a plate."

For the pine needle powder, dry fresh pine needles from the tender tips of the branches overnight at 120°F (50°C) in a Combi or dehydrator. Grind them in a spice grinder, adding salt, a drop of pine needle absolute and citric acid to taste—it will enhance the natural acidity of the pine.

To make the purée, peel and cook the potatoes in well-salted water until just tender. Don't overcook them, as they will become dilute, and the starches will dissipate. And don't undercook them either, because undercooked potatoes are gross. Strain the potatoes, reserving the water. In a Thermomix, blend the potatoes, potato water, olive oil, cream and pine absolute to make a smooth, thick purée. Add the pine absolute by the drop—it's strong! It's also not very liquid, so dip a toothpick in the absolute, and then into the potato as it is blending. Taste and repeat as necessary (with a different toothpick each time). Season a little high to compensate for the aeration. Strain through a chinois into a siphon. Charge twice and hold warm.

Trim 2 small pieces off of the outside of 4 matsutake caps to make them flat on the sides, and then slice through the middle of the stem to make 2 even pieces about ½-inch (1-cm) thick. They should be clean, even cuts. Season with salt on both sides, and then grill on either a charcoal grill, a plancha, or in a cast iron pan (they all work). The surface of whatever you're cooking them on should be lightly brushed with pure olive oil. Grill them until just cooked and juicy inside, to preserve their distinctive texture and flavor.

To serve, thinly slice the remaining matsutake into 8 nice pieces. Dispense a little pool of potato purée on the plate, and dust with some of the pine needle powder. Place 2 slices of shaved matsutake on top, and garnish with wood sorrel. Lay 2 pieces of cooked matsutake on the side.

*Wood sorrel is the common name and oxalis is the Latin name. Here they call it sour grass, and kids grow up chewing on the thick, juicy, sour stems. It's a Nor-Cal childhood memory plant.

PARSLEY ROOT SOUP
snails, green garlic, pickled watermelon radish

This soup started with snails. Special snails.

I was talking to a friend in 2007, when he told me about Mary Stewart, a snail rancher in Swarthmore, a small town in California's Central Valley. "They're the same kind they raise in Burgundy. She feeds them basil. They're incredible." Weirdly, I had to call an East Coast distributer to buy them, at which point they were shipped directly from California. But when they arrived, I forgot all about how they got there. The little pests came vacuum-sealed in a plastic bag, completely clean and purged of all grit. They were delicious, with a sweet, earthy, gently herbaceous flavor that hinted at mushrooms. They were even non-awful raw (yes, I taste everything I lay my hands on, cooked or not. I'm very curious. This is undoubtedly going to get me in real trouble someday, like the time I drank warm, fermented masato, in an open-air market on the Peruvian Amazon. I felt the after-effects for weeks . . . but that's a story for another time).

I'd never worked with snails before, so I did what I often do in moments of complete disorientation: I went back to tradition. I cooked them with lightly browned butter, shallot, garlic and mushrooms. Not mushrooms, exactly—mushroom dashi. The katsuobushi and seaweed notes in the stock gave the dish a haunting complexity, a whisper of fermentation, smoke and ocean. The flavor of the snails integrated perfectly, and when they were cooked to tenderness I couldn't stop eating them.

Tradition dictates parsley. (It also, at least in this country, dictates serving them as chewy, flavorless little bits, acrid with old garlic butter, out of decorative shells. I'm not *that* traditional.) Mariquita Farm in Watsonville grows terrific Hamburg parsley, a variant cultivated for its white, aromatic root. I made a simple soup, and then served the snails in the bowls with some of their cooking liquid; a little bit of puréed green garlic, which had just started showing up in the markets; snipped parsley; and something to bring acidity and to tie to the vaguely Japanese feeling lent by the dashi: pickled watermelon radish. Snails with parsley, garlic, mushroom. Understandable flavors, tuned to my sensibilities.

I was so excited that I pitched a story about snails to my editor at the *New York Times Magazine*. The exact response, as I recall, was "Eww." I took the dish off the menu when the parsley root faded. Several months later I tried to order more snails, but they were out. I forgot about them for a while, and when I called again the distributor had stopped selling them. I couldn't find them anywhere, and no amount of Internet searching yielded any direct contacts.

And then one day in 2012, there they were: in the *New York Times* food section ("Hmmph!" I thought). She was working with a new distributor, Mikuni Wild Harvest in Seattle. I already had a relationship with the company, so I gave them a call to order some snails almost immediately. I made exactly the same dish, and it was just as good as I remembered. It is now, I guess, my own tradition.

If you're going to clean the snails yourself, I can't help you. I've never done that. I'm really not a general snail fan, just a fan of these snails, which arrive already purged of their grit and funk. Dump them out of the bag and give them a rinse. Lightly brown the butter in a heavy sauce pot, and then add the minced shallot and green garlic. Cook for 1 minute, stirring often, and then add the snails and cook a minute more. Add the wine, reduce by two-thirds, and then add the mushroom dashi (see page 112). Bring the liquid to a bare simmer, cover and cook for about an hour and a half, until the snails are tender. Remove the snails and strain the liquid, discarding the shallot and garlic. Combine the snails and liquid and correct the seasoning with salt. If you're going right into plating then keep the snails at room temperature, otherwise cool in an ice bath and refrigerate until needed.

Heat the water, rice vinegar, champagne vinegar, salt and sugar to a boil, and pour over the watermelon radish. Let cool at room temperature.

You might have noticed how little garlic we use in this book. Garlic, generally, is not my favorite ingredient. It has its place, but in my kitchen that place is a small one. Green garlic, on the other hand, I love. It is the fresh, uncured, more polite version of the plant, before the bottom coalesces into its familiar papery bulb. To make the purée, cook sliced green garlic (just the white and light green parts) with butter and salt over low heat, covered, stirring occasionally, until very tender. Purée in a blender and season with salt.

For the soup, peel and slice the parsley root into ½-inch (1-cm) thick pieces. Simmer with the vegetable stock and butter until very tender. Blend and pass through a chinois. Season with salt.

Most of our soups are composite soups. The parsley root soup by itself is a simple and pure expression of the ingredient. We put all of the garnish elements in the bowl, and then pour the broth in front of the diner. That gives them the aromatic experience of soup hitting the warm plate that is normally kept in the kitchen, but it also allows the various components to be kept separate until just before eating. You could mix them together in advance, but that would diminish the individuality of each, creating the kind of blended flavor you would typically find in a stew.

To serve, warm the snails in their liquid and place 6 in each bowl, along with a spoonful of their cooking liquid. Add 6 dots of green garlic purée, and 6 pieces of pickled watermelon radish. With scissors snip some parsley over everything. Pour the soup just before eating.

2008

EARTH AND SEA

new harvest potatoes, cucumber, coastal plants

The year before I opened Coi, Alexandra and I moved to the western edge of the city. The end of the continent. It was a place out of time, constantly shrouded in ghostly fog, with forests of giant trees bumping up against rolling grass, and moss-covered hillsides cascading down to rocky beaches. Beyond the dunes, the Pacific Ocean sprawled endlessly towards the horizon. Growing up on the East Coast I was used to living by the shore, but this felt different, more untamed, the moment where earth meets sea more vivid. I walked the trails along the coast frequently, finding herbs and flowers in forests and by the beach, and that connection to the place where I lived seeped into my cooking.

The first Earth and Sea dish had spiny lobster and wild mushrooms. It wasn't very successful, and I have mostly banished it from my memory. The second one was beets with a sauce of cauliflower and seaweed. I liked that better. But it was in spring 2008 that I stumbled onto the dish that suggested a different path for our cooking.

It started with ice plant flowers, the bright pink blossoms that pop up everywhere in the spring. I found them while walking near my house, and thought about using them in a dish. This was right as the first new potatoes and cucumbers were appearing at the market, and I imagined a dish that combined them with coastal plants. We used agretti, sea beans, and little herbs, along with the ice plant flowers.

I grated the cucumbers on a wooden Japanese grater called an oni-oroshi. A friend brought it to me from Japan and it quickly became a favorite grating tool. Its blunt wooden teeth break soft vegetables into coarse pieces, and turn cucumbers into irregular, stone-like shapes. I thought it would be fun if the sauce under the potatoes was very dark and bumpy, to contrast with the smooth, light-colored potatoes on top. I made a fluid gel of vegetable stock and squid ink, and then seasoned it with a ton of lemon juice and champagne vinegar, and just a little dried chile, so it looked dark and foreboding but tasted light and fresh, especially once the grated cucumber was stirred in.

The final dish, which we served as the second course on the menu, was striking, both visually and in terms of taste. The searing acidity of the cucumbers in vinaigrette was balanced by the dense sweetness of the potatoes and lots of good olive oil; the crunchy, saline coastal grasses and flowers perched on top.

The focused, simple presentation of a conceptual idea was exciting, and for a while we tried giving dishes more evocative names. We've mostly moved on from that idea, but we continue to develop dishes that we call Earth and Sea. Our coastline is always inspiring something new.

Go to the farmers' market really early when the new potatoes begin to arrive. Pick through every box they have to get the tiniest ones, choosing all different cultivars. There are so many kinds available now. I like Ozette, grown hundreds of years ago by the Makah Indians in Washington; rose finn apple from England; la ratte from Denmark; and bintje from Holland. Ignore the funny comments the other chefs make about size obsessions. Bring them back and steam them at 185°F (85°C) until tender–they should be a little softer than seems correct, as they'll harden a lot as they cool. Peel and toss them with fruity olive oil and salt. Store at room temperature, covered.

Bring the vegetable stock, squid ink and agar to a boil, and then cool in an ice bath until firm. Blend with salt, piment d'Espelette, rice wine vinegar, champagne vinegar and lemon juice. Use the champagne vinegar for sharpness, and round out the rough edges with the rice wine vinegar and lemon juice. It should be bright and fresh, neither aggressive nor timid.

Peel the cucumbers and grate them on an oni-oroshi. Refrigerate them stored in a basket strainer set over a bowl for at least an hour to get rid of excess liquid, which would dilute the dressing.

Cut the coastal plants into nice shapes with scissors, looking for tender and flavorful pieces, mostly the shoots and tips. Borage and other sprouting greens work as well, as do wild radish leaves, pods and flowers.

To serve, dress the cucumber with the squid ink fluid gel, adjusting as necessary with salt and acid. Put a large spoonful on a plate, and place several tiny potatoes on top. Drizzle with fruity olive oil and a sprinkle of piment d'Espelette, and arrange the coastal greens on top.

EARTH AND SEA

steamed tofu mousseline, yuba, mushroom dashi

San Francisco's importance in California soared in the years after the Gold Rush. The miners would come down from the northern hills and rivers flush with money, looking for good times. San Francisco provided just that. In the 1800s the edge of the city was just a few blocks away from Coi, and the buildings that now house posh design studios and galleries were home to flop houses and saloons.

As the town grew, it became more than just a playground for the newly wealthy; it was home to a growing population of immigrants who settled here, helping to build the city and shape its culture. The settlers came from Europe and Asia, Central and South America, bringing their traditions and products and ideas. Their influence shapes our cuisine as much as the natural setting around us.

San Francisco is a port town, and although the use of locally grown ingredients is one of the organizing principles on which our cuisine is based, we also buy dried goods like salt, coffee and spices from around the world. The next version of Earth and Sea, developed later the same year, incorporated more Japanese influences.

At the bottom of the bowl is steamed tofu mousseline, a purée of tofu, ginger and white soy, bound with egg, that sets like a custard when steamed. On top of that, a lightly thickened broth of mushroom dashi, yuba and fresh seaweed.

Mushroom dashi is a broth that I've made for years. It's something like a regular dashi—an infusion of dried seaweed and katsuobushi—but based on mushroom and vegetable stocks. It's sweet and savory, intensely umami but balanced. It's also an incredibly hard broth to get right. Both stocks need to be well made, with clean flavor and good concentration. The infusion needs to be done correctly. And then, in the end, it's still wrong half the time and requires adjustment. This technique—making stocks separately and then combining them at the end—is something we do a lot. It allows us to adjust each element of the sauce more precisely, based on how each component tastes that day.

You know how milk forms a skin when heated for a while? That's how yuba is made, except with soy milk. If the soy milk is great quality, the abundance of protein will form skin with a tender but chewy texture, unlike anything else. We cut it into strips and float it into the broth, along with different kinds of fresh seaweeds and pickled turnips. We thicken the broth with agar, so everything stays in suspension, and the flavor lingers on the palate. It's light, deeply flavored and elegant.

To make the dashi, heat the vegetable and mushroom stocks with the kombu to just below a simmer. Cook for 15 minutes, then add the katsuobushi. Cook for 2 minutes, then pull from the heat and let stand until flavorful. Strain through cheesecloth, then season with salt and shiro dashi to taste. Generally speaking, using more katsuobushi for a shorter time gives a fresher, more delicious flavor. After a while it starts to taste dull and fishy. While still hot, separate half of the liquid and add the agar. Bring to a boil, whisking rapidly. Transfer to a metal bowl sitting in an ice bath. Cool completely, then blend until smooth–this will thicken the broth, causing it to linger on the tongue, making the taste more powerful. Cool the other half of the broth separately.

To pickle the turnips, cut them in quarters, sixths or eighths, depending on the size, and put them into a metal container. Bring the water, rice wine vinegar, sugar and salt to a boil. Pour over the turnips and let cool to room temperature. Keep the turnips in the liquid for at least a half hour and until you need them.

Clean several kinds of fresh seaweeds, like bull kelp, alaria, sea lettuce, eel grass, purple laver, Turkish towel, sea grapes and giant kelp. Cook the ones that require cooking in unsalted water until tender. Cool and cut into small shapes. Cut the other kinds into similar size pieces. Combine the trimmed cooked and raw seaweeds and soak in cold water, changing the water occasionally and rinsing them each time, to remove the sliminess.

To serve, place the medium tofu, silken tofu, egg white, and ⅛ teaspoon finely grated ginger in a blender. Purée and pass through a fine mesh sieve. Season with white soy and salt. Put a large spoonful of mousseline in 4 ovenproof ceramic bowls and dust lightly with shichimi togarashi. Place the bowls into a water bath in the oven at 300°F (150°C) for 15 minutes, until just set. Remove from the oven and add 5 small pieces of drained pickled turnip. Warm equal parts plain and thickened dashi (you will need about 400 ml) until warm but not hot (otherwise it will lose its texture). Add the yuba, 4 spoonfuls of seaweeds, and grated lime zest. (Mushroom and lime is a happy combination. The lime is also there to brighten all the deep, dark flavors, so use a decent amount.) Heat through. Spoon the mixture over the baked tofu mousseline.

OYSTERS UNDER GLASS
yuzu, rau ram

This is a play on a classic French dish, "Pheasant Under Glass." I should, at the outset, say that I have never eaten that dish, nor have I made it. Here's how I learned about it.

When I was twenty-three years old and working as a sous chef at a restaurant in Sonoma, I befriended one of the cooks. He was a blond-haired, blue-eyed California boy, and we bonded over tennis. As we sat on the bench after one match (in which, I seem to remember, he pretty much cleaned the court with me—he was one of those ranked juniors who never quite made it), he told me that he was leaving to take a job in the city. At a classy new strip club, which would be swathed in marble and have a proper kitchen, serving a proper menu.

I looked at him pityingly. Such a sweet boy. "You know they're all mafia controlled, right?" I told him.

He laughed. "I doubt it. Anyway, I'm going to be a chef, not a bouncer!"

I caught up to him several months later. He looked a little less naïve. "That thing that you told me about," he said, looking around warily, "You were right."

He left eventually to be the chef of another restaurant in town, which was reviewed in the local paper. Featured in the review was "Pheasant Under Glass," which involved a warm roasted bird in cognac sauce, served under a glass dome. I never went to the restaurant and never ate the dish, but I loved the idea, which stayed with me for about fifteen years.

The funny thing is what happened to that recollection—it morphed in my mind, until I was certain that the review had actually described cold pheasant under clear gel. My imagination often does what it wants with what I see and read, treating memory and experience as fungible building blocks for creative development. That false memory simmered for years, the idea growing and evolving until eventually it became the inspiration for this dish.

It's really quite a traditional preparation: Oysters with lemon, parsley and mignonette. But instead of the lemon, we use yuzu, an Asian citrus fruit that reminds me of a wildly aromatic and vaguely funky lemon, that we turn into a sheet of gel that covers the oysters. Instead of parsley, we use rau răm, a Southeast Asian herb that tastes like the love child of coriander, shiso, lemon balm, and parsley. Under the oysters, instead of a proper mignonette we make a mixture of vegetables and apple, sweet and sharp with vinegar. In my mind the exotic flavors that surround the oyster seem totally normal, because their origin is so close to what I'm used to.

Oh, and the strip club? It went out of business. They tore out all the marble and everything that made it fancy, and turned it into a fully nude place. It's the one right next to Coi.

To prepare the oysters, buy very fresh, plump, briny-sweet ones with lots of liquor. The Virginica oysters that we get from Taylor Shellfish Farms in Washington might be the best all-around oyster in the country. It's an East Coast transplant grown on the West Coast, so it has the plumpness of an East Coast oyster combined with the briny taste of our waters. Remove them from the shell, and strain the liquor through cheesecloth. Rinse the oysters quickly in a bowl of ice water, and store them in a quarter of their own liquor.

Use the remaining three-quarters of the oyster liquor to make the oyster gel. Season the liquor with yuzu. Add salt if necessary. If they're already scary salty, dilute with a little water. Keep the oyster flavor on top, the yuzu is just to balance the brininess and create a little connection with the gel sheet. Weigh the liquid and set with 2.3% gelatin. Refrigerate.

To make the gel sheet, boil the vegetable stock with the agar. Off the heat, whisk in the gelatin until melted. Let the mixture cool to warm room temperature, and then add the yuzu juice and zest, and season with salt and champagne vinegar. The agar and the cold will knock down the seasoning quite a bit, so season it a little higher than you think it should be, and use the vinegar to push the yuzu and really make it sing—but always keep the yuzu flavor in front. Check the seasoning by cooling a spoonful on a plate before setting the entire batch. When it's right, pour out the liquid onto a plastic sheet tray. Use a blowtorch to burn off any bubbles on the surface. Keep the sheet tray very level until set. A 12 x 18-inch (30 x 45-cm) tray requires 225 g of gel to achieve the right thickness. Refrigerate. When cold, cut into 3-inch (7.5-cm) squares, 2¾-inch (7-cm) if the oysters are a little small.

Before you cut the vegetables for the mignonette, put the vinegar, oil and some salt in a bowl. Start by mincing the radish and move on to celery and then apple, and as you cut them add immediately to the bowl and mix—the oil and vinegar will keep everything from oxidizing. Season with salt and black pepper. It takes a surprising amount of salt, and as it sits it will need more, because the juices will leak from the vegetables and dilute the dressing. Refrigerate.

To serve, spread a spoonful of mignonette, sans liquid, on the plate in a small circle (you tasted it first and adjusted the salt, right?). Place 2 oysters on top, next to each other. Blot any excess juice so it doesn't drip all over the place, but do it fast and gentle—oysters should be shiny and juicy, not dry and dull. In between the oysters, spoon a little oyster gel. Snip some pieces of rau răm. Cover with a sheet of yuzu gel, plastic side (which will be the shiniest) up. See, it looks like oysters under glass! Whatever that is.

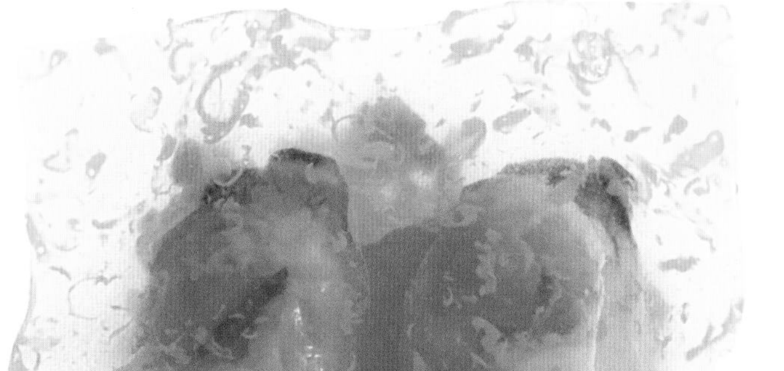

TOW-AWAY
NO PARKING
ANY
TIME
SHOWGIR
SPECIALIZED

SAUTEED MONTEREY BAY ABALONE
escarole, sea lettuce-caper berry vinaigrette

The fall before we opened Coi, I took a trip to Japan with Alexandra and Scott Kester, our designer. It was my first time there, and the food knocked me out. It was the discipline, the depth of flavor, the refinement and balance, the consistency. From cheap noodle shop to high-end sushi, everything was great.

I loved the aesthetic sensibility just as much. There was a level of imagination and distinctiveness in the design which belied the underlying cultural uniformity. I had, then as now, a bit of a pottery fetish, and I came back with two extra suitcases full, some of which we still use at the restaurant. I also came back with a burning desire to use seaweed.

At the Nishiki market in Kyoto there was a shop that sold eighteen kinds of fresh seaweed, laid out in bowls at the front counter. I was fascinated. Fresh seaweed is common in Asian cooking, but not at home. When I returned to California I found that they were impossible to find. I used the dried version for a while, and then let the urge lapse.

A few years later it returned. I was in Dénia, Spain, visiting Quique Dacosta at his restaurant. I had just participated in a food conference in Madrid, and Alexandra and I drove down after, through vineyards and orchards of orange trees that reminded me of California. We had many amazing dishes at El Poblet (since renamed Quique Dacosta), but the one that stayed with me was grilled fresh loin from pigs that roam among ancient oaks, stuffing themselves with acorns, before being turned into the famous Ibérico de bellota hams. He served it accompanied only by different kinds of seaweeds. I went home more determined than ever to find a source.

We were using abalone, and it suddenly dawned on me that abalone eat seaweed. Why can't I buy fresh seaweed from the abalone guys? So I asked, and they said yes, which started a long and fascinating process of learning how to work with fresh seaweeds.

This dish uses only one kind of seaweed: sea lettuce. The flavor profile itself starts with traditional French. Flour, brown butter and lemon on the abalone. A little bed of cooked escarole. And the sauce is a variant on an emulsified vinaigrette, with shallot, caper and parsley. But instead of parsley we use sea lettuce, which we blend into a smooth sauce. The sea lettuce brings a fresh, clean, ocean tone that connects to the escarole and the abalone, a harmony born in nature.

Use mature escarole with a very pale yellow interior. Cut away the tough dark green outer leaves, dark green tops and core. Cut the escarole into small pieces of about 1¼ inch (3 cm).

Cure the shallot in champagne vinegar and salt for 20 minutes. Combine the shallots and liquid with all the other ingredients in a blender, and blend until smooth and bright green. Use just enough xanthan to make a smooth emulsion, about the texture of a thin mayonnaise.

To serve, cook the escarole with a little water, 10 g butter and salt in a covered pot until tender. Season with salt and rice wine vinegar. Drain on a paper towel.

While the escarole is cooking, season the abalone with salt and pepper and dust lightly with flour, shaking off any excess. Brown 30 g butter fairly deeply—the abalone will take its color from the butter, not from the cooking, since it spends so little time in the pan. Add the abalone, top side down, and move it around by shaking the pan. After about 30 to 45 seconds, flip the abalone and cook another 30 seconds or so. Add a spoonful of lemon juice, swirl it into the butter, and flip the abalone again, basting it with the sauce off the heat so it has a nice glaze. Flip it back, glaze it again and remove to a paper towel.

Spoon a pool of sauce in the center of the plate. Place some escarole on top of the sauce, and the abalone on top of the escarole. Garnish with a wild mustard flower.

GOAT
wheatgrass-raw almond puree, sprouted seeds, beans and nuts

Cooking refined food at a high level relies on ritual. Consistency comes from practicing the same techniques over and over, until the process and understanding are so internalized that the execution is flawless, dish after dish. The down side of that kind of repetition is that it can have a deadening effect on creativity. Special requests can be a jolt to the system, forcing new ideas. Sometimes it's good to be pushed.

This is a meat dish that started with vegetables. I ran into a friend who was on a raw food diet and I invited her in. I knew what I was getting into.

We don't cook raw or vegan food per se, but much of our food is just that, so I was not totally lost as I thought about what to make. I didn't want to raid the typical raw food pantry; that would be too easy. But I did like one idea that I found, of soaking nuts and then blending them into a purée. I wanted to include wheatgrass in one of the dishes, and I wondered what would happen if I used soaked raw almond to thicken it. It was amazing. Most everything I made that night has faded from my memory, except that component, which became the basis for this dish.

Around that time Bill Niman started raising goats. Bill is one of the pioneers of the local grass-fed beef movement, and one of my meat suppliers as far back as the early '90s. I liked his new product, and as I began to think of a dish, I thought about the grassland in Western Marin where the goats were raised, which somehow put me in mind of the wheatgrass-almond purée, which then somehow made me think about the sprouted seeds, beans and nuts that the wheatgrass guy at the market sold. Kind of a socio/eco-system connection.

And it played out like this: some of the loin was poached and thinly sliced; the leg was roasted and sliced more thickly; the tough parts were braised. It was all mounded on top of the wheatgrass-raw almond purée, and then the sprouted seeds, beans and nuts were sautéed with olive oil, seasoned with champagne vinegar and spooned over the lamb. The sauce was a vinaigrette made from the braising liquid. Then a few more sprouts on top.

This was the first time that we used wheatgrass in a dish on the menu. I managed to avoid the stuff for the first fifteen or so years that I lived in California, until Alexandra bought me a shot at the farmers' market. I was deeply skeptical. I was also wrong. It was delicious, intensely sweet with anise/licorice notes. I started experimenting with it at home, and it has since become a staple seasoning in our kitchen, like parsley or chives—now we even grow our own.

This was also the first time that sprouted beans, seeds and nuts entered the kitchen. As good as the goat was, it was the raw food elements which energized the dish, giving the meaty components life.

We use whole goats, about 50 pounds dressed weight, when they have developed some flavor. For smaller amounts you may want to buy pieces. If you can't find goat, lamb works great as well.

The day before season the shoulder, shanks and miscellaneous tough bits with salt and pepper. Heat a cast iron pan to almost smoking, add pure olive oil to cover the bottom of the pan in a thin layer, and add the pieces of goat, being careful not to crowd the pan. Brown the goat on all sides and remove to a braising pan. Add the vegetables to the same pan that the goat was seared in and cook for 5 minutes until softened. Add to the braising pan, along with the white wine, AP stock and thyme. Bring to a boil and then cover and set in a 250°F (120°C) oven, covered, until tender, 2 to 3 hours. Let the meat cool in the cooking liquid, preferably overnight. The next day bring it back to room temperature, remove the meat and cut into smaller pieces, holding them in a covered container moistened with some of their cooking liquid.

Soak the almonds in water overnight, and then discard the water. Peel the almonds and blend them with the wheatgrass juice, pure olive oil (for texture) and salt. Your blender won't be happy. It will take a while to get something smooth, and, even so, it will look a little grainy. Don't let it heat up, which would cook the juice. Refrigerate until needed.

To serve, season the leg (leave it whole, no shank, for lots of people, a smaller piece for a few) with salt and pepper and let it stand for 20 minutes at room temperature. Heat 20 g pure olive oil in an enameled cast iron pan over medium-high heat. When it's hot, add the leg and sear. Once it's browned, remove the leg and add the onion and carrot. Cook the vegetables for 5 minutes to soften them. Turn off the heat, add the leg back to the pot, cover and put in an oven set to at 250°F (120°C), and cook, turning often, until rosy pink. Remove to a tray to rest.

At the same time that you roast the leg, heat enough pure olive oil in a metal container to submerge the loin and set in a water bath held at 130°F (55°C). Clean the piece of loin, tenderloin or rib-eye of all silver skin and connective tissue. Season with salt, let stand at room temperature for 5 minutes, and then put in the oil. Cook until the interior is pink and juicy.

Reheat the braised pieces. Strain about 500 g of braising liquid and reduce to sauce consistency. If it starts getting salty then stop reducing and thicken with xanthan. Season with champagne vinegar (which will reduce the salt level quite a bit) and good olive oil to make a broken vinaigrette.

Warm the wheatgrass-raw almond purée and place a mound in the center of the plate. Place slices or pieces of the different kind of meats around. Sauté the sprouted seeds, beans and nuts in a little pure olive oil for 30 seconds, just enough to soften their taste, and then season them with vinegar. Spoon over and around the meats. Spoon some sauce over and around the meat, and garnish with top sprouts here and there.

Fri
GOAT MILK
8/17

APA

2009

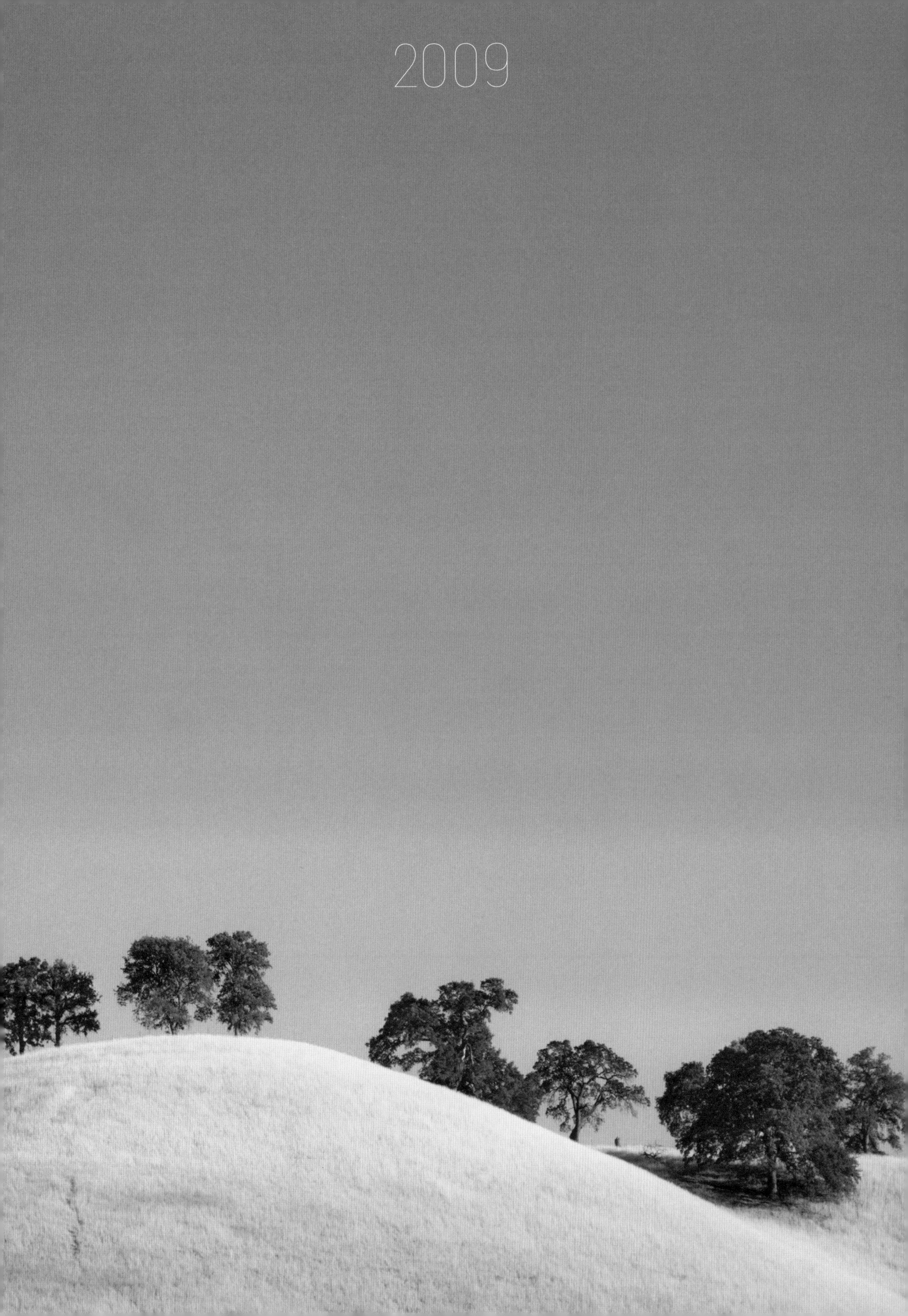

INVERTED CHERRY TOMATO TART
black olive, basil

I've always liked including a tart as part of our menu. I love their construction and intricacy, the way they show classic technique and respect for tradition. A bad tart is really, really dreadful; a great one is transcendent. I remember vividly an amuse bouche I had at Michel Bras in 2002: A tiny piece of perfectly crisp dough covered in shingles of barely cooked cèpes, brushed with oil redolent of garlic, dotted with just a few grains of coarse salt. So simple. So perfect.

For years we rotated tarts through the menu, but after a while I started to feel like the form didn't quite fit the rest of the menu—it was *too* traditional, the energy too staid. So I turned it upside down, floating a thin, wavy disk of olive tuile over goat cheese mousse. And thus, the inverted tart was born (at least as it's understood in our kitchen): the crust is on top, a texturally creamy midsection, and the garnish on the bottom. It eats well, and allows for a lot of latitude in combining different flavors and textures.

The second one we made was notable for its complicated construction. It was late spring, and we used about twenty different kinds of raw, cooked and pickled herbs and young vegetables, grounded with an acidulated onion purée on the plate, and topped with a vinaigrette mousse—a vinaigrette made with vegetable stock, oil and vinegar, bound with gelatin and forced through a siphon. The riot of different colors and flavors was kept tight by an ultra-precise rectangle of the same black olive tuile, which gave the plate definition. We kept it on our menu until we went on our summer break at the end of June.

While the restaurant was closed I worked on the menu. In theory everyone takes a vacation twice a year, but in practice it never seems to work out for me. There's always something to do—remodel the dining room or kitchen, clean the rugs, refinish the floors. Little by little we've upgraded from our humble beginnings.

By the time we re-opened the cherry tomatoes were just getting good, so I adapted the form of the tart to accommodate them. It turned out to be one of our most well-loved dishes, a classic combination of tomato, basil and olive. The rectangular olive crisp is delicate and crisp, yielding easily to an intense tomato mousse, made the same way as the vinaigrette, a raw purée bound in gelatin. Underneath there were peeled cherry tomatoes, and at the bottom an almost traditional pesto. Familiar, comforting flavors in a different form.

Dehydrate some black olives at 140°F (60°C) until completely dry. Chop fine.

Freeze the mortar and pestle so the heat does not discolor the basil when you use it.

Blend the whole tomatoes and pure olive oil. Season with salt (a little high, as it will lose seasoning from gelatin, cold, time), and strain through a chinois. Warm 100 g of the mixture, and melt the gelatin. Stir the gelatin mixture into the rest, and chill in an ice bath. When the gelatin is set, place the mixture into a siphon and add two charges. Refrigerate.

To make the tuile batter, combine the ground isomalt, flour and salt. In a separate bowl, mix the olive purée with the egg whites, and then add the melted butter and half of the dry mixture. Whisk until half-incorporated. Add the rest of the flour/isomalt mixture and mix just until incorporated. Refrigerate for 30 minutes. Spread thinly on a baking sheet in 5 x 1½-inch (12.5 x 4-cm) rectangles. Make sure that the batter doesn't heat up too much, as it will become impossible to spread. Bake the tuiles at 350°F (180°C) for 20 minutes or until crisp. Keep rotating in the oven and watch for hot spots. Because the batter is very dark, you won't be able to tell about doneness by color—go by smell and taste. They should be crisp, half sweet and half bitter. When they're done, set aside to cool.

Make the pesto as on page 58.

Wash and stem the cherry tomatoes, then pat dry. Remove the skins.

To serve, spread the pesto thinly on a flat plate in the shape of the olive tuiles (we use the same template to spread the pesto as we do to spread the tuiles). Place 8 cherry tomatoes in a line on top of the pesto. Add 2 grains of sel gris and 3 grains of dried black olive to each tomato. Cover the top of the cherry tomatoes with the mousse, then place a tuile on top of the mousse. Garnish with basil sprouts.

BEET AND GOAT CHEESE TART (BROKEN, INVERTED)
rye, dill

As the summer turned to fall, we felt like we weren't done yet with the idea of the inverted tart, so we turned to fall flavors. More precisely, we turned to common San Francisco flavors.

There are different theories about the origins of the beet and goat cheese salad, but what cannot be argued is its subjugation of the local culinary landscape. Even now it's hard to avoid. In 2011, while preparing for a talk at MAD Food Symposium in Copenhagen, I did an experiment. I gathered a dozen restaurant menus from around the city. On every menu was some variant of beets and goat cheese. The local appetite for the combination is, apparently, insatiable.

One way to look at it is as a cliché, but that's only part of the story. Beets and goat cheese are not only delicious together, but they have a special place in local diners' hearts. The combination brings with it a strong emotional association, which is incredibly valuable. It's a great challenge as a chef to take something so familiar and make it new again, without losing the qualities that make it great.

This is my version, a tart that's upside down and broken, with seasoning that leans towards Scandinavia: beet, dill, rye. It took some similar elements from its predecessor, like the pesto (in this case made from dill and walnut). In appearance, though, it's more loose, organic, the pesto smeared across the plate in a way that resembles a spontaneous gesture. The beets that sit in little piles on top of the pesto are roasted, minced and dressed in their own (thickened) juice, topped with a mousse of fresh goat cheese. On top are crisps of rye bread, which have been dehydrated, ground, and re-formed into delicate crackers that dance on top of the cheese like little hats.

Blend fresh goat cheese with a touch of goat's milk (cow's milk will also do, you will use very little) until smooth. The texture should be very thick, barely pourable. Season with salt. Transfer to a siphon and charge twice. Refrigerate for at least 2 hours.

Peel the roasted beets. To make the fluid gel, bring the vegetable stock and agar to a boil. Off the heat, stir in the roasted beets and cool. Blend until smooth and season with champagne vinegar, lemon juice and salt. Pulse the remaining beets in a food processor to grind them. Add enough fluid gel to make a nice texture, both nubbly and creamy. Season with salt, lemon juice, champagne vinegar and sugar if necessary. It should be bright, sweet and sour but still keeping the flavor of the beet at the forefront. Refrigerate at least an hour, and adjust the seasoning before serving. It will change a lot.

Grind all of the ingredients for the crisps together in a Thermomix, or a spice grinder (preferably one that doesn't smell like coffee or spices). Using a basket strainer, shake an even layer over a sheet tray lined with a Silpat, and bake in the Combi at 340°F (170°C) with the fan on one bar for 8 minutes. Remove the Silpat from the tray (Yeah, I know, it's hot. Sorry about that.) and invert onto a piece of parchment paper. Let it cool for a minute, and then peel the Silpat back from the crisp. Break the crisp into manageable pieces, and store in a tightly wrapped container until you need them. They absorb moisture like no one's business, so don't do them too far in advance.

Make a dill pesto the same way as a basil pesto (see page 58), except substitute dill for basil, and walnuts for pine nuts.

To serve, spread the dill pesto on the plate in an organic, streaky line. Use a small offset spatula so that it doesn't look too organic. Position 3 small piles of beet on the pesto, and top each with goat cheese. Perch a piece of crisp (broken into an irregular shape just bigger than the pile of beets) on top of each serving of goat cheese.

CHICKEN AND EGG
poached scrambled egg, chicken jus infused with katsuobushi, radish, seaweed powder

I first served this as a meat course. It was not very successful. To our customers eggs—no matter how good—are not an adequate substitute for meat. And, although a jus is a full expression of an entire animal (or at least it should be), it's not a substitute, in people's minds, for the flesh of the animal. So I let the dish go for a while and this year I brought it back, a little earlier on the menu. It makes a delightful spring mid-course.

Eggs are one of our favorite ingredients, utterly familiar yet capable of taking on an astonishing variety of forms. They can be an enrichment or a binding agent, and they play nicely with vegetables, meat and fish.

In this dish the eggs take center stage—the egg cookery is actually the most interesting part of the dish. It is a lightly beaten, very fresh egg, poured into simmering water and cooked for twenty seconds. The bubbles in the egg expand at almost the same time as the proteins set in the relatively high heat. The water is drained, and the result is an egg that is fully cooked, but incredibly light and fluffy. It is a very different texture than conventional egg cooking techniques can provide. I published the recipe for the eggs before Coi opened, but it took a few years to figure out how to replicate the process in a restaurant setting.

I designed the technique for home cooking, and in fact it's fast, easy and delicious. I highly recommend adding it to your Sunday morning egg repertoire. In the restaurant kitchen, on the other hand, it's a major pain. It can't be scaled, so it's one pot, one lid, one strainer basket per person. It requires full attention, and a lot of room. Nothing about it is particularly well-suited to a professional environment. Which makes it just the kind of challenge I love.

Once we'd worked out the egg cooking details, the rest of the dish was easy. The chicken and egg thing is more than an intellectual construct—a savory sauce of browned chicken bones, infused with smoky, fermented katsuobushi at the last minute, gives the dish intensity and depth. The eggs are seasoned with seaweed powder—more umami flavors —and balanced with a bright salad of spring radishes, sprouts and flowers.

It took almost seven years from the conception of the technique until it found a comfortable place on our menu. Along the way we worked with the same elements, and kept tweaking them until they settled into a final form. Sometimes it takes a while to get a dish right.

To make the seaweed powder you need 3 days. Hydrate dried kombu overnight in the liquids, then simmer gently in a small pan over low heat for about 2 hours until the liquid is absorbed, and the seaweed is tender. Dehydrate at warm room temperature for a few days, until completely dry. Grind in a spice mill.

For the chicken jus, deeply brown the backs and necks in pure olive oil in a wide pan. Add the sliced onion and carrot, and cook until softened. Deglaze with white wine, scraping up any bits that cling to the bottom of the pan. Reduce until almost dry. Add the AP stock, and bring to a light simmer. Cook for a few hours, without skimming, until the stock is redolent of browned chicken bones. Strain through a chinois, and reduce, skimming frequently, until light sauce consistency (i.e. before it gets tacky). Add the seaweed, and cook on medium-low heat for about 15 minutes. Add the shaved katsuobushi, remove from the heat, and cover for 5 minutes, until the flavor is balanced–smoky and savory, but never losing the flavor of the chicken. Strain through cheesecloth and season with a little champagne vinegar, just enough to balance the sauce. It should not be sour.

To serve, crack an egg into a bowl. If it's not super-fresh, first rest it in a narrow-slotted spoon, letting the thin white drain away, and then transfer the remaining yolk and thick white to a small bowl. Beat the egg vigorously with a fork for 30 seconds. Set a medium saucepan filled with 4 inches (10 cm) of water over moderate heat. Put a strainer in the sink. When the water is at a low boil, add a few large pinches of salt, then stir in a clockwise direction to create a whirlpool. Pour the egg into the moving water, cover the pan and count to 20. Turn off the heat and uncover the pan. The egg should be floating on the surface in ribbons. While holding back the egg with a spoon, pour off most of the water over the strainer. Gently slide the egg into the strainer and press lightly to expel any excess liquid. Season with salt, and then overturn onto a small plate. Season with a little more salt, and then sprinkle seaweed powder over in an even layer.

Cut the radishes in different shapes and textures. The most peppery ones, leave raw. Any tough ones like black Spanish radish, cook in salted water until crisp-tender. Season the other pieces with rice wine vinegar and salt. There are no right answers–taste the radishes and season them the way that seems to best highlight their special qualities. Top the egg with the radish pieces, and transfer to a shallow bowl. Garnish with wild radish flowers, pods and sprouts if you have them. Spoon some jus around.

YOUNG CARROTS ROASTED IN HAY
aged sheep's milk cheese, radish powder

Fall was my favorite time of year when I was young. I loved the clear, quiet light and the feeling of loss that came with the end of summer, a kind of sweet, painful ache that I could neither understand nor explain. Every year there was the ritual: the leaves turning color and falling, the cleaning of gutters and organizing of drawers, buying new clothes to prepare for the long, frigid winter ahead. It always felt like a moment in between seasons, when anything was possible.

After I opened my first restaurant in Sonoma, fall came to mean something entirely different. It was when the rains came, and the tourists went away. The first year the bills piled up on the mantelpiece at home, one pile per week, carefully bound with a rubber band, the total owed marked on a Post-it on top. At first there were two, then four and later eight piles, sitting there as a constant reminder of our empty dining room. The rain cut off roads and flooded fields, seeping into our subterranean bedroom at home, filling it with the smell of damp concrete and mold. Subsequent years were never as bad as the first, but every fall after that, as the days shortened and our bank account dwindled, my heart broke a little as we dug in for an isolated, depressing winter. That was some time ago, but the scars still remain. Every year, even now, when I step outside and feel that the light has changed, that it is fall and that summer is gone, I fight down a rising panic. It will be all right, I tell myself, over and over, until eventually I believe it enough to keep going.

This dish is about a moment sometime after summer surrenders, when the harvest is done and the farms are muddy. There's wind-blown detritus scattered about, the neat rows of tender greens given way to masses of sodden earth. The way the plate looks, messy but still beautiful, reminds me of walking farms just before winter.

We cook with alfalfa and clover hays. We also use sprouts from the same plants, the first tender growth mingled with an infusion of dead husks. Radishes are dried and ground into a pink, subtly pungent powder, which blankets the plate. On top, the sweet smell of cooked carrots and the nutty complexity of the shaved sheep's milk cheese. When the dish is finished the aroma is evocative of pasture, of loamy soil and smoke.

It's almost enough to make me love fall again.

The idea of roasting the carrots in hay came from my then-sous chef, Nico Borzee. Nico was born and raised in France, where cooking in hay is quite traditional. We were talking about new ways to cook carrots, and he thought back to a typical fall dish that he had made before, pork cooked with consommé and hay. Why couldn't we apply that to carrots? A few days later I found myself at the farmers' market, shoehorning a bale of hay into my not-very-big car. A bale is bigger than you'd think.

One of the best parts of the dish is the hay stock, which was a revelation: deep, sweet and aromatic. To make it, soak the hay in water for 5 minutes. Strain off all excess liquid, place the damp hay on a flat top or a plancha and char slightly. Seal it in a bag with the water and steam in the circulator at 197°F (95°C) for an hour. Strain through a chinois.

For the gel, season 500 g of hay stock with salt. Boil with the agar. Remove from the heat, pour into a storage container and refrigerate for at least an hour, until firm. The gel should be brittle, almost crunchy, and break into jagged-looking pieces when cut with a spoon. It's not a texture that we use very often, but in this dish it plays well against the crunch of the sprouts and the tender carrots.

For the radish powder, thinly slice the radishes. Spread them on a sheet tray lined with parchment paper, and place in the dehydrator at 130°F (55°C), with high fan setting, until dry. Grind in a spice grinder.

To prepare the carrots, cut the tops, leaving ½ inch (1 cm) of green. Scrape with a knife to remove all dirt and extra roots. Wash well–by which I mean, immaculately. One grain of dirt will ruin the entire dish.

Toss the carrots with pure olive oil, and season with a generous amount of salt. In a heavy, medium-size roasting pan, place 100 g of the hay stock and 50 g of hay, and nestle the carrots on top. Cover, bring to a boil on the stovetop, and then roast in the oven at 250°F (120°C) for approximately 30 minutes, shaking occasionally, until the carrots are tender (check with a cake tester, which should pass through without resistance).

To serve, dust a plate with radish powder. Scoop 5 irregular, dime-size pieces of hay gel onto a paper towel, let them weep for a minute, and then place here and there on the plate. Season the alfalfa, clover and radish bottom sprouts with champagne vinegar and salt, and spread over and around the hay gel. If they're thick, cut in half lengthwise. Cut about 1 inch (2 cm) off the bottom of the cooked carrots on a short diagonal. Three reasons: (1) to check the seasoning; (2) the thin ends cook more than the thicker tops; (3) to create a moment of visual preciseness in an otherwise organic-looking plate. Arrange on top in a natural way. Finish with several shavings of aged sheep's milk cheese and 5 to 6 radish top sprouts.

Eggs

MELON AND CUCUMBER
aroma of mint

Sensory memory is the most important attribute of a cook. Without a database of experiences to contextualize flavor, a good palate means nothing. I had a cook recently who could mechanically reproduce the food, more or less. He looked good doing it. But, day after day, he just couldn't get the taste right. Either Andrew or I taste everything before it leaves the kitchen, and there was almost never a time that we let something go from his station without adjustment. A professional cook should be able to get the seasoning down for a dish within the first three or four tries. The amount of salt that flows from your hand onto a piece of abalone, the exact amount of butter and lemon to deglaze the pan, should all be connected to a specific taste. You make the dish, taste, adjust, and then it's locked in, dish after dish, the same all night, the same the next day. A cook should know by feel how the dish will taste, because the physical act of making it triggers a taste memory. Without that connection there can be no good cooking.

I remember apricot tarts and bread and butter in France, when I was a kid. Beef tongue and borscht and apple pies at holiday parties at my grandmother's house, the first time I had foie gras at Maison Robert in Boston as a teenager, my first real restaurant meal in San Francisco, at Zuni in 1990. I can taste all of those things in my mind, perfectly preserved, exactly as they were. Now I have to force myself to forget things, to keep my mind from getting cluttered with meaningless experiences. That overwrought dish of scallops and eighty-five herbs and flowers? Gone. That pizza that tastes like a million other pizzas I've had? Into deep storage. But remarkable tastes and textures—good and bad—remain easily accessible, lined up in my memory, like a warehouse with neatly organized rows. My recollection of personal experiences is strangely inaccurate, almost dream-like, but I have a photographic memory for tastes and smells. I use those remembrances as touchstones to connect to the people I cook for.

Sensory memories matter just as much to the diner. The way an American, a Dane and a Russian understand the taste and context of a cucumber, for example, can be wildly different. We have to make food that somehow triggers primal memories in all of them, using shared experience to create something new, something that will linger long after the dinner is over. After all, what's more important—the three hours they spend at the table, or the ten or twenty years the memory stays with them, glowing in their mind?

Here, two preparations of melon and cucumber—biological cousins—are served on a plate scented with the aroma of mint. The taste of the melon melds with the cucumber to create a new flavor, neither fully one nor the other. At first the mint is a separate component, but its aroma quickly becomes entangled with the melon and cucumber and over time it becomes impossible to tell whether you are eating or smelling the herb.

What makes the dish work is not the strangeness, but the familiarity. Cucumber and melon are common flavors, easily understood on their own but peculiar in combination, changed by the aroma of mint into something unexpected that draws you along a different path, creating a new memory.

Put the cups for the consommé in the refrigerator to chill. For the consommé, juice the cucumbers with the skin on. Peel, seed and juice the melon. Combine the juices and season with lime juice and salt–it will take a lot of both.

Cut ⅔-inch (1.5-cm) cubes from the center of the yellow and red watermelons. Place the cubes of each color of melon into separate bags. Peel and juice the remainder of each melon, strain and add to the bags. Compress on a gentle setting in a Cryovac machine. Let sit for an hour and then drain excess liquid.

For the mint spray ... well, I can't help you here. Mandy concocted something for me that had both mint absolute and essential oil, but she never told me the ratio. It was diluted in pure alcohol, so you could play around with making your own.

To serve, place 40 g of consommé into a chilled cup. Toss the coarsely grated, peeled cucumber with rice wine vinegar and salt. Place 1 tablespoon of seasoned cucumber in a small bowl. Arrange 2 cubes of each color of melon on top of the cucumber. Add 2 grains of sel gris to each piece of melon. Finish with 2 borage leaves and 1 borage flower. Serve the consommé and salad side by side on a plate that has been lightly sprayed with mint.

Mint

SUMMER, FROZEN IN TIME
plum, frozen meringues, yogurt

The first taste should not tell the whole story of a dish. When we teach cooks here to taste, we teach them to take more than one bite, in order to understand how salt and acid aggregate and grow, or how some flavors start strong and then dissipate. Our food changes a lot, not only bite to bite, but from the beginning of a bite, from that first blast of flavor, to the aftertaste. We pay a lot of attention to the tail end, to the way that flavors change and evolve, to how a dish can echo for minutes after.

This is a dish of memory triggered by form and smell, with points of reference that are so varied that they defy easy categorization. I created it thinking about the way time seems to move differently during the warm months—one minute lasting an eternity, the next passing in a rush.

Ripe, aromatic stone fruit capture the essence of summer for me, especially the flavor of plums. If I can get them I use elephant hearts for their deep, intense flavor, and because they remind me of discovering them for the first time, from the same farm in Sonoma where I picked my own squash blossoms and corn every morning for Babette's. The taste of that plum, eaten by hand in the waxing summer heat, under an ancient tree in the center of the farm, is one of those memories that has stayed with me all these years. I've never tasted anything quite like it since (which I attribute partially to surprise, that moment of discovery that you get once and is then lost forever, leaving behind only the lesser pleasure of fulfilled expectation).

On the East Coast, summer meant frozen foods, like ices and popsicles. So I took egg whites, a little sugar and different essential oils to create frozen meringues—cold, crunchy air scented with summery notes (rose, ginger, pepper, citrus). Interspersed with the frozen meringue are dots of aerated yogurt, and slices of seasoned plum. Everything is covered in intensely flavored plum ice and scattered with salt—the salt keeps it a first course and not a dessert. It's sweet and sour, each bite changing in temperature and texture, the central flavor of plum mingling with fleeting floral notes that rise, entwine and fade into an aftertaste that lingers for several moments and slowly disappears.

Pit and blend the plums with a little water—just enough to stretch the pectin, because otherwise it won't freeze properly. Use the most aromatic and flavorful plums you can find, as the freezing process will sap them of some of their vitality. I do like elephant heart plums, but the Santa Rosa variety has its own charming story. Created in 1906 by Luther Burbank, perhaps the greatest horticulturalist in the history of the United States, they were named after Burbank's adopted hometown. For a time they were the most widely grown plum in California. To this day at their best they are unbeatable for density of flavor and sweet/sour balance, and for their remarkable aromatics.

Back to the base for the ice. Season with lime juice, salt, and sugar if necessary. Pour into a metal hotel pan and place in the freezer, breaking with a fork every 20 minutes, until the flakes are pleasantly crunchy.

Season the yogurt with a little bit of salt, just enough to bring up the flavor. Transfer to a siphon and charge twice.

Place 4 half sheet pans lined with parchment paper, a cutting board and 4 containers in the freezer. Divide the egg whites into 4 bowls, and season each one with a different oil (except the citrus, which gets a mix) and salt. The salt will push down the sweetness, but they shouldn't be salty. Charge them once in a siphon and shake for 2 minutes, until you can't feel any moving liquid. Charge again, and then spray out the meringue onto the frozen sheet pans in an even layer, about ¾-inch (2-cm) high, and put immediately back into the freezer until frozen solid. One sheet tray at a time, overturn onto a frozen cutting board, peel away the paper, and cut the meringue into ⅔-inch (1.5-cm) cubes. Transfer immediately back to the freezer on the cutting board, and then, once the meringue is completely solid, to the frozen containers. This is a trick, a sleight of hand. Without the stability that liquid nitrogen brings, any warming at any step of the process is fatal. (This goes for the entire dish. I once watched a chef let the dish sit in front of him untouched for several minutes while he talked to his date, and by the time he picked up a spoon it had turned into a weird slushy. I had a small heart attack, fighting back the urge to remove the plate from the table before he could taste it and make another one. So here's the warning: If you let this warm up, this dish will disappear. There is nothing to the meringues except air and aroma, which is their charm, and their downfall. If the ice is not properly frozen, or if it sits after it's made, the whole thing becomes a disaster.)

To serve, place the serving bowls in the freezer. When they're frozen, add 2 of each flavor of meringue. Thinly slice a plum—about ⅔-inch (1.5-cm) slices in diameter—and season with rice wine vinegar and salt. Dispense 4 dollops of yogurt here and there around the meringues. Add 6 pieces of the seasoned plum, and spoon a few tablespoons of ice over the top, covering everything but allowing the ghostly expression of the shapes underneath to show through. Season with Murray River salt and sprinkle with alyssum flowers. Eat immediately. Seriously.

2010

CLAM
bull kelp, wild fennel, meyer lemon

The drive down Highway 1 from San Francisco, heading south, is breathtaking. The jagged coastline plunges towards the sea on one side, and on the other rolling hills, forests and farmland tumble by. On a summer morning the sky is shielded by a thick layer of grey mist; by afternoon it burns off and the air is filled with the smell of wild fennel baking in the sun mingled with saline grasses and ocean. After the fall rains everything turns bright green, bathed in bleached-out light. This is a dish about the feeling of that stretch of coastline, at the moment when fall turns to early winter.

Geoduck—giant clams indigenous to southern Washington—are cleaned, cut into small pieces, and seasoned. The clams firm up a little, becoming sweeter and more flavorful.

To amplify the clam flavor we steam manila clams with shallots, garlic and white wine, and then stir squid ink into the cooking liquid. After discarding the clams we set the liquid into a thin sheet of gel, which we cut into strips.

There is a kind of seaweed that is wonderful in late fall called bull kelp, commonly known as kombu. (I call the dried version kombu throughout the book, as that is its more common name, especially when purchasing it.) Fresh bull kelp is worlds different than dried, more like a vegetable than a flavoring and thickening agent, the texture thick and snappy. We cook it briefly in boiling water, until it turns bright green and toothsome, and then cut it into the same size strips as the clam gel. The green and black strips are combined with the geoduck, all enlivened with fragrant Meyer lemon, like sunshine in winter.

The seaweed and clam tumble and curve around each other, a little like the highway, and perched on top are the first tiny shoots of wild fennel. Every year the plants are reborn after it rains, the new growth poking out of the base of the dried husks of last year's plants. They're sweet and delicate, with an intense licorice flavor. The fennel fronds capture the fleeting feeling of the dish, here for only a few weeks a year.

Kill the geoduck by dunking it in boiling water for 10 seconds, and then plunging it into an ice bath. Remove the shell and capture the juice. Clean and dice the body meat in ½-inch (1-cm) pieces. Peel the skin off the neck of the clam (I'll just say it–it's a little creepy, like removing saggy skin from a prosthesis) and dice the neck meat. Toss body and neck meat with salt and shiro dashi to taste, and refrigerate for at least a few hours. (The body meat is fatty and a little gamy–in a good way–the neck meat clean and delicate. I like them together.) It should be assertively seasoned, still sweet but with a whisper of ocean.

To make the vinaigrette, combine all of the ingredients and season with salt. If the Meyer lemons aren't sweet enough, add a pinch of sugar. It's an alluring vinaigrette, the shiro dashi adding a bump of umami where you don't expect it.

For the clam gel, sweat the shallot, garlic and piment d'Espelette in the olive oil until tender. Add the squid ink and cook for 2 minutes. Add the white wine and Manila clams, cover the pan, and steam until clams are opened. Cook 2 minutes more and strain the liquid through cheesecloth. Discard the clams, and cool the liquid in an ice bath. Season with Meyer lemon juice and the juice from the geoduck, which is salty, in place of salt.

Bring a 150 g of the clam juices to a boil with the agar, and then off the heat whisk in the gelatin to dissolve. Add to the rest of the clam juices and check the seasoning–it should taste dark, briny and bright, like clean coastal waters. Pour 218 g for a 12 x 18-inch (30 x 45-cm) sheet tray, and let cool in the refrigerator. Cut into 1 x 3-inch (2.5 x 7.5-cm) strips.

Cook the bull kelp in simmering unsalted water until just tender. Cool on a sheet tray lined with parchment, and cut also into 1 x 3-inch (2.5 x 7.5-cm) strips. Soak in several changes of water, drain and refrigerate.

To serve, toss 48 pieces of geoduck and 12 strips of bull kelp with Meyer lemon vinaigrette, salt and black pepper. Arrange in a bowl, interspersing with strips of clam gel. Garnish with tiny wild fennel shoots and Meyer lemon zest.

SAVORY CHANTERELLE PORRIDGE
pig's foot, wood sorrel

One day in 2007, I bought a grain mill. The motivation for the purchase is a little fuzzy, but not its aftermath. I started running anything that was dry and resembled a grain through that thing. We used the resulting powders in pasta, bread and cakes. Then I discovered that I could mill rice on the coarsest setting and break the grains. The rice, as it cooked, released its starch in a really pleasing way. I made a rice porridge, which set off a long series of dishes based on this technique.

There is no new discovery here. Peasants in China and Vietnam—the ones who knew better than to waste the less premium, broken pieces leftover from the threshing and winnowing—have been making broken rice porridge for thousands of years.

This is a fancy way of doing it, and one that, like its humble inspiration, allows for a lot of variations. As a base for a squash dish, I once folded in a squash purée seasoned with fermented vadouvan and lime, turning the rice a vivid yellow. It had a creamy mouth feel, bright acidity, and no fat except olive oil. It has worked well with carrot purées, beet purées . . . anything, really. It involves cooking the rice, letting it rest, and then adding the purée and bringing up the heat. That's it.

For this dish, I cooked the rice in chanterelle stock instead of water, and then folded in chanterelles sautéed in lots of brown butter. Soft-cooked and chopped garlic and shallot deepened and rounded the flavor, giving the dish a savory, mouth-filling quality. On top, to cut the richness, was the sour ping of wood sorrel and raw chanterelles. On the side, crunchy root vegetables.

Oh, and then there's the pig's foot. It was poached, finely chopped and then folded into the rice, as an enrichment (as if the dish needed it), the gelatin and fat of the meat combining with the starch and butter to create a voluptuous texture.

This is a humble dish with earthy, woodsy flavors that evoke the peasant food for which the grain mill was meant.

Put the pig's foot, carrot, onion and thyme in a large pan, cover with water, add salt and bring to a light simmer. Cook until the foot is very tender, about 3 to 4 hours. Let cool to warm room temperature in the cooking liquid, and then remove the bones. Getting all those tiny bones out is painstaking work. Take your time. Your knife will not like it if you leave any bones, and neither will your guests. Refrigerate the pig's foot, and then when fully cool, chop finely.

To prepare the chanterelles, set aside the tiniest, nicest ones for shaving, and clean the rest by brushing or rinsing them in cold water and laying them out on a sheet tray lined with towels to dry. (It's OK to wash wild mushrooms in water. Really.) Cut the chanterelles for sautéing, if necessary. Make the chanterelle stock by simmering the fresh scraps and dried chanterelles with the mushroom stock and vegetable stock.

Vacuum seal the garlic and pure olive oil and steam at 185°F (85°C) until tender. Cool, drain and mince.

Simmer the shallots with the vegetable stock, butter and vinegar until tender. Remove the shallots, cool and mince. Reduce the remaining liquid in the pot and then introduce the minced shallots back into the syrupy liquid–taste to make sure it's not too salty. Season with salt or more vinegar if necessary, and cool.

Brown the butter slowly until a medium deep brown and cool in an ice bath, stirring constantly, to keep the butter solids evenly suspended throughout.

Thinly slice all of the root vegetables. On some, like the salsify, slice in rounds. On others, like the young parsnip, shave lengthwise. Create a nice mixture of shapes. Heat the vegetable oil to 350°F (180°C) and fry the root vegetables one at a time until crisp. Drain on paper towels and season with salt. Hold warm.

To serve, cook the broken rice with the chanterelle stock by bringing to a low simmer and cooking, covered, until the stock has been absorbed and the rice is tender, about 25 to 30 minutes. Let stand off the heat for at least 5 minutes, and up to 30 minutes. Sauté the chanterelles in butter, seasoning with salt once they're coated in fat. When they're tender add some chanterelle stock to stop the cooking of the mushrooms. Add the cooked rice, 2 spoonfuls of chopped pig's foot, 1 spoonful each of minced shallot and garlic, and a little brown butter. Cook over low heat until the mixture is creamy, and add whatever aromatic ingredients (brown butter, shallot, garlic) you think are needed to make the rice delicious. Top with shaved chanterelles, wood sorrel and, depending on the month, a few of whatever kind of winter flowers you can find, like oxalis or radish. Serve the root vegetable chips on the side.

EARLY SPRING

buttermilk panna cotta, cherry blossom, first fronds of wild fennel

Spring comes early in Northern California. The new crop of artichokes at the end of January, the oxalis flowers and sudden spring days amongst the cold, all whisper of its arrival. But it really starts in February, when the fruit trees begin to blossom. They appear first at flower markets and then at farmers' markets, their wispy branches laden with white and pink flowers, saying that the end of the rainy season is near.

This dish captures the feeling of early spring, when the cherry blossoms are in bloom and the milk is sweet and herbaceous from the cows' diet of winter grasses. The spring vegetables have not fully arrived, and the larder is still (for California) relatively bare.

There is a gently set custard of our buttermilk infused with cured cherry blossoms, which we make the year before and store in salt; an agar-thickened sauce of cherry blossom, lightly sweetened; pickled fennel bulb; the young, tender shoots of wild fennel. We serve it next to a branch of fresh cherry blossoms, to amplify the aroma.

It's a polarizing dish. It's delicate, ethereal, difficult to contextualize. Buttermilk is European. Cherry blossoms reference Japan, where you will find very few dishes made with buttermilk. It fits perfectly into our style, and uses one of our best products, the buttermilk that we make ourselves. The transitory nature of the season is captured in the dish, maybe too well. I thought it was delicious, but reliably there would be someone every few nights who just could not stand it.

We always seem to have at least one dish on the menu that is not a unanimous rave. It could be a strange texture (abalone) or a foreign flavor (redwood). I accept that as an unfortunate side effect of the way that we cook. Part of what allows us to grow and evolve is a constant curiosity, a willingness to try something new. Even if it sometimes gets lost in translation.

You'll need to start the dish a year in advance. Sorry. Or, you could buy some Japanese preserved cherry blossoms, which if you spend enough will probably be better anyway. They've been doing it for a while there, and they've figured it out pretty well.

However, if you're in a DIY mood, combine the cherry blossoms with 20% salt by weight. Press them with a weight equal to the blossoms for 48 hours. You can cure the leaves the same way. After pressing, pack in salt and hold in a cool, dark place for a year (we use our wine cellar). The flavor and aromatics develop over time.

To make the panna cotta, combine the buttermilk with the blossoms and leaves, and refrigerate for 2½ hours. Strain, but reserve the blossoms for the next step. Bring the heavy cream, reserved blossoms, sugar and a pinch of the salt from curing the cherry blossoms to just under a boil. Remove from the heat, and melt in the gelatin. Taste for intensity, and let it stand for a few minutes if the flavor needs more time to develop. Strain and combine with the infused buttermilk. Season with cherry blossom salt and pour into bowls. Refrigerate for at least 3 hours until set.

For the fluid gel, vacuum seal all the ingredients in a bag and refrigerate for at least 3 hours. Strain and weigh the liquid. Bring the liquid to a boil with the agar. Cool until hardened and blend. Season with sugar, lemon juice and salt. The blossoms can be a little bitter, so the sugar and lemon juice will balance the flavor.

For the pickles, bring the vinegar, water, sugar and salt to a boil, and pour over the fennel (which should be in a metal container). Cool at room temperature.

To serve, spoon 2 tablespoons of the fluid gel over the buttermilk panna cotta. Garnish with pickled fennel and tiny, tender wild fennel fronds. Place the bowl on a plate next to a blossom branch.

MOREL/FAVA
angelica root, tarragon

Cooking is a lot about waiting. Some of the most extraordinary flavors, like fermentation, happen painfully slowly. The aromas of a roast or a cake baking permeate the kitchen long before they can be eaten. And, when it comes to ingredients, they happen when they happen, and not before. Like morels. Every year I start thinking about them in March, and every year they're ready in mid- to late-April, with the best ones coming later. In between, I wait.

This is an early May dish. The fava beans are still small and sweet. The tarragon is new, with tiny, intense leaves. And it's the time that we harvest angelica root. Everything in the dish is at peak flavor.

I discovered angelica through a local herbalist. I had cooked with what the French call "réglisse," or licorice root, which I had bought in little jars at Fauchon in Paris in the late '90s and brought back to California. I loved it, but when it was gone I never found a local substitute. Angelica is it, our licorice root, powerfully aromatic with a dusky, earthy edge. We dig it in the spring, when the green tops point the way. Later in the summer the greens die off, the roots are harder to find, and the flavor changes for the worse.

A little angelica root goes a long way. After we harvest it we bring it back to the restaurant, cut away and discard the tops, and wash the roots well. Then we slice and dry them overnight at room temperature—fresh angelica root is not so delicious, although we use the green leaves to make infusions. The next day, or when they've dried fully, we vacuum seal them and store them for the year. We use them like a spice, in either ground or whole form.

This is a classic spring combination of favas and morels, transformed by the angelica into something new. The licorice note of the angelica is amplified by tarragon, which makes the combination pop. Ironically, after all that waiting, the dish is one of timing and quickness, rushing the favas from plant to plate so as to not lose the sweetness and tender texture. There's some cooking in the moment and a bit of sauce making, both of which require careful coordination.

Professional kitchens are a strange blend of patience and urgency. A cook's days are measured in tiny increments, governed by a list of tasks that borders on insurmountable. We rush through our preparations only to arrive at the crush of service, where seconds delineate the fine line between success and failure.

I never cared much for the idea of cook as rebel or insouciant artist. Cooking is an act of generosity, not of private, inward contemplation. It is a traditional craft that requires practice and dedication, like building cabinets or throwing pottery. Pure imagination, the romantic side of creativity, is easy. Execution is hard.

If the morels are the size of your pinky finger, keep them whole. Index finger or bigger, cut in half. Remove the white stems. In a metal bowl, pour warm water over them, agitate and wait a minute. If there are any worms, the warm water will force them out. Drain and cover again with cold water, agitate, drain. Repeat until the morels are clean. Spread on a towel to dry.

Make the morel stock by simmering the mushroom stock, vegetable stock and morel scraps for 30 to 45 minutes, until the flavor is light but clear.

To make the fava bean purée, shuck and peel the fava beans and cook them in salted water until tender. Drain, and while the favas are still hot blend with salt and a little water to make a smooth purée. Cool in an ice bath, and adjust the seasoning after it's cooled. Transfer to a squeeze bottle and hold at room temperature.

To serve, heat 2 tablespoons of butter over medium heat until melted and foamy. Add the morels and a pinch of salt. When the morels are about half cooked, add 3 to 4 spoonfuls of morel stock and more butter. Cook over high heat, adding 40 small fava beans at the end, just barely cooking them. Reduce the liquid so that it glazes the morels and the favas.

While the morels are cooking, make the sauce. Cook the morel scraps in a spoonful of butter and a pinch of salt. Add the morel stock and reduce by half. Whisk in the rest of the butter to make an emulsified sauce, and season with a pinch of angelica powder and a few drops of champagne vinegar. Strain through a chinois.

Place 7 dime-size drops of fava purée around the plate, and scatter the morels and favas over the plate. Pour sauce over and around the morels, and garnish with tarragon leaves and a sprinkle of angelica powder.

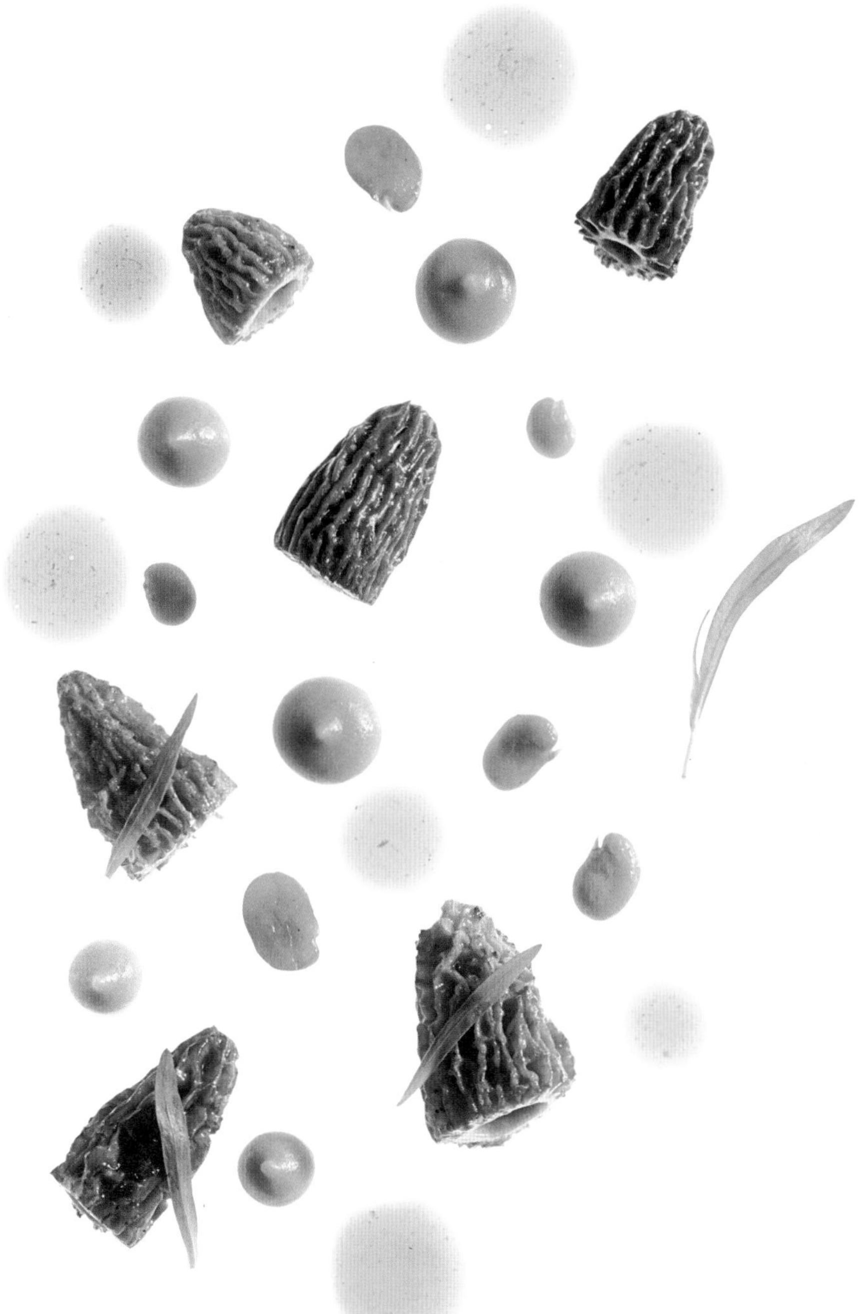

ASPARAGUS COOKED IN ITS JUICE
seaweed powder, meyer lemon sabayon

"Who made this?" my son often asks, holding out a carrot or a piece of fruit. Since he was tiny I've brought him to the farmers' markets, where he learned that ingredients come from people. Also, that there are hot dogs and pizza there.

There is a farmer that I only see in the spring named Roscoe Zuckerman. On a patch of land in the San Joaquin Delta that his family has farmed since the 1930s, Roscoe grows the only asparagus we've ever served. Sure, there are plenty of good farms around, but I have yet to taste anything better. And besides, I like the guy. Sometimes it's hard not to link the value of a food to the person who grew it.

This is an asparagus dish that has been evolving for a while. It began in 2000, on one of the first menus at Elisabeth Daniel. It was three thick spears of asparagus, steamed to order and served warm, with Meyer lemon sabayon, green olive oil and nothing else. We got more than a few comments that it was a little *too* minimal.

In 2010, I was looking for an asparagus dish for the season. I remembered that dish, but it still felt too simplistic. We had just developed the seaweed powder recipe, so I thought about contrasting the sweetness of the asparagus with something savory and fermented. I also liked the visual contrast of the black powder against the vibrant green grass.

I wanted to keep the sabayon, a strange version of a traditional sauce. It contains no sugar, except the natural sugar of the vegetable stock. It has a lot of lemon juice. It's cooked directly over a flame, giving it a lighter, less substantial texture, with clear, direct lemon favor. It's a tricky sauce to make, but when done right and then drizzled with good olive oil it makes a harmonious accompaniment. Still, the dish needed something else.

So I made a sauce of asparagus juice, seasoned with a little champagne vinegar just before serving. For the oil, a mix of different citrus essential oils infused into pure olive oil, their aromatics balancing the darkness of the seaweed and bringing complexity to the lemon. Three sauces, working in unison.

These days the market duties have mostly been passed on to Roscoe's son, Carlos, who shares his father's impish smile and wry sense of humor. Carlos is great, but I still like seeing the old man. On Saturday mornings I slip behind their stand, kids in tow, to pick up the asparagus that he made. We stand by his truck in the gentle spring light, talking and laughing while the kids play nearby.

Three days before serving make the seaweed powder as in Chicken and Egg (see page 136). Also at that time, combine the essential oils with the pure olive oil. Start with two drops of each oil, and then tune the mixture to your own taste–it's fun to see how they interact with each other. It's best if the oils sit for a few days so they can all get to know each other.

For the sabayon base, whisk all of the ingredients to combine, and strain. Season with salt.

For the asparagus vinaigrette, boil the vegetable stock and agar and cool in an ice bath. Break into smaller pieces. Blend 100 g of asparagus juice with the vegetable stock gel, a piece at a time, until you achieve a smooth sauce consistency. Compress in an open container to remove bubbles. Refrigerate until serving–if you add the vinegar in advance it will discolor the sauce.

Choose very large asparagus. Using the tip of a sharp paring knife, remove the little shoots and scales on the side of the stem, and a few at the top, to make a nice conical shape. Still using the knife, carefully peel the very outer layer of skin, so that only the layer of pale green subcutaneous flesh is exposed, and not the white underneath. This is an extraordinarily tedious and difficult task. When you get peeled asparagus that glow iridescent green, you can be sure that the cook worked very hard to make something beautiful. Do this right before serving–if you do it in advance, cover them with a moist towel.

To serve, heat a small amount of pure olive oil in a sauté pan. Add the asparagus and sear for 10 seconds, shaking the pan and seasoning with salt. Add enough asparagus juice to come halfway up the asparagus and cook, covered, shaking the pan occasionally, until the asparagus is just tender. (There's a moment when it's still raw in the middle, and one when it's slightly overcooked. In between, there is a fleeting moment of perfection. If you pay attention you will find it.) Towards the end of the cooking remove the lid, reduce the juice, and glaze the asparagus. This is also tricky–it involves a perfect synchronicity of salt in the liquid and timing, so that the asparagus doesn't get overcooked. You can also remove the asparagus and reintroduce it into the pan when the liquid is at glaze consistency. Transfer the asparagus to a plate lined with paper towels, and cut a tiny bit off the end to standardize the size, and also to check for seasoning. Adjust with salt, but not too much, as the seaweed powder is fairly saline. Sprinkle a line of seaweed powder on top.

While the asparagus is cooking, put a few tablespoons of sabayon base per serving into a small heavy pot. Over medium-high heat, whisk vigorously with a small whisk, turning the pot frequently to avoid hotspots. The idea is to build up bubbles while the proteins are setting. This, I am sorry to say, is also a bit challenging, and takes some practice. If the heat is too high then it will curdle. Too low and the proteins won't set properly. And the whisking must be constant and vigorous. (One of my old cooks had a special dance he did while making the sauce. It was a lot of fun to watch.) Once you get the hang of it, it's an easy and fast sauce that can be used in many savory applications. Pull it from the heat when it's cooked but a little soft, it will continue to set up.

Season a little thickened asparagus juice with rice wine vinegar and salt, and spoon onto a plate. Pour the sabayon over and around it, drizzle with several drops of citrus oil, and place the asparagus spears on top of the sauces.

CRAYFISH AND SPRING VEGETABLE STEW

spicy crayfish jelly

Cultural context plays a big role in how we perceive value and quality. Crayfish—aka crawdaddies, mudbugs, and so on—are an undervalued ingredient in many parts of the United States, at least in haute cuisine. Where I grew up, in fact, they weren't considered an ingredient at all, just something fun that we could catch by the shore in freshwater New England lakes. When Americans do eat crayfish, it's usually in casual settings, like the outdoor parties based around crayfish boils, in New Orleans and environs.

In Europe, on the other hand, crayfish are the basis for many famous dishes, past and present (like Fernand Point's *gratin de queues d'écrevisses*, a crayfish gratin). In Scandinavian countries the freshwater crayfish are fat and sweet, a spring/summer delicacy. In Australia crayfish are abundant in both fresh and saltwaters, and so tasty that they hold a prominent place on fine-dining menus.

Crayfish run wild in the quiet waters of the Sacramento delta, a few hours north of San Francisco. They are not, if we're being entirely honest, as good as the ones that live elsewhere. But handled correctly, they're still pretty great.

I've used crayfish for years, quite happily. We almost always create dishes that involve some sort of liquid infusion. This is because, for our crayfish, broths, stocks and oils are their best expression. As a bisque their flavors evoke Old World elegance, like a more gentle and precisely flavored version of lobster. When I was much younger I set a crayfish bisque with gelatin to make a panna cotta. I served it with caviar from the same area and a sauce of sorrel and crème fraîche. Very Troisgros circa 1973.

This stew of crayfish and young, tender vegetables went in a completely different direction. I call it a stew, but really all of the components are made separately and brought together at the last moment, which makes it cleaner, brighter and more energetic than the long-cooked dish that the name connotes. There is a deeply flavored broth, infused with lemongrass and ginger and seasoned with lime; a spicy crayfish jelly set with gellan, so it can withstand some heat; and a crayfish oil, liberally spooned over everything.

I like crayfish best in the spring, when we can use all manner of vegetables at the height of their sweetness and delicacy. The vegetables and herbs balance the spice and acidity and bring freshness and life to the broth. It's a refined and intensely flavorful expression of a common ingredient that deserves a second look.

Reserve 12 crayfish for steamed tails, and kill the rest by cutting them in half. Cut through the head first and then through the tail, humming the executioner's song. Crayfish are angry little creatures, so you should probably plan on being nipped at least once. And keep an eye on them, they're escape artists that will die a slow and stinky death under your kitchen table. Spray out the insides that you exposed and drain them.

For the crayfish broth and oil, heat the pure olive oil to smoking in a wide (non-reactive, heavy-bottomed) pan, and add the crayfish. Sear stirring often, until they turn bright red. Remove the pan from the heat, and grind the crayfish slightly by pulsing in a food processor. Your machine will hate this, by the way, and it probably voids the warranty, but your sauce will be the better for it, by exposing as much surface area of the crayfish as possible.

To make the crayfish oil, combine 200 g cooked crayfish and the pure olive oil and cook for 2 to 3 hours at a bare simmer, until the oil tastes deliciously of crayfish. Strain through cheesecloth.

For the broth, add the rest of the seared crayfish back to the pan, and add the wine to deglaze. Reduce by three-quarters, and add the rest of the ingredients. Simmer for 1½ to 2 hours, partly covered, until flavorful. Strain the broth, reserving 250 g of liquid for the jelly. For the rest, add lemongrass (smashed with the back of a knife and then chopped) and ginger (sliced), and cover. You're making an infusion, like a tea–keep it hot and covered but don't cook it. When the flavor is right–the aromatics present and fresh, but not overwhelming, about 20 minutes–strain it through cheesecloth. Season with salt, lime juice and rice wine vinegar.

For the jelly, reduce 250 g reserved broth to 200 g, and season with salt and chile powder. Season it high, because the gellan will diminish the seasoning. Cool. Weigh and blend with the gellan LT and gellan F. Bring it to a good, rolling boil, and then pour into a metal container to set at room temperature (don't jiggle the container while it's setting).

Steam the reserved whole crayfish at 212°F (100°C) for 3 minutes, or until cooked. (You may be tempted to try this at a lower temperature. Let me assure you that we have done it for you. The texture is not nice. 212°F [100°C] is good.) We use the Combi oven for this, as it's the only way to get an exact temperature, although you could certainly steam them in the usual way, in a basket set over a pot of boiling water. Cool the crayfish in the refrigerator, and then shell and clean the tails.

We use up to 10 different spring vegetables–here's a selection below. The main thing to remember is that each vegetable should be handled sensitively, based on its flavor and texture. Tiny Tokyo turnips might be good whole, but if slightly larger they should be cut in half or sliced. Cook them as much as you think they need to reveal their fullest flavor. It's spring, so at least some of the ingredients should be delicious raw.

We like to use vegetables like little, new onions and young fennel, which should be cooked in salted water, set aside to cool, and then trimmed as necessary. Cook the young artichokes with vegetable stock and olive oil in a bag at 185°F (85°C). Cool and trim. English peas and fava beans should be peeled and cooked to order. Pea shoots, fava flowers and shaved turnip should be raw.

To serve, heat the broth with peas and favas until just cooked, about a minute. Add the cooked onion, artichoke and fennel, and warm through. Off the heat, add 3 crayfish tails and 3 scoops of crayfish jelly, cover for a minute until they're warm, then transfer the vegetables and broth to the bowl. Drizzle a large spoonful of crayfish oil over everything–the oil will balance the acidity in the sauce, and add another layer of flavor. Garnish with pea shoots, shaved turnip and fava flowers.

THANK YOU FOR VISITING...

2011

DUNGENESS CRAB ENCASED IN ITS CONSOMME
buttered crab broth, wild winter herbs

I was raised in Manchester, a small town on the north coast of Massachusetts. I grew up listening to the clang of lanyards slapping against hollow masts, the breath of gathering waves eddying against the shore, the squeak of sand under bare feet. There was the smell of seaweed drying on sun-warmed rocks, of lobster and clams steamed over a fire dug into the beach, of smoke mingled with sweat and suntan lotion and something more mysterious that's hard to put my finger on now.

My father owned a 19-foot O'Day sailboat that he moored in the harbor, and I learned to sail not long after I learned to walk. At the end of the pier by the boat was a little shack that sold live and cooked lobsters for $4 a pound, and one of my vivid childhood memories is lobster boiled (for too long, although I didn't know it then) in seawater and then served with drawn butter. To this day lobster and butter bring me back to that harbor, back to the town where I grew up.

There is no lobster in Northern California. Instead we have Dungeness crab, one of the most iconic and delicious seafood ingredients of our area. Every year around Thanksgiving the season starts. Every year, the crabbers strike for more money. And every year, inevitably, they come to an understanding, and we put crab on the menu, where it stays until the season fades around February or March.

This dish started as a simple, primary taste memory. Some fancy stuff happened along the way, but the whole time we were developing the dish, Evan and I kept saying the same thing: crab and butter. Crab and butter.

We wanted the best of everything—texture, flavor, ease of eating. The form took a while to get right. It's crab that's cooked in salted water and cooled. The meat is picked, and the shells are used to make a savory consommé. Part of the consommé is made into a gelatin gel that binds the meat. Part is made into a temperature-resistant gel that forms a thin coating around the meat, creating a neat little crab-square. And the rest of the consommé is mixed with lightly browned butter and served as a broth.

When gently warmed, the squares of crab, glazed with their own consommé, liquefy inside, firm enough to hold their shape, but soft enough to be completely yielding when cut with a spoon. It's like cracked crab carefully picked out of the shell and then dipped in butter, but better. And easier to eat.

To the crab and butter I added some wild winter herbs for accent: sheep sorrel, chickweed, oxalis and alyssum flowers. It was a dish that made me think of my old home, and my new one as well.

Cook a crab for 8 to 10 minutes in simmering, salted water, and then cool on a sheet tray until you can handle it. Remove all the meat, breaking up the big pieces and carefully removing all bits of shell. If you own a black light, you can use that in a darkened room to illuminate the tiny pieces of shell. (Also, if you own a black light, I have other questions for you.) You can also drop the crab as you're picking through it on a metal sheet tray, and any bits of shell you've missed will make a distinctive clacking sound. In no case should you ever, ever, serve your guests pieces of shell. It will ruin the dish, the meal and probably your friendship. Break the big pieces up a little. Season with salt if necessary, and refrigerate.

For the broth, smash the shells. Sear them in pure olive oil, and then add the white wine and reduce by half. Add the water and vegetable stock. Simmer over low heat for 2 to 3 hours, tasting as it cooks, until the broth is concentrated and delicious. Strain through cheesecloth, season with salt and cool. Let the broth stand 2 hours, and then decant the very clearest liquid on the top.

For the crab squares, bring the crab broth to a boil with the agar. Remove from the heat and stir in the gelatin. When the gelatin is melted, stir in the crab and spread on a 12 x 18-inch (30 x 45-cm) sheet tray to cool, making sure that the thickness is exactly uniform. Let it set in the refrigerator for 2 hours. Remove and cut it into scant 1¾-inch (4-cm) squares. Transfer the squares to the freezer for 30 minutes.

Meanwhile, make the consommé gel by blending the crab broth with the gellans, and then bringing the mixture to a hard boil to hydrate. Keep at a bare simmer while you glaze the crab squares. If you take it off the heat it will set, and you will have to throw it out and start again—it won't remelt. Using a fork or a pair of tweezers, dip each square, one by one, into the gellan broth. When the gel has set, which will happen almost instantly, dip it again. Remove it to a sheet tray lined with parchment paper.

Lightly brown the butter, just barely past the clarified stage. Strain the butter solids, and then add some to the reserved broth and season with salt.

To serve, warm the crab square on a sheet tray under a medium broiler until just warmed through. Place in the center of a bowl. Spoon some buttered crab broth around, and garnish with the wild greens and flowers.

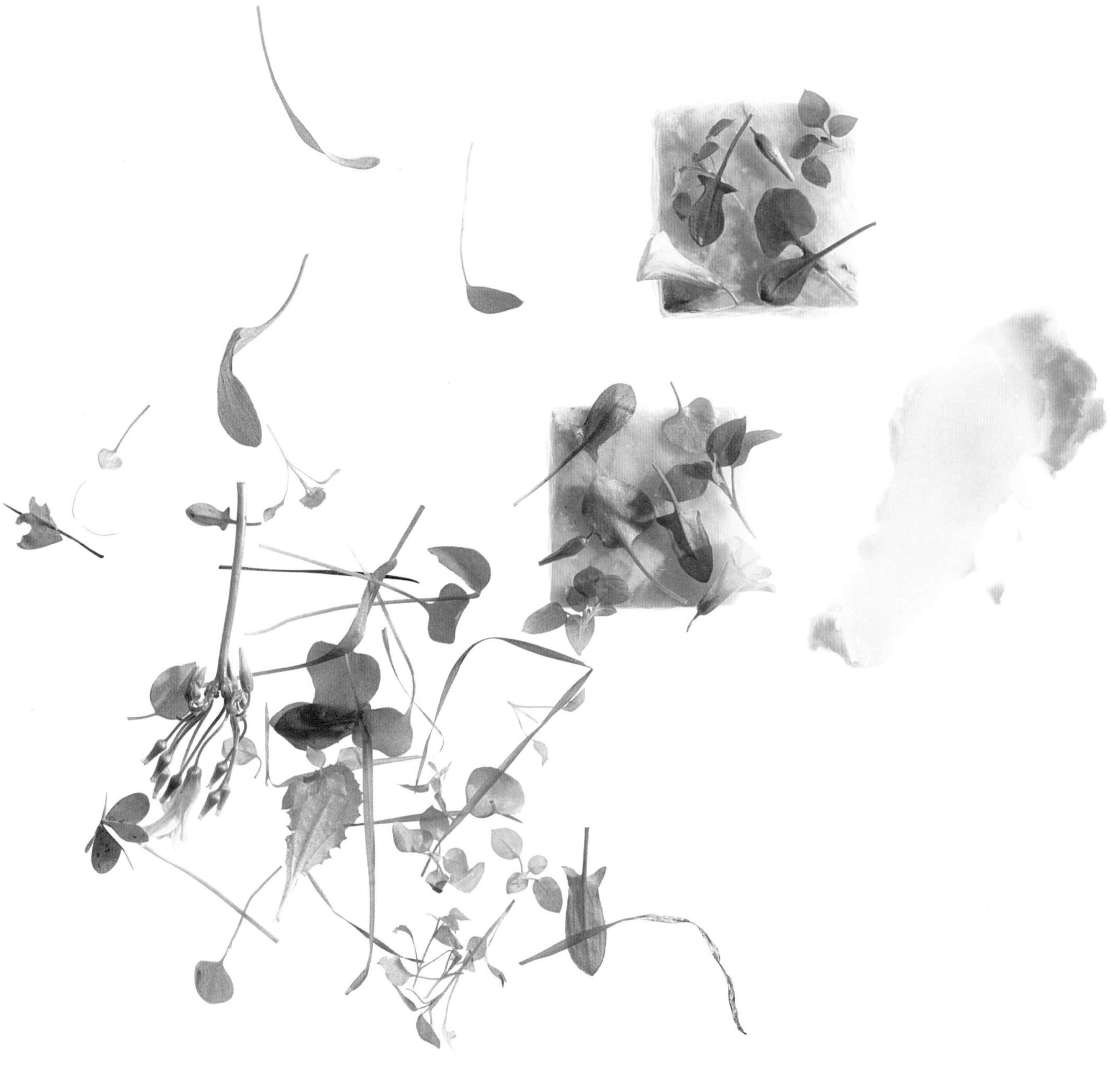

WOMEN

FRIED EGG (NOT FRIED)
brassica, smoked oil, herbs

In writing, it's called voice. In music, it might be called sound, the combination of tone and rhythm that makes a performance unique. But in food, there's no word for the quality of distinctiveness that makes a chef's work his or her own. "Everyone's using the same ingredients," I've heard chefs say. "That's why all the food tastes the same in the Bay Area." Not so! There are only twelve notes that all musicians use. It's their sound—*how* they play them—that distinguishes each artist.

This dish started with a conversation I had with the Italian chef Massimo Bottura about one of his best-known dishes, *Bollito Misto no Bollito* (Boiled Meat, not Boiled). In it he reinterprets a classic dish from his region of Emilia-Romagna in a modern way. The dish, at first regarded with some skepticism in his area, came to be one of his best-known—and most-copied—creations. "They're even making *Fritto Misto, no Fritto*," Massimo told me, laughing.

When Massimo came to my restaurant, I thought I'd create a dish in his honor. Fried Egg (not Fried), I called it. I cooked the yolk of a farm egg slowly in oil, and then covered it in smoked breadcrumbs, so it looked like a breaded and fried egg. I steamed the whites and emulsified them into a ravigote-ish sauce, seasoned with caper and shallot and herbs, enriched with smoked oil, and electric with acidity from champagne vinegar. It is not a subtle sauce. To go with the egg, we took whatever sort of brassica we could find in the markets, and grilled them.

We tend to sauce in a way that's hard to replicate from dish to dish, that exactly reflects the motion of the hand, like calligraphy. One mistake, a wavering, a disruption of the fluid motion of the sauce, and there's no fixing it, it needs to be redone. It's a form that is handmade, human, an expression of craft. This dish I sauced like a crazy person, a pool at the bottom to season the egg, and then in swirls and drips all around. It's a kind of saucing that, even in my own kitchen, is hard to recreate.

The dish ate well, intense, rich and exciting at the same time. Massimo loved it, my little joke about the line between inspiration and re-creation.

Steam the egg whites at 185°F (85°C) until they are set. Cool. Blend the steamed whites with the herbs, champagne vinegar, water, pure olive oil and smoked oil until emulsified. It should be smoky and intensely acidic, with plenty of salt. It should, on its own, seem like too much of everything—the egg yolk needs it for balance.

For the smoked breadcrumbs, tear a loaf of levain bread into chunks, and dry out in the oven at 480°F (250°C) until dry. Grind in a food processor with smoked oil until they become breadcrumbs. Season with salt and more smoked oil, if necessary.

Clean, cut and cook the brassica leaves, stems and florets, as in New Olive Oil on page 224.

To serve, cook the egg yolks in pure olive oil held in a 150°F (65°C) water bath heated with a circulator for 45 to 60 minutes until the yolks are thickly creamy and not runny at all, with an almost waxy quality. It's an unusual and appealing texture. If you need to, you can hold the eggs, turn the temperature of the circulator down to 120°F (50°C), they'll hold a few hours without changing much.

Remove an egg yolk with a slotted spoon (so that the oil drains away) and transfer to a bowl containing the breadcrumbs. Cover in the crumbs, and pick up the yolk, packing it tightly into the crumbs, gently pressing them in so the yolk is completely covered. Season the brassica with pure olive oil and salt, and grill them on the plancha. Remove to a sheet tray lined with paper towels. Add the sauce to the bowl with a spoonful in the center, and then thin lines around, in whichever way you think looks good. Place brassica on top of the sauce, and the egg on top of the brassica, making sure that the crust is completely covering the egg.

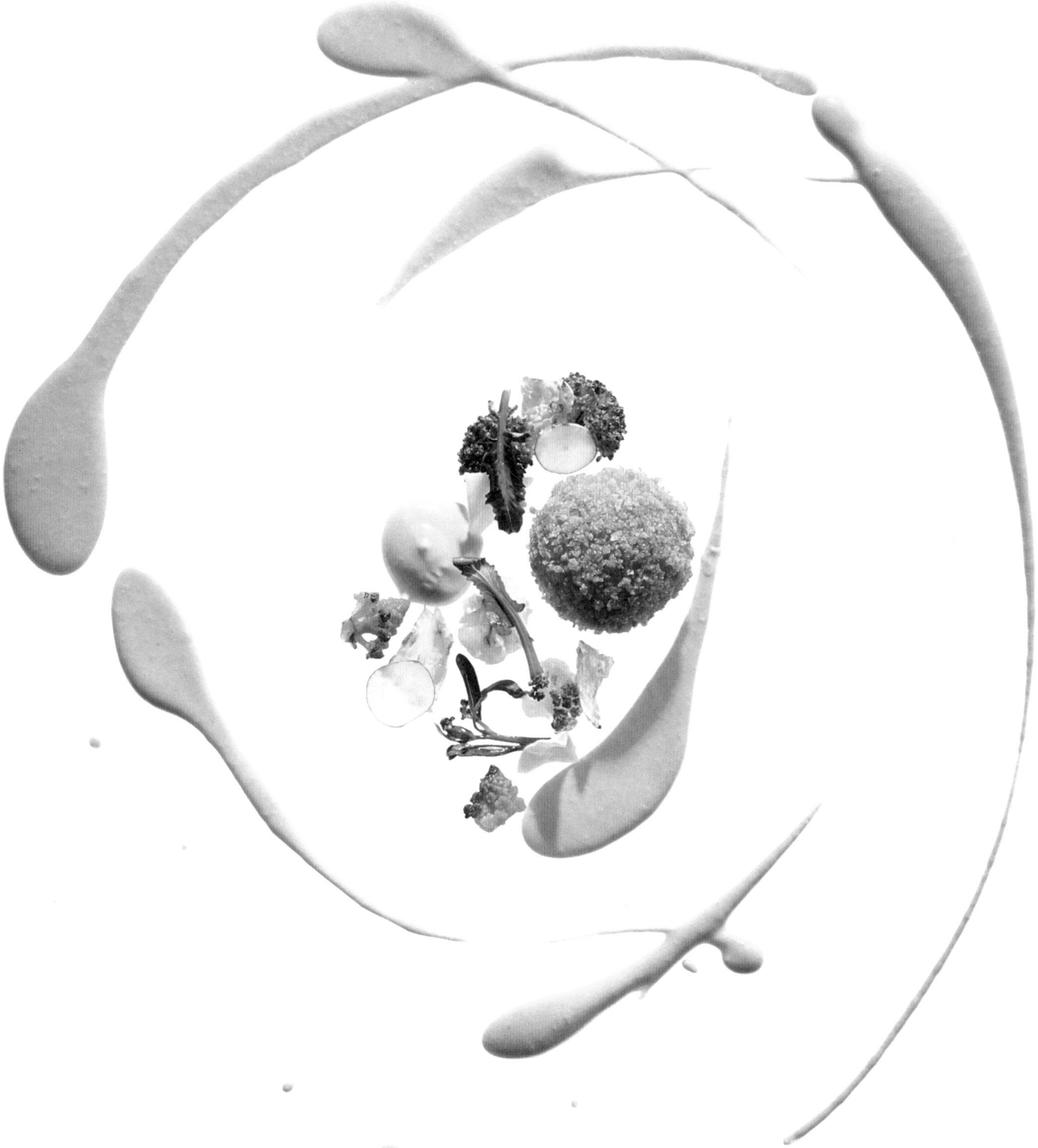

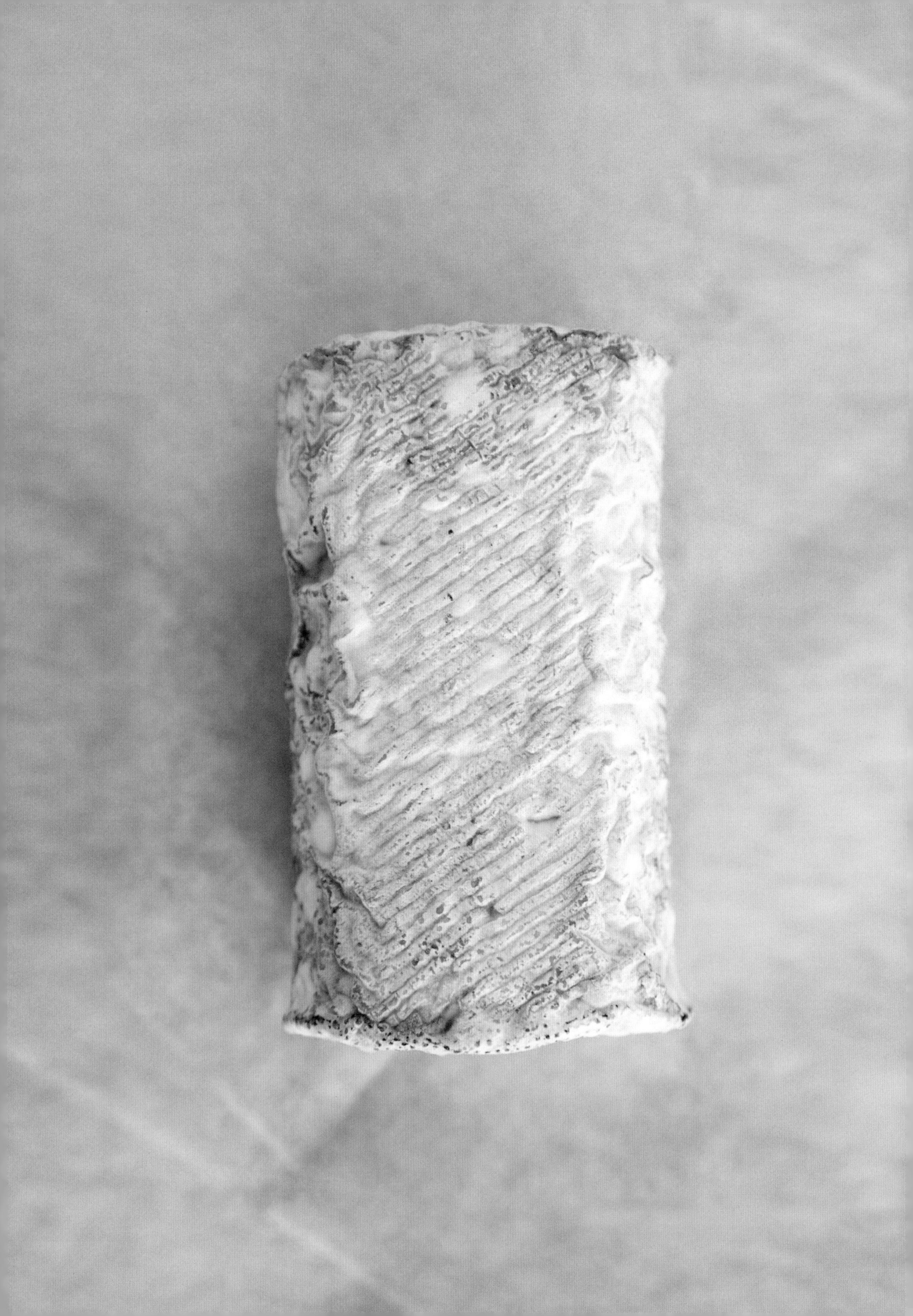

BEET ROSE
yogurt, rose petal ice

This dish started as a combination of two flavors—beet and rose. For some reason I immediately thought of a beet that looked like a rose. It could have been the apple rose that Albert Adrià made at an event we did together, or maybe the idea of a rose evoked some long-forgotten memory, but in any event I immediately fixated on how I could make a beet look like a rose.

My staff, who know me pretty well, shook their heads when I told them what I wanted to do. It seemed improbable. I could have used molds and gels, surefire ways of creating form, but I wanted something more natural, something that tasted intensely of beet. A hyper-real beet. The seasoning came immediately to mind—compress the roasted beets in reduced beet juice seasoned with a little rice wine vinegar to balance the sweetness. But the form was elusive.

You can take a vegetable peeler and shave a continuous piece from the sides that can then be fashioned into a rose shape. It wouldn't eat quite right though, and anyway it's been done. But after some messing around I found that a small piece cut in that manner worked well for the center. I trimmed the rest of the beet into cylinders, flat on one side so they slightly resembled a tunnel, and then sliced them thinly (not too thin, or they lose their texture; not too thick, they won't bend properly). After compressing them I dipped the flat bottom of one in a purée of roasted beets and a little reduced juice, and then pressed it against the center piece, the purée working like a glue. I continued in a circular pattern, gently pulling the petals outward until they formed a rose shape. I then put it in the refrigerator, where the flavors melded in a magical way.

When a dish is right, there is synchronicity between form and substance, idea and execution. This is a dish that was meant to be challenging to make, impractical to reproduce. There is something about its unreasonableness which made it more impactful. For it to work, everything has to be perfect. The beets must be flavorful and properly cooked, sliced and seasoned. The aerated yogurt beneath, clear and bright. The rose ice, sweet and sour, with enough salt to make it jump; it should be like a cold soda on a hot day, so refreshing you keep wanting more.

But I came to love it most for what it represented to me: intuitive, handmade cooking. Each rose is a little different, and I can pick out who made which one every night. The seasoning is finely tuned, wobbling on the edge of sweet and savory, always close to tumbling into failure. The recipe, such as it is, has no amounts, no times, very little specifics—it's all cooking by feel and taste.

And it's stubbornly ephemeral. It's not enough for everything to be prepared perfectly. The bowls must be frozen, every component added quickly and cleanly. And then, if you let it sit for one minute too long, the dish is ruined. The ice loses its texture, the temperatures run together, it becomes not bad, but boring.

After a few months I took it off the menu, as winter became spring. No matter how good a dish is, keeping it on too long leads to boredom and complacency; the energy of the kitchen requires a steady supply of new dishes and ideas. But every once in a while I bring it back, to remind the cooks, and myself, how hard it can be to produce a simple form.

First make the rose petal ice. Infuse the petals in hot, but not boiling water, like making a tea. Strain through a chinois. Season with the honey, lemon juice, sugar and salt. Pour into a frozen pan and transfer to the freezer. Break with a fork every 30 minutes until it becomes completely frozen and crunchy, adjusting the seasoning with salt and lemon along the way.

Roast medium to large beets, skin on, with water, olive oil, salt and pepper. While the beets are roasting, reduce the beet juice by about half. Cool and season gently with salt and rice wine vinegar. When the beets are tender, cool, peel and cut into 2 sizes of cylinders. Cut a sliver off one side of each to slightly flatten them. Slice approximately ⅛-inch (1-mm) thick to make the petals–you will need about 30 petals per beet rose, and about twice as many large as small. Make extra because some will break in the process of seasoning them. For the centers, peel some strips with a vegetable peeler and cut into ¾-inch (1.5-cm) lengths.

Toss the different size beets with reduced beet juice and season with more salt, rice wine vinegar and sugar if necessary. Keep the different shapes separate. Compress in the Cryovac on high in open containers. Remove and adjust seasoning–the goal is vibrant, well-seasoned beets, neither salty, sweet nor acidic. Purée the trimmings with a little reduced beet juice until smooth, season with salt and rice wine vinegar.

To assemble the roses, start by rolling a strip of beet and placing it on a working surface. That is the center. Tweezers come in handy here. Dip the bottom of a small petal of beet into the purée, and press against the centerpiece. Repeat, overlapping the first petal with the second by half, moving always in a clockwise direction. Occasionally press the petals together from the bottom to keep them tight. Gradually make the petals larger, until the rose is about 1¾-inch (4-cm) wide. Gently spread the petals outward so it looks like a rose. Refrigerate for at least 2 hours.

Season the yogurt to taste with lime juice and salt. Put in a siphon and charge twice.

To serve, place a dab of beet purée in the center of a frozen bowl, and dispense a dollop of aerated yogurt on top of that. Spoon some of the rose petal ice around the yogurt. Place the beet rose in the center of the yogurt. Serve immediately.

Cucumber
buttermilk +
verbena
&
Melon
Spot Prawn
pepper corn
Avocado
Popcorn cuke
Grits buttermilk
tart
Piquillo
Eggplant
little onions
garden sorrel
Radish
Mint
Onion
lettuce
Potato
Sorrel
Abalone
with grains
lamb
Sunchoke
black olive
Beef
Fresh cheese
Pear
Beet
Peach

AGED DUCK BREAST COOKED ON THE BONE
sprouted wheatberries, radish, redwood tips

When I was four our house burned down. It's my first memory, watching the chaos and confusion from our neighbors' yard while bright flames clawed at the sky. Funny, I guess, that I ended up working with fire for a living. My sister was hurt and spent the next few years in and out of hospitals, and for a while my parents were a little distracted. They rebuilt a new house in the same place, and that's where I spent the next several years.

Behind the house was a small pond, surrounded by a forest. That forest was where I spent a lot of my time, walking, playing, hiding. The woods were comfort and solace, something dependable when other things weren't. I learned to lie still and listen to creaking branches and the rustle of birds, to see patterns in spider webs and bark, to know the smell of pine and forest floor after a summer rain. To this day, the calmness and quiet of a forest soothes me in a way that nothing else does.

That forest behind our house was filled with evergreens, but I never thought about eating them. Then one day in 2007 Connie Green, the famous forager who founded Wine Forest Wild Foods—and from whom I've bought mushrooms from for eighteen years—surprised me with a present. It was a small bag of Douglas Fir tips, the tender, pale green shoots that grow out of the tips of these evergreen branches every spring.

The taste of the fir tips was incredible, kind of Christmas-like, with orange notes and a sour undertone, like sorrel. We used the tips in a salmon dish, and made a green oil from the mature needles to accentuate the flavor. We eventually moved on to other local trees, like Monterey cypress and redwoods.

Few trees here are as iconic as the California redwood. Massive stands of them dot the coastline, some thousands of years old. They've become a symbol of the environment, and more than once they've stood in the way of development. Every spring they throw out their little shoots, and in 2011 I decided to make a dish to celebrate them.

I can't explain the combination, but trust me, it works. Duck, aged until it's gamy and flavorful, is cooked on the bone, which maintains the juiciness and integrity of the texture. It's not an easy way to cook the duck, but the result is fantastic. Next to the duck is a salad of sprouted wheatberries and radish, garnished with the redwood tips; underneath, a duck jus shot through with champagne vinegar, and balanced with bright green redwood oil.

I still live near a forest, where on Sundays I sometimes take my kids for walks. They pick sour grass and I break open bay leaves for them to smell. Their voices flutter in the air in front of me as they run ahead, the stillness punctured every so often by their cries: "Papa! Look what I found!"

We hang the whole ducks for 2 weeks or more in a refrigerator. The meat should have a pleasant funk, but should not smell rotten. Rinse the duck well before you cut it up, and leave the breastbone on the breasts. The bones might not taste great for stock, because of the aging. You will need to find something else to do with the legs–we serve them to our staff for dinner.

Wheatberries take about 2 days to sprout. Put them in a glass jar, cover with twice as much water as wheatberries, and let stand at room temperature for 24 hours, covered. Drain them the next morning, and cover the top of the container with a wire screen. Rinse and drain the wheatberries (without removing the screen) at morning and at night, and they will be ready, their wispy little sprouts poking out of the ends, in 1 to 2 days. The sprouting softens the texture and makes them edible–and delicious–raw.

To make the redwood oil, blend the redwood needles with pure olive oil for 45 seconds on high, until it becomes a smooth purée. Prepare a bowl in an ice bath, with a chinois close at hand. Heat a wide stainless steel pan to almost smoking. Pour in the redwood oil carefully, stirring constantly, for about 10 seconds, until the color deepens. Pour through the chinois into the bowl in the ice bath and stir constantly until cool. It should be a deep, vibrant green.

Make a duck jus by browning some fresh duck bones, adding the carrot and onion and stirring until soft, deglazing with white wine and then simmering for a few hours in AP stock until flavorful. Strain and reduce, skimming, until the sauce is limpid and thickened to sauce consistency–if you run your finger through it on a plate, the channel should take a few seconds to close. Season with champagne vinegar and salt–it should have fresh, clean acidity.

For the vinaigrette, combine the minced radish, redwood oil and champagne vinegar to make a balanced but slightly sharp vinaigrette. It should be a little liquidy.

To serve, bring the duck breast to room temperature, and season it 20 minutes before cooking, salting heavily on both sides, and with pepper only on the bone side. Start the duck in a cast iron pan, skin side down, to render the fat. Cook at a moderate heat, and as the fat renders and heats up, spoon some over the bone to cook it. Flip the duck and keep cooking and basting, repeating a few more times, turning often, until the meat is cooked and rosy, and the skin is nicely browned. Sprinkle some more salt on the skin and rest just until the meat is warm to the touch instead of hot–the juices shouldn't run, but the meat should be juicy. Remove the bone, trim the top, bottom and sides of the meat to make a rectangle, and then slice the duck in half lengthwise. There will be some fat on your cutting board. I like to swab the cut side in the fat to give it a nice sheen, barbecue-style.

Mix some sprouted wheatberries with radish vinaigrette, radish bottom sprouts, salt and black pepper. The salad should be brightly seasoned. Spoon some sauce on the left side of the plate in a random pattern, and drizzle some of the redwood oil into the sauce, to make a broken vinaigrette of sorts. Place a piece of the duck in the center of the plate, and the wheatberry salad next to it. On top of the wheatberries place some shaved breakfast radish and redwood shoots.

INVERTED FROMAGE BLANC TART
fennel, wheatgrass

Much has been said about the proper role of a chef in the modern era of television shows and endless promotion. I think that our job is much the same as it was a hundred years ago: Make sure that the food that comes out of the kitchen tastes great.

How that happens is different for every restaurant. At Coi we serve about six hundred dishes on a busy night, with up to seventeen cooks working hard for many hours. Either Andrew or I will select every product that we use, and then we monitor the progress of the cooks' work. Sometimes I'm in the kitchen a lot during the day, other times less, but we always get together to taste every dish on the menu before we open, to fine-tune the components. A good night is when a few out of fifteen dishes are perfect and need no adjustment. During service one of us tastes every salad, sauté or sauce that is cooked or seasoned to order. And still things slip through from time to time.

We rely on the passion, talent and intelligence of our cooks. Without a strong team, we cannot work at the highest level. But there are some things that cannot be delegated. One is inspiration.

The last inverted tart came about in the late winter of 2011. There was some wheatgrass around, and some fromage blanc, and I had the idea that the combination would be electric: It was. I added a buckwheat tuile on top to balance the dish and give it an earthiness, and fennel in different forms to play against the anise notes in the wheatgrass. It's the least accessible, most exciting version of the inverted tarts.

This is a dish that can be made any time of year, but it's best in winter to early spring. The milk is sweetest and most delicious then, when the animals graze on new, tender herbs and grass. I tried making it in the late summer and couldn't figure out why I didn't like it as much. When it went on the menu again the following winter I found in the cheese the power and energy the fall version lacked.

It's a hard dish to make perfectly, and when it's not perfect it's pretty ordinary. There are a million ways that it can go wrong. If the crisp on top is too thick then the texture is jarring, too thin and it sogs, collapsing into the cheese. The fennel fluid gel dressing needs a round sweet/sour balance—not enough sweetness and the taste is tinny and unsatisfying, not enough acid and it's boring. The wheatgrass has to be the right texture to interact with the cheese—too thin and it disappears, too thick and it's disgusting in the way that only over-xanthaned sauces can be. But, in the end, it's a cheese tart, and the cheese has to be extraordinary, the flavor of sweet milk balanced by the sour culture.

Sometimes, when we're tasting before service, I feel that there is something a bit off with a dish. The seasoning is fine, everything seems to be in the right place, but there's a diminishment that's hard to put my finger on. It is one of the most frustrating parts of my job, that vague sense that something's not right. It's a nagging feeling that stays with me through the night and often into the next day, occasionally longer, like living in a grey cloud. No matter how good the cooks are, no one else is ever going to have as sensitive, as personal a relationship with the dishes as I do.

I had that feeling for over a week last winter before I figured out what was wrong. One night, as I tasted the tart before service, I suddenly realized that there was too much whey in the cheese. The foam was a touch too airy and insubstantial, the taste too sour, and the center of the dish was gone. So then I drained the cheese again, too much this time, which made it dense and dominating. A bit looser and it was just right, with an intense, commanding flavor that held the dish together, and a texture that bridged the delicacy of the crisp and the crunch of the fennel.

The first inverted tart was clever but, as a friend pointed out, it seemed familiar somehow. The second tart I broke apart, literally, but it was still bound by the commonness of the beet/goat cheese combination. In this iteration, finally, the form morphed into a dish with many antecedents but few reference points. That's a role that I hope will never change, stubbornly pushing ideas forward for years until I arrive at something new.

Dice perfect ½-inch (0.7-mm) squares of fennel, and cook half in salted water until they are tender. Drain and cool on a plate. Keep the rest raw. With the scraps of fennel you will inevitably generate turning a multilayered root into cubes, make the fennel stock and the burnt fennel oil. For the burnt fennel oil, roast the fennel scraps at 400°F (200°C) until half-burned. Dehydrate at 140°F (60°C) and then blend with pure olive oil to make a smooth, black oil. Burnt fennel oil sounds like it would be bitter, but it's not.

For the stock, simmer the scraps and water until the flavor is sweet and concentrated. To make the fluid gel, strain the stock, measure the appropriate amount and boil it with the agar and the reserved cooked fennel. Cool until solid, and then blend until smooth. Season with dried fennel pollen, champagne vinegar and salt.

We get the fromage blanc undrained—that is, sitting in its whey—and then we drain what we need every day. Drain it enough to make a thick purée, and season with salt. Transfer to a siphon, and charge twice.

Combine all of the ingredients for the buckwheat crisp—it's similar to the rye crisp on page 132. Transfer to a fine strainer and shake over a Silpat in an even layer. Bake in the Combi at 340°F (170°C) and medium fan for about 8 minutes, rotating at 4 minutes, until lightly browned. Turn the Silpat onto a piece of parchment set on the counter, and peel back the Silpat. Break into pieces and store in a tightly covered container.

Blend the wheatgrass juice with the pure olive oil and xanthan to make a nice sauce. The wheatgrass juice should be very fresh, juiced within a few hours. If you want to juice it yourself, I encourage that, but it needs a special juicer. An expensive one, of course.

To serve, toss the raw and cooked fennel in some of the fennel gel, just to coat and season. Taste and add champagne vinegar or salt if necessary. Place 6 each raw and cooked pieces in the center of the plate, with a little of the fluid gel. Place a drop of the burnt fennel oil on each corner (shake the bottle first). Drizzle the wheatgrass juice around it, dispense some fromage blanc from the siphon on top of the fennel, and place a buckwheat crisp on top of the cheese. Garnish with a piece of chervil.

CARROTS ROASTED IN COFFEE BEANS
creme fraiche, oats, cilantro

I was standing in my kitchen at home, looking at my coffee grinder, thinking about making an espresso. I often think about making espresso—something about restaurants and kids and no sleep. In this instance I was in the middle of a two-day cooking session for a magazine story with René Redzepi, who had traded his kitchen at Noma for my mid-'60s electric range, and all of a sudden, it occurred to me that we should cook something with coffee. So I said that. René, who happened to be holding a small winter squash at that moment, looked at it and proposed that we roast the squash buried in coffee beans. And that's how this dish began.

The interaction between the carrots and the coffee is magic, a totally new taste, the two flavors so entwined it's impossible to tell where one picks up and the other leaves off. The carrots have to be sweet, and the coffee beans freshly roasted and dark, for it to work, otherwise it all tastes bitter and disappointing.

I've always had an uneasy relationship with traditional cheese courses. Even in France, they are never my favorite part of the meal. Yet they do perform a function, bridging the gap between savory and sweet. The carrots turned into a kind of cheese course with no cheese. We served them with thick blobs of crème fraîche, oats toasted with honey and chicory (which some people call granola), green olive oil and cilantro. It's kind of sweet, kind of savory, and in the end it tastes oddly like tiramisù.

While I made this dish (and others like it, as on page 70), René went back to his restaurant and started burying roots in whole spices and roasting them. There are so many variations—carrots in coriander, fennel in fennel seed, rutabaga in black pepper.

Ideas are never the end of the story, but the beginning. We take promising lines of inquiry and follow them to their conclusion, often over a period of years. Some techniques, like fermentation, are never-ending sources of experimentation. The first idea is intuition and luck. The subsequent ones are hard work.

Put the oats in a metal bowl. Cook the brown sugar, butter and honey in a small saucepan until melted and simmering, then pour over the oats. Add the chicory and salt and mix to combine. Spread the mixture in an even layer on a baking tray lined with a Silpat and bake at 325°F (160°C), stirring occasionally, until golden brown. Cool and store in a well-covered container.

Cook the carrots as in Carrots Roasted in Coffee Beans (see page 70), and cut into different shapes.

To serve, sprinkle a plate with a little finely ground coffee. Throw crème fraîche at the plate with a spoon. Be liberal with it, and use great crème fraîche, cultured slowly, so that it has a thick, almost elastic texture. Place carrot pieces around the plate, and sprinkle with the oats. Dot the plate with a few drops of green olive oil, sprinkle some coarse salt on the carrots, and garnish with pieces of cilantro and cilantro flowers if you have them.

QUINOA
almond, cauliflower, popped sorghum

This began as a dinner that I cooked at a friend's house. We had arrived in the early afternoon, and the kids were hungry. We were hungry. Our friends had a vintage popcorn machine, so we fired it up and tried out some great heirloom popcorns. We got to talking about popcorn, and our friends brought out a small jar filled with little seeds. "Do you know what this is," they asked. "A friend who's allergic to corn gave it to us. It supposedly pops like popcorn, but it's not corn." Of course I wanted to try it out immediately. We put some in their magic machine, and a few minutes later, voilà, popcorn-that-wasn't-corn. In miniature.

I was fascinated, but I still had no idea what it was. The kernels were tiny and sweet and nutty and delicious, with no corn flavor. So I did what the kids do nowadays: I posted a picture and a query on Twitter. I got an instant response: sorghum, the seed of a grass. It's common in the South, often used for syrups and moonshine. And, apparently, popping.

Later that day, I made dinner. A salad of vegetables from the garden and whatever wild things I found nearby. Some beef, and a side dish of quinoa and cauliflower topped with popped sorghum, a creamy, nutty, highly textural combination of grains, perfect for the fall. It was so good that I put it on the menu the following week.

The first time we made it at the restaurant I was excited. A friend who ate there that night, less so. "Everything was great," she told me, "But that quinoa dish . . . It doesn't seem finished."

It wasn't. The next day I added toasted, chopped new crop almonds and minced chives to the quinoa to give it the texture and complexity that it needed. The crunch of almond against the popped and cooked grains was exciting, and the onion flavor gave the dish something green, fresh and alive. Now, the dish was complete.

I love home cooking, but that's not what we do at the restaurant. The line can be a fine one, and sometimes the hardest part of the creative process is finding that one grace note, that little twist of technique, seasoning or texture, that lifts a dish, making it extraordinary.

Cut small florets out of a head of cauliflower—they should be spoon-size when shaved. Cut the rest of the cauliflower into medium-size pieces and toss with the olive oil and salt. Put into a pan and roast in the oven at 400°F (200°C) until tender, stirring occasionally so they are lightly browned and barely tender. Pull out of the oven and onto the stove top, and add the water. Simmer until the water is absorbed and the cauliflower has collapsed. Blend until smooth, thinning with milk as necessary, and adjust seasoning with salt. The texture should be smooth and luscious, thick but just pourable. Pour into a siphon and charge twice. Keep warm. (This makes a terrific purée even without the siphon, it's just a little more dense.)

Cook white and red quinoa in separate pots of salted water, and simmer until tender. Start with 5 parts water to 1 part quinoa, and keep the simmer brisk but below a boil. Cook until the little white string-looking thing appears around the ball of the grain, and the texture is just tender. The texture of the quinoa is crucial—the grains should be cooked but perceptibly individual. Strain, rinse under cold water and drain.

Heat the vegetable oil in a large pan until almost smoking. Add a thin layer of sorghum and cover. Shake the pan occasionally, keeping the heat a little higher than you would with corn. When the popping sound diminishes considerably, empty the sorghum into a colander with holes just smaller than the size of the popped sorghum, and shake the colander to get rid of any broken or unpopped seeds. Season the popped sorghum with salt.

Toast the almonds deeply and cut into pieces slightly smaller than the popped sorghum.

To serve, make a salad of the white and red quinoa, toasted almonds, shaved raw cauliflower (use small inside florets) and snipped chive. Season with rice wine vinegar, fruity olive oil, salt and pepper. Don't make the salad acidic—use the vinegar only to brighten the earthy/nutty tones. Dispense a bit of the cauliflower purée in the bottom of the bowl. Cover with the salad, and top with popped sorghum.

PRATHER RANCH BEEF ENCRUSTED IN LICHEN
wild spinach, chanterelles, bordelaise infused with native spices

I was always a sensitive kid, highly aware of my surroundings. Some of it was my nature and some was my home environment, which trained me to pay attention to the littlest details, to subtle shifts in energy or circumstance. As I grew into a cook, and later a chef, that hyper-sensitivity translated into an intense focus on the smallest things. I see wisps of dust on a baseboard, a corner of an herb a millimeter out of place, the barest suggestion of fraying edges on a mushroom as if they were under a microscope. Sometimes I forget that other people don't see the world the same way, and when cooks miss details I think it means that they don't care, which is usually not true. They never had to study the world with an intensity born of self-preservation rather than pleasure.

Foraging, like cooking, rewards that kind of obsessiveness. When we opened I incorporated only a few wild plants on the menu. As I learned more about the local eco-system, that number increased, and eventually I was going out every morning, often to the same places, year after year. I saw the life cycles of the plants, from tiny sprouts to flowers, how their taste and texture changed over time and the moments when they were most delicious. I grew to understand the seasons and micro-seasons instinctively, developing a degree of intimacy with the plants and where they grew that is hard to explain. I always felt that some part of that emotional connection made its way into the food.

There is an incredible amount of flavor variation among wild plants. My favorite California bay tree has an exhilarating, penetrating eucalyptus/menthol aroma, but the tree twenty feet away has gamy, cat pissy notes that make its flavor totally different (and for me, unusable). That awareness is everything about how I cook. It's also how this dish came to be.

I was in a photo shoot in a forest. For some reason, the photographer wanted me to hold branches covered with lichen, in spite of the fact that I insisted that they were not one of our cooking ingredients. That's just how those things go sometimes. I smiled a lot, and eventually, because I tend to eat everything I get my hands on, I popped a piece of the lichen in my mouth. I chewed. It tasted like nothing at first, but gradually the flavor came out, mushroomy and earthy and interesting, like a mouthful of forest.

I'd just been to an event where I'd learned to boil lichens, so I cleaned and boiled them in several changes of water, until they gave up their bitterness. I dehydrated the cooked lichens, and ground them into a powder, which tasted like a cross between black trumpet mushrooms and black truffles. I covered the outside of a piece of beef in the powder, wrapped it into a neat little cylinder and then cooked it in a low oven until it was pink and juicy. The flavor of the lichen fused with the beef in an incredible way, bringing out deep, aged notes in the meat.

From there the dish fell into place naturally. It's a dish of tradition, although it doesn't seem like it at first glance. It is based on a classic *boeuf bordelaise*: beef with marrow sauce, spinach and mushrooms. Except the spinach is a wild coastal spinach, the predominant mushroom flavor comes from lichen, and the bordelaise sauce is the weirdest iteration you've ever tasted, infused with native forest spices and pumped full of acidity, so it looks dark but tastes green and fresh and bright.

We only cook with grass-fed beef. Beyond the ethical and environmental reasons, I prefer the flavor. Cows that are fattened on corn and grains can be delicious, but they do not reflect the taste of the place where they were raised. Since we opened we have used beef from Prather Ranch. Their animals graze on cool, lush Sierra-Nevada mountain fields in the summer, and Sacramento Delta pasture in the winter. Prather is a small, closed-herd ranch that can trace their roots to the nineteenth century. They grow their own hay, breed from within their own herds and, most unusually, operate their own slaughterhouse, where they process the animals. They control every aspect of the operation.

The care they take in raising the animals shows in the flavor. Prather dry-ages the meat, and the taste is intensely beefy and direct, the way beef used to taste before feedlots were invented. I have found the flavor to be particularly accommodating to wild plants. This dish is evocative of the forests near the coastline, and the meat a platform on which those flavors are expressed.

If, for some crazy reason, you decide to make this dish, then we'll need to have a talk about the lichen powder. It's not that much fun to make. First, you have to go find the lichen. You will find that it grows well and tastes great in certain spots, and not at all in others. You will need to find not just a piece or two, but an area where it exists in abundance, because you'll need a lot of it. Did you bring a bag and a sharp knife? Good. Start by chewing on a piece. It should have a nice earthy/mushroomy aftertaste, not right away but towards the end. It shouldn't be wildly bitter. If it doesn't taste appealing raw then it won't be that good when it's cooked. Scrape the lichen off the branches. It will contain varying levels of moisture, and they're all fine, even if it's dry. You'll need a small grocery bag full to get any kind of quantity of powder. What starts as a lark in a beautiful forest will turn quickly into drudgery. (This is an almost perfect metaphor for haute cuisine.)

Once you get the lichen back to civilization, you will need to clean it. That involves taking a paring knife and tediously removing all bark, pine needles, dirt and other foreign matter and dropping the lichen into cold water, where it will go through a few changes, agitating the lichen each time. Then boil the lichen in unsalted water. Depending on the state the lichen is in, this will take anywhere from 1 to 3 hours, boiling the entire time. Change the water if it gets too dark and/or bitter. There's a moment that's hard to describe, when the lichen changes into something extraordinary. I noticed it right away, the first time I cooked it. Cooking is not, in the end, about recipes. Recipes are the breadcrumbs left behind so that other people can more or less retrace the path that the cook took in the first place. But even that can't happen without something that neither I nor anyone else can teach: Intuition. Intuition is the product of skill, knowledge and experience. Without intuition there can be good cooking, but not great cooking.

This is an example of a dish that relies on intuition. The instinct that says that there's something special in the lichen in the first place; the instinct that says that it should be boiled; and the instinct that knows exactly when it's done. As the lichen cooks, it spends a lot of time almost ready, when the taste is still a little bitter and unresolved. And then, all of a sudden–improbably, after cooking for hours, by which time the taste should have been obliterated–the bitterness disappears, and the flavor is watery, but earthy and round. Whenever the process goes wrong at the restaurant, it's either because the lichen was pulled too soon, or because someone picked lichen that didn't taste good in the first place. Drain the lichen and dehydrate it overnight at 140°F (60°C) until it's completely dry. Grind in a spice grinder.

Trim the tenderloin of all fat and sinew, and cut into a long piece that is more or less cylindrical. Dust it with the lichen powder and transfer to the center of a large piece of plastic wrap. Wrap it tight, tying off the ends. Repeat, until the cylinder of beef is perfectly round. Cryovac, and cook in a water bath at 140°F (60°C) for 8 to 10 minutes, depending on thickness, then cool in ice water. This will not actually cook the beef, but it makes the lichen flavor more pronounced, and helps the crust adhere.

To make the marrow stock, simmer the marrow bones with water until flavorful, 4 to 5 hours. Don't skim. Cool.

For the sauce brown the beef scraps in pure olive oil, then add the vegetables and cook until lightly browned and softened. Deglaze with the red wine, reduce by a third, and then add the other liquids. Simmer and reduce, without skimming, until the flavor is concentrated. Strain the sauce through a chinois and reduce, skimming occasionally, until the flavor is clear and powerful. At this point, add the aromatics. It's really hard to explain this part; it takes a little bit of alchemy to get the balance right. The most important seasoning is the wild bay, but be careful because it's strong, and it can take over. The angelica is the bass note, grounding and earthy, but it should be subordinate to the bay. The fennel and cypress fill out the middle, green notes–you won't be able to distinguish them, but if they're not there the sauce will feel hollow. Add some lime juice and a little rice wine vinegar (not too much at first) during the infusion process, and if the sauce seems too thin, add a little xanthan. Adjust as the sauce is cooking, and then finalize it once it has been strained–it will take what we call colloquially in the kitchen a shit-ton of acidity, which means way more than you'd expect. And yet, it doesn't taste acidic, just green and bright. It's a strange sauce, even more so because of what happens after it's strained–an hour later, as if by magic, the aromatics will fully resolve, and become a cohesive whole.

To serve, remove the plastic wrap, season the beef with salt, and let it sit at room temperature for 20 minutes, until the salt dissolves into the crust. Cook the beef in a medium-hot pan, 5 to 10 seconds on each side, not to brown it but to form the crust and to bring out the aromatics. Transfer to a baking sheet and put in the oven at 250°F (120°C) until cooked, turning often. The beef should be rosy pink and juicy. Remove from the oven and prepare the vegetables.

Sauté the chanterelles in pure olive oil with salt, and then when they're done add the spinach and a splash of water, and cover until wilted. If the spinach is tough, it may need an extra 1 or 2 minutes, but keep it moist. Remove the cover and season with salt and a little rice wine vinegar. Transfer to a sheet tray lined with paper towels. Cut the beef in thick rounds and place on the plate. Place the chanterelles and spinach around, and add a few pieces of shaved raw chanterelle. Sauce generously.

SALSIFY
black trumpet, wood sorrel, salsify-milk curd

When we took the Prather Ranch Beef Encrusted in Lichen (see page 203) off the menu, we still had some lichen powder left. It was early winter, and black trumpets, one of my favorite mushrooms, were in season. Then, at the farmers' market, I found some salsify, which we seldom work with. The dish began to take shape in my mind.

The salsify looked gnarled and black, and for some reason it put me in mind of a log. What if I made it really look like a log? My first thought was the black trumpets. I cut them in tiny strips and cooked them quickly in butter. But they needed a way to adhere to the salsify.

I'd cooked the salsify in milk. It's a classic way to keep it white, and I like the sweetness that it brings, the way the milk flavor entwines with the vegetable. I took scraps of mushroom and salsify and some leftover milk (now flavored with salsify), and made a purée. I lightly browned the salsify in butter to bring immediacy and depth of flavor. Then I applied dots of the purée all over the top of the salsify, and painstakingly covered it in slivers of cooked black trumpet mushrooms, so they looked like bark on a log. A few more dots of purée on top, to which I adhered some perfect pieces of wood sorrel.

The surprise was what was left after the salsify cooked—milk curd that tasted like salsify. I put a little on the side and then sauced the plate with a vinaigrette made from the lichen powder.

To me late winter is the most beautiful time of year here, when everything is covered in a thick blanket of green. On a nice day the sunlight, generous and kind, sparkles through the high branches of the trees, illuminating the grass and plants below. The dish, when I was done, was black and green, the way a forest looks in the Northern California winter.

Blend lichen powder with warm water, and refrigerate overnight. The next day mix with pure olive oil, champagne vinegar and salt to make a vinaigrette.

Peel and trim the salsify. Clean off any dirt or debris, rinse in clean water, and then place immediately into a pan filled with cold milk, enough to cover, to avoid oxidation. Make sure the strips are long enough to be divided into 4-inch (10-cm) increments. Heat the milk to barely simmering with a little salt and cook the salsify until just tender. Continuously skim the milk curd that forms on the top, and place the skimmed curds in a container. Add salsify milk if necessary to achieve a creamy texture, season with salt and refrigerate. Once the salsify is tender, cool and then cut on a bias into 4-inch (10-cm) pieces, reserving the off-cuts.

To prepare the black trumpets, remove the very bottom of the stems and discard. Cut the curling tops (the part that gives the mushroom its name) from the straight bottoms, and with scissors cut them into thin strips ¾-inch (2-cm) long. Tedium alert: It takes a while, because the mushrooms lose a lot of volume when they're cooked. One cup of cut black trumpet tops is enough for about 10 portions. Reserve the stems for the purée. Wash the cut mushrooms in cold water, drain and lay out on a paper towel to dry.

To make the black trumpet purée, clean the reserved stems and sauté them with butter and a little bit of salt. Add the salsify scraps and the skimmed milk left over from cooking the salsify. Reduce by half, then blend until smooth, cool, and season with salt. It should be a thick purée, so hold back some liquid and then add it until the consistency is correct.

To serve, sauté the salsify in butter, seasoning with salt as it cooks (even if it was perfectly seasoned cold, it will need a little more salt when it's hot—things tend to need more seasoning when they change state). Brown the salsify very lightly and unevenly. Remove to a plate lined with a paper towel, and add more butter and some thin strips of black trumpets. Cook with salt until tender and place next to the salsify. Dot the salsify all over with trumpet-salsify purée, and then cover with the mushrooms, so it looks kind of like bark. Place a few more dots of purée on top, and then stick a piece of wood sorrel onto each dot. Transfer to a plate, 2 pieces per serving. Sauce with a little lichen vinaigrette, and put a small spoon of salsify-milk curd on the side.

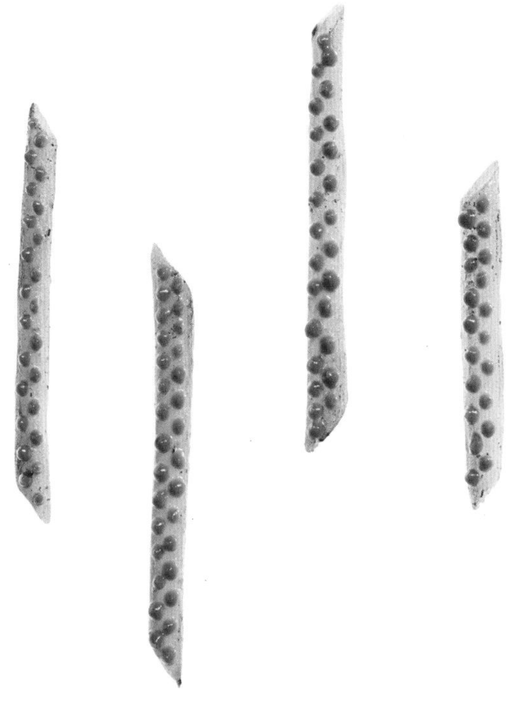

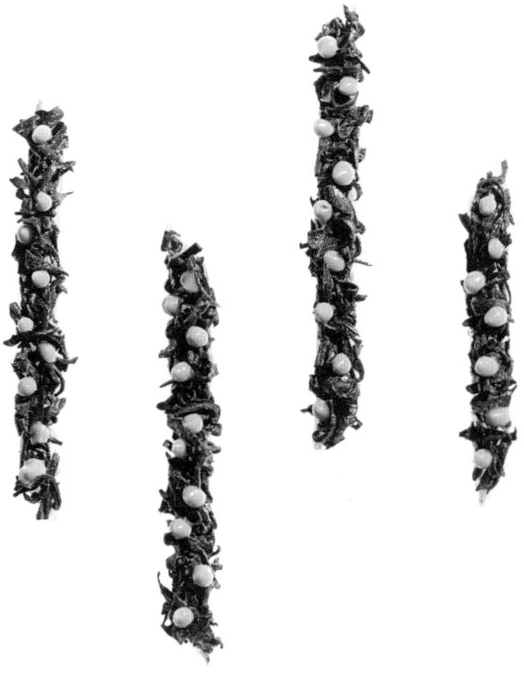

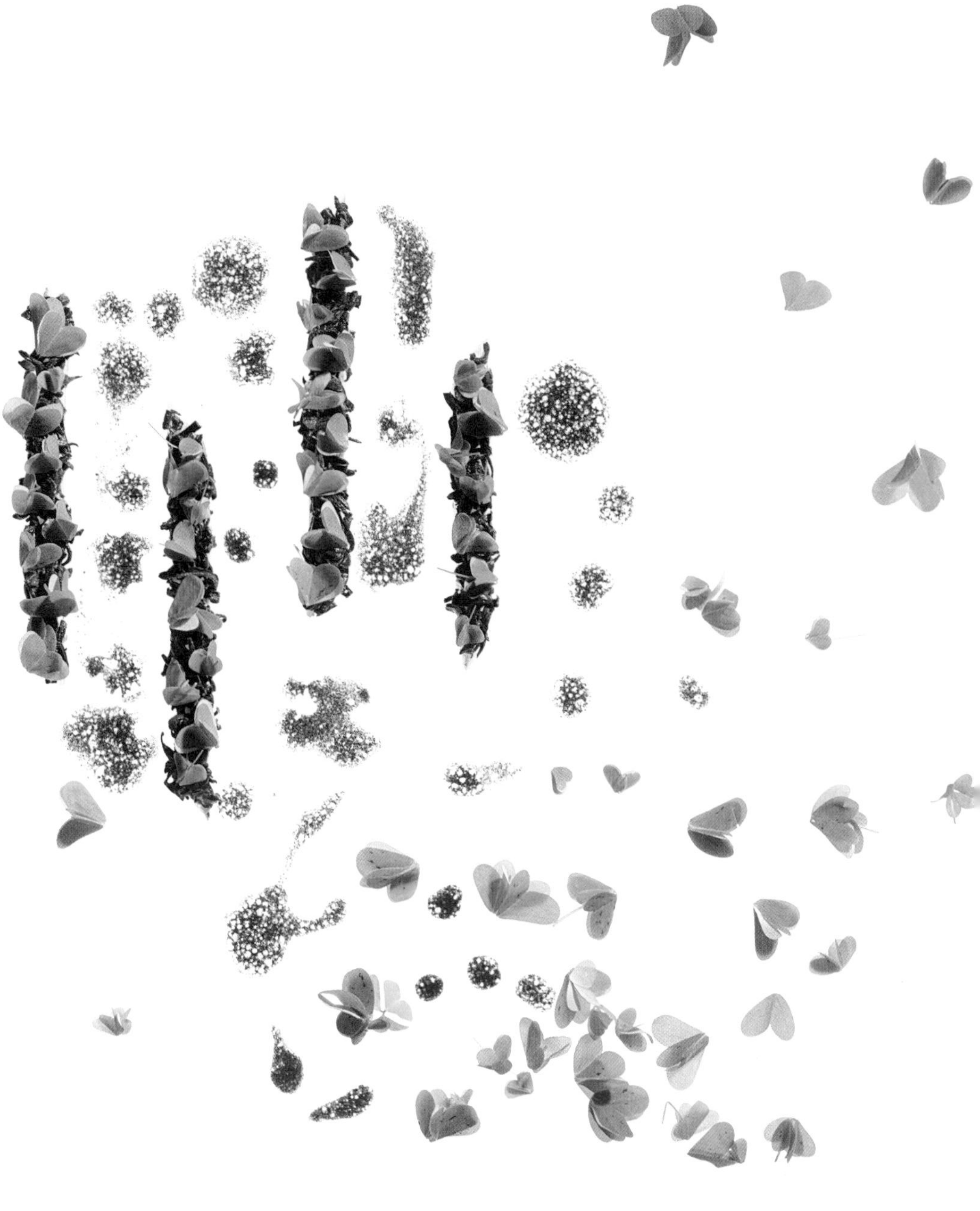

ABALONE/DUCK TONGUE

little gem, sprouts, mint

In 1994, just after Babette's opened in Sonoma, I was introduced to a local farmer name Phillip Paine, who raised squabs. I started buying them, and also duck eggs from his ducks. He eventually grew tired of having the ducks around, being more of a squab guy, so he gave them to his neighbor across the street, Shelley Arrowsmith. Shelley was new to the area and interested in gardening. When I called her to work out the duck egg situation, I got a whole lot more than I expected. She told me she would take our green waste every week to use as compost for her garden. And she introduced me to sprouts.

By sprouts, I don't mean those scary worm-like things that fester in plastic vats in bad salad bars. I mean the first new growth of a plant. Shelley had just taken a class with a semi-famous local farmer named Bob Cannard, who showed her how to grow tiny heads of greens in ultra-rich soil. She brought a flat of arugula by the restaurant the first time we talked, and I was amazed at how much flavor was in those little leaves. I ordered a bunch of different things and I built a few shelves out back of the restaurant. For the next five years, I cut what I needed just before service.

By the time I opened Elisabeth Daniel sprouts had become a *thing*. They were called "micro-greens," shipped in plastic containers from all over the country, and they started showing up on every plate in town. They took on a bad connotation for me, and I stopped using them.

After Coi opened I had a different sort of problem. We weren't very busy. We didn't use a lot of herbs. And I refused to use old herbs, which meant that I was always buying too many and then throwing most of them away. I had found Shelley again at a farmers' market, and I had an idea: What if I used herbs grown in flats, which I could cut as needed? No waste, and I could use the herbs in whole form, because the leaves would be so small. It wouldn't work for everything, but for some herbs, like cilantro, it would capture the energy of the plant at the moment of inception.

It worked so well that now we grow our own sprouts. During the summer our greenhouse is full of many different kinds, and they all go into this dish, plus whatever flowers we can find.

This is a dish of texture. Toothsome slices of abalone are cooked quickly with soft, gelatinous duck tongues. They're tossed with little gem lettuce, radish and mint to make a warm salad, and garnished with all manner of sprouts and flowers. The duck tongue carries the softness of the dish, and the rest is a riot of different sensations.

Americans tend to have a narrow window of textural acceptability, and this dish can be a little challenging for some. I call it the revulsion barrier, the line that demarcates what is pleasurable to eat, and beyond which lies physiological opposition. The line is different for everyone, and it's linked to culture as well as biology. We can all agree that mother's milk is at one end of the spectrum and cannibalism at the other, but everything in the middle is subjective. An ingredient like duck tongues is not only strange for textural reasons—blubbery and yielding in all the wrong ways—but it conjures disconcerting visions of a gaggle of very quiet ducks. I am always mindful of the strangeness of our cooking, of the diversity of its influences and inspirations. It is American food, true, but America is not a homogeneous society. So I always try and ground a dish in an element of comfort and familiarity. In this case, a simple salad. The little gem lettuce and the brightly flavored sprouts and herbs provide the normalcy that makes the other components understandable. And delicious.

Season the duck tongues with salt mixed with 10% sugar. Cure for 3 hours. Vacuum seal them in a Cryovac bag with a large spoonful of duck fat. Cook for 10 hours at 185°F (85°C). Cool to room temperature. Remove the tongues from the bags and remove their bones.

Thinly slice the abalone and toss with pure olive oil.

To serve, season the abalone with salt. Prepare a small bowl with julienned little gem lettuce, shaved radish and thinly snipped mint leaves. Oil the plancha, and add the abalone and duck tongue at the same time, stirring often. When the abalone is cooked, about 10 to 20 seconds, remove both abalone and duck tongue to the bowl of lettuces and herbs. Season with lemon juice and rice wine vinegar, and place in a serving bowl. Garnish with as many kinds of sprouts and flowers as you can find.

CELTUCE
brown butter, burnt hay, tarragon, comte

American farming has changed a lot over the last hundred years. Through consolidation of land and seed sources, the diversity of vegetables and cultivars has plummeted. It used to be that every farmer saved their seeds from year to year, resulting in plants that were not only adapted to their particular eco-system, but that all had a slightly different taste. Now it's hard to find more than one kind of carrot or one kind of onion in a supermarket.

Little by little, the farming community is changing in Northern California. Pioneers like Star Route and Full Belly have inspired a new generation by combining sound ecological practices with delicious food. The farmers' markets, where producers can sell directly to consumers, have helped make small-scale farming more sustainable. These farms are bringing back the kinds of flavorful, interesting varieties of vegetables and fruits that make cooking a joy.

This dish started with celtuce, an ancient member of the lettuce family that is seldom grown in California. I saw it for the first time when a gentleman farmer who was into seed saving and heirloom varieties brought it to me, not long after we'd opened. The Chinese wait for the plant to bolt before harvesting, as it is prized for its stalk. The green leaves on top were tasty, but recognizable. The stalk was something new. When peeled and gently cooked, it turned iridescent green, with a snappy texture and a flavor unlike any other vegetable, with echoes of the sweet/bitter taste of romaine.

Now we get ours from Fog Line, a newish farm on an historic property in the Santa Cruz Mountains that's been owned by the Manildi family for three generations. It's hard to find a good source for celtuce, so when they started harvesting their crop in 2011 I had to put it on the menu.

Working with the natural shape of the stalk, I shaved it into slices and briefly steamed them in butter. To make a sauce I stirred burnt hay into brown butter, adding salt and champagne vinegar to make a warm vinaigrette. The greenness of the celtuce needed a partner, so I added steamed new potatoes and tarragon, which lifted the taste and made it more exciting.

The combination was good the first time that we tried it, but it needed something to connect the disparate parts. Then I remembered Soyoung telling me about a very special aged Comté she had on hand. It seemed like it might work, so I gave it a try. It was brilliant. The sweet, vegetal taste of the celtuce, charged up by an intense purée of the leaves and tarragon, was smoothed out and enriched by the complex pastoral aromatics of the Comté. The vinegar in the sauce cut through the smoky richness of the burnt hay and brown butter.

This dish, based on an obscure, ancient vegetable, turned out to be one of our most popular.

To make the burnt hay powder, set some hay on fire and let it burn until all that's left is the blackened remains. If you're considering doing this in your kitchen, I wouldn't. Outside is probably a better idea. Grind the blackened hay in a spice grinder. Brown the butter deeply, leaving the solids in, and whisk in the burnt hay powder. It should be jet black. The taste should be strong, because the vinegar added later will diminish its intensity. Cool in an ice bath, stirring, so the solids remain evenly suspended in the liquid.

To prepare the celtuce, separate the bottom stalks from the leafy tops. Remove the tiny inner leaves from the top–they will be served raw. Cut the bottoms–checking for fibrousness–into 3-inch (7.5-cm) lengths. Square off 3 of the 4 sides, and then shave the exposed flesh (opposite side from the remaining skin) into ribbons 1/16-inch (2-mm) wide. Trim a few of the thin, tender pieces of the stem where it narrows at the top and reserve. Peel and save the most tender of the reserved pieces for shaving raw, and cut the rest into small pieces to cook with the strips.

For the celtuce leaf purée, coarsely chop the big leaves from the top and cook them in salted water until tender. Rinse under cold water to cool, and then squeeze out the liquid. Blend with the tarragon leaves, pure olive oil for texture and to carry flavor, and ice, to keep the temperature down and to provide the necessary water. It should be a thick purée, redolent of tarragon.

Steam the potatoes at 185°F (85°C) until tender–they should be a little softer than seems correct, as they'll harden quite a bit as they cool. Peel, punch with a small ring mold if they're more than ¾-inch (2 cm), and cut into ½-inch (1-cm) thick rounds.

To serve, cook the celtuce–both ribbons and pieces–with a small amount of water, a little butter and some salt, covered, until just tender. They're the whole dish, so don't overcook them. At the end, add the potatoes and remove from the heat when they're just warmed through.

Warm some burnt-hay butter and season with champagne vinegar and salt. It should be very acidic, like a warm vinaigrette. Spoon some sauce on the plate, then add 4 small dots of the celtuce leaf-tarragon purée. Place 4 rounds of potato next to the dots of purée, and then cover the potato with pieces of shaved Comté (we use 24-month-old cheese from Marcel Petite). Put 3 pieces of cooked celtuce on top of the cheese, and then 5 to 6 pieces of the cooked strips, which should wrap around each other like ribbons. Garnish with 3 pieces of shaved raw stem, 3 pieces of small leaves, and 3 small leaves of tarragon.

MORELS ROASTED IN BUTTER
just-harvested potatoes, popcorn, basil

The genesis of this dish was adequately covered in the description of its progeny, Popcorn Grits (see page 66). But there's another story as well.

It was the summer of 2011. Evan had left to open his own restaurant. He would come back later that summer for another stretch, when his opening was pushed back, as they always are. But at the moment that this dish went on, he was gone, and I had no replacement.

It was the most challenging few months that I've had since we opened. We remodeled the restaurant for the third time in five years, spending far more money than we had, and putting incredible pressure on the business. Our service staff was disjointed, led by an inexperienced manager. We were busy. And the kitchen was woefully understaffed. The staff that we did have did not have the skill to execute at our level.

In restaurants, trying is seldom enough. Everyone, or almost everyone, tries. Success is a mixture of talent, timing and luck. I have been fortunate to have a long string of terrific cooks to work with, and many of them went on to be chefs and open their own restaurants. But that summer, for whatever reason, I couldn't find qualified staff to save my life. I had a new baby at home, and I was exhausted and fighting depression, which didn't help. And I was working a station. This dish came off my station.

I love to cook. Taking a station, even now, is in theory a joy. But if I'm on a station, it means that I can't see everything—to be a good line cook, you need blinders, complete focus. With a new restaurant, two more on the way and a million other things jockeying for attention in my brain, I ended up going home at the end of every night defeated, knowing that I had given less than I was capable of. The dishes that summer were wonderful, some of my best. The execution, erratic. And it was all absolutely, unequivocally, my fault.

This is a great dish, but I won't make it again. To me it tastes like failure.

Clean and cut the morels as in Morel/Fava (see page 164). Make a morel stock the same way as described in that recipe.

Make the popcorn grits according to the instructions on page 66. Blend the grits with the remaining cooking liquid until smooth, adding more butter as necessary. Refrigerate until needed—it will get thicker as it sits. Make some buttered popcorn.

Steam the potatoes at 185°F (85°C) until tender—they should be a little softer than seems correct, as they'll harden quite a bit as they cool. Peel and toss in butter and salt.

Trim the basil sprouts so that they still have some stem attached. I like them a little larger, with 2 well-formed leaves, and even the beginning of the third. Or, pick out the smaller leaves from a bunch of mature basil.

To serve, heat a spoonful of butter to bubbling in a sauté pan, and add the morels. When they're coated with butter, season them with salt, stirring often, over medium-high heat. Add stock. If the morels are very wet, add less and if they're drier, add more. Simmer until just tender, and add the potatoes, cooking until they're warmed through. The butter on the potatoes will melt into the sauce, and the liquid left in the pan should be just enough to glaze everything. Watch the salt—it creeps up fast with morels, and especially as the liquid reduces.

Warm some sauce and spread a few spoonfuls in a bowl. Arrange the mushrooms and potatoes on top. Garnish with kernels of buttered popcorn (you will treat this the way you do any other garnish, and choose only the beautiful, perfectly popped ones, yes?) and basil sprouts.

NEW OLIVE OIL
brassica, charred onion broth

California once had a thriving olive oil business. All up and down the state, missionaries planted olive groves, and by the 1800s olive oil was an important local product. That all came to an end in the early 1900s when Italians flooded the market with less expensive oil. Over time most of California's olive groves were torn out, leaving only trees that grew low-quality fruit destined to be sliced into the sad little washer rings that you see on mass-produced pizza.

Money can't buy everything, but when it comes to an expensive hobby like fine olive oil, it helps. There was B.R. Cohn, founded by Bruce Cohn, who managed the Doobie Brothers to fame (and not a little fortune). With the help of Helen Turley, they made wine at first, and by the early '90s they were also making very good—and wildly expensive—olive oil. Around that time, Ridgely Evers, who created the accounting software QuickBooks, started DaVero Sonoma with his wife Colleen McGlynn. They brought in cuttings from Italy and grew them on their Sonoma estate, making fantastic Tuscan-style oil. In 1991 Nan McEvoy, scion of the de Young family (founders of the *San Francisco Chronicle*) bought a massive tract of land near Petaluma. There was a zoning requirement to have some agricultural production, and, Nan, a fan of Italian food and culture, chose olive oil. She brought trees over from Italy, along with a stone press and a building's worth of equipment. She also brought an olive oil consultant from Italy. She then proceeded to make some of the finest olive oil in the state.

Now there are many small producers making wonderful oil. Every year, in the Italian tradition, they release their new oils in the fall, just after they're pressed.

New oil (Italians call it *olio nuovo* and throw huge parties when it arrives) is one of the most special products that we work with. It's full of sediment and solid matter that hasn't been allowed to settle. The flavor is the freshest, most vibrant expression of olive oil: Intensely peppery and green, redolent of artichokes and fresh cut grass. Every year I buy as much of the new oil as I can afford, and every year I create a dish to highlight it.

I have made variations on this dish almost every year since 1994, refining along the way. For this iteration, we go to the markets, which are filled with all manner of brassicas in the winter, and buy whatever we find that is delicious. We use leaves, stems, florets, flowers. Underneath, a bright green purée of dandelion greens and potato, seasoned with a little lemon. And a broth of charred onions, sweet and roasty, scented with aromatic lemon leaves and sharpened with a generous amount of Rosa's vinegar. Over everything, an even more generous amount of the new oil, which mingles with the purée and the broth in a delightful way.

After many years of putting charred onions into the vegetable stock, I tried making a stock based solely on them. It was amazing, sweet and smoky, and with the addition of Rosa's vinegar it made a great foil to the new olive oil. Char the onions (see page 49), coarsely chop them and simmer with the water until the flavor is intense, about 2 to 3 hours. Strain and pour over the cut lemon leaves. (When we moved into a new house, we inherited a lemon tree. I've tried many lemon leaves over the years, and didn't much care for them. These, however, are extraordinary, the kind of exhilarating citrus notes normally found in makrut lime leaves. The leaves are actually better than the fruit.) When the flavor of the leaves is present but not overwhelming, strain again through cheesecloth and season with champagne and Rosa's vinegars.

For the dandelion-potato purée, peel and slice the potatoes and boil in salted water until tender. Cook the dandelion greens in salted water until tender, drain and cool by rinsing under cold water. Squeeze out all excess water and coarsely chop. Blend with the potatoes, pure olive oil and lemon juice to make a smooth, thick purée. Season with salt.

Take all the brassicas you can find and trim them all differently (reserving some stems to shave raw) and cook them in well-salted water, or sea water. We use: purple, white and gold cauliflower; romanesco (the genetic antecedent of cauliflower and broccoli); broccoli and broccolini; cabbages; kales and mustards. Use any little leaves you find attached as well, and trim and use the stems.

Heat the pickling liquid and pour over the finely julienned red cabbage. Let cool at room temperature.

To serve, warm the dandelion purée and place a spoonful in the middle of a bowl. Cook the brassicas very briefly on the plancha (just to warm, but not to darken too much, as the charred onion broth will add that roasty note), and toss with the raw, shaved stems. Put on top of the dandelion-potato purée. Garnish with pickled red cabbage and any flowers you can find, especially rosemary. Pour the broth around, and drizzle a generous spoonful of new olive oil over the vegetables and the broth.

MONTEREY BAY ABALONE
grains, fresh seaweeds, raw turnip

Water is one of the most important elements in cooking. It is much of what makes up our ingredients. In dairy—butter, milk, cheese—the water content is as critical as the fat. Water carries and melds flavors. It's the basis for all stocks and sauces. And yet, for many years, I never really talked about it in the kitchen.

Now I talk about water all the time. When we talk about water at Coi, we're often talking about concentration. If there's too much water in a sauce then it becomes dilute. Too little, and the flavors stack on top of each other, creating a muddy taste. It's a little like playing an instrument. If you play too many notes, too close together, it all runs together into a solid mass of sound. If you stretch out those notes a little bit and take away a few, all of a sudden you can hear them, and they become music instead of noise. Controlling that density in cooking has everything to do with controlling the water.

Water is the best cooking medium for many—I would say most—grains and vegetables. The shop-worn practice of simmering everything in animal stock makes everything taste like, well, stock. Water allows the clearest expression of ingredients. The richness can come in other ways, like a flavorful oil or fat introduced at the end of cooking.

When we make a gel, we are controlling water in a different way. The qualities contained within that water, once bound into a viscous or solid fluid or a gel, express themselves differently. We manipulate the texture of water so that we can fine-tune the precise flavors that we need for a dish.

In a cultural and environmental sense, water has defined California. The region with the world's fifth largest economy is also a drought state, always teetering on the edge of disaster. From year to year we wait through the long, dry summer to see what the winter rains will bring, praying that the snow pack will be deep and the reservoirs full. Meanwhile vast sloughs of water flow constantly from the Sierra Mountains and the Sacramento-San Joaquin Delta to the manicured lawns of Beverly Hills, as if there were an endless supply. It's a little like building a skyscraper on top of an eggshell.

When you live on the coast, a lot of dishes become, in a literal way, about water. Here, the abalone and the seaweeds they feed on are the basis for the dish. The sauce is seaweed, white soy, garum and vinegar, savory from the fermentation and sharpened with the iodine edge of squid ink.

The grains are the earth and they ground the dish, the balance for all of the water elements. We use several different kinds to vary texture and flavor, and season the mixture with the lemon and brown butter left over from the cooking of the abalone.

As little fresh water as there is in California, its geography is defined by the Pacific Ocean, the final resting place of the American frontier. It's still alive, in this place of big skies and fertile land and constant reinvention, the idea that anything is possible. It's not true, of course. The convertibles and mansions and never-ending beach parties drift silently by as though in a dream, and the ocean is always there, waiting.

To make the seaweed sauce, simmer the kombu, fresh seaweeds, vegetable stock, water, garum, olive oil and white soy until the kombu is tender. Add the squid ink and cook 5 minutes more. Blend–the seaweed will serve as a natural thickener, so you may need to loosen the sauce with some water. Season with champagne vinegar and salt. Don't make the sauce too acidic, and add more garum or white soy if it needs more savory notes.

Cook the farro, wheatberries and barley in separate pans of salted water until tender. Drain and cool. Season each individually, and then combine them.

Trim and clean several kinds of fresh seaweeds, like bull kelp, alaria, sea lettuce, eel grass, purple laver, Turkish towel, sea grape and giant kelp. Cook them if necessary, cutting after they've been cooked. Soak the seaweeds all together in cold water, changing occasionally and rinsing them each time, to remove the sliminess.

To serve, season the abalone with salt and pepper and dust lightly with flour. Brown a few spoonfuls of butter fairly deeply–the abalone will take its color from the butter, not from the cooking, since it spends so little time in the pan. Add the abalone, top side down, and move around by shaking the pan. After about 30 to 45 seconds, flip the abalone and cook another 30 seconds or so. Add a spoonful of lemon juice, swirl it into the butter, and flip the abalone again, basting it with the sauce off the heat so it has a nice glaze. Remove to a paper towel.

Combine the grains and fresh seaweeds in a pot and warm with a little water. When the abalone is done cooking, add the butter and lemon that remains in the pan, and season with more lemon and butter if necessary. It should be balanced, rich, earthy and ocean-y. Make two piles of the grain mixture on the plate, and then pour the warmed seaweed sauce around. Cut the abalone in half and place on top of the grains. Garnish with shavings of raw Tokyo turnip.

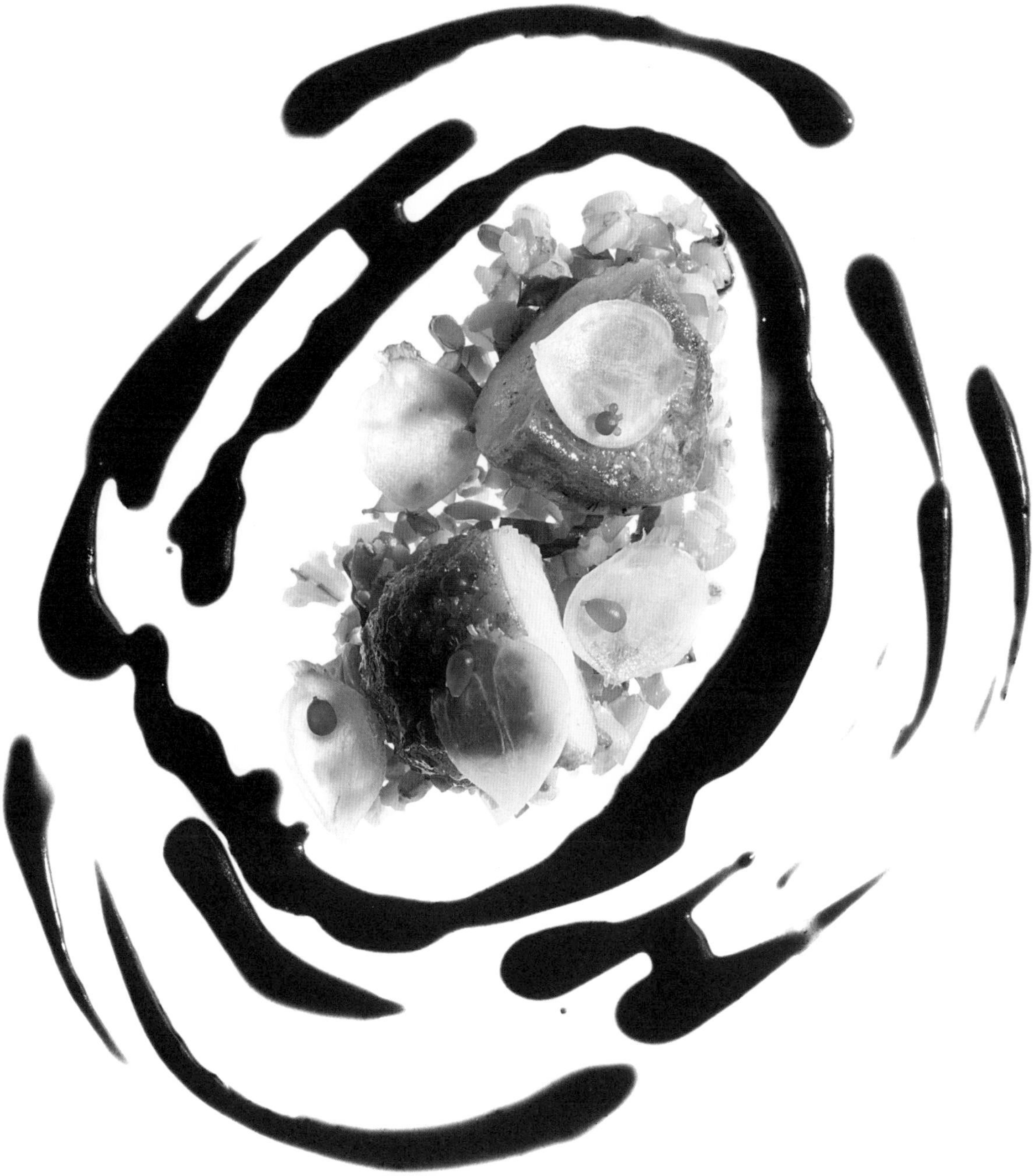

DUNGENESS CRAB AND BEEF TENDON SOUP
asian pear, finger lime

Coi, pronounced *kwa*, is an archaic French word that used to mean "tranquil" or "quiet." It came from the Latin root *quietus*. It was last commonly used hundreds of years ago in middle French, and it migrated to middle English, where it became "coy." Quietus, of course, took on a completely different meaning in English—to bring quietus is to kill someone. I guess that makes sense, because dead people are pretty quiet. Coi is often confused with the Japanese word koi, pronounced *coy*, which is a kind of fish (occasionally, even after all these years, arriving guests are disappointed to learn that we're not a sushi restaurant). New guests seldom know what our name means, nor how to pronounce it. It fits us perfectly.

When it comes to what a marketing wonk would call "brand clarity," we don't do ourselves any favors. We forage, but we're not a foraging restaurant. We pioneered the use of essential oils in cooking, but we're not an aroma restaurant. We use modern equipment, but also a mortar and pestle. We're Californian, but not. When someone asks, "What's the food like?" the best thing I can come up with is, "Um, hopefully delicious," my voice rising at the end in a note of uncertainty.

I have very diverse tastes, in art, music, architecture, people. I also have a very polyglot palate. My French background and appreciation of pastry and butter, of refinement, is balanced by an Italian-like attraction to bitterness and sharp acidity. I am comforted by the Eastern European peasant food I grew up with: beets and tongue and cabbage and onions. I love all kinds of fermented flavors, the spices and depth of Mexican food, the textural diversity and purity of Japanese food, the complexity of Chinese cooking, and everything about the flavors of Thailand and Vietnam. We have all those things and more in our area. And they're all in my cooking.

In other words, this cultural mash-up of a dish makes perfect sense to me. It's a deep, savory, spicy and sour crab broth, built on stock from simmered beef tendon. Beef tendon, common in Asian cooking but not so much in fine dining, is the stuff that connects muscle to bone. When simmered for hours, it becomes soft and unctuous. The tendon is thinly sliced and mixed with crab meat, crunchy Asian pear for sweetness and caviar-like finger limes. Finger limes, originally from Australia and now grown here, are little oblong pods that hold a multitude of crunchy pale green spheres. When you bite one it explodes with lime-times-ten flavor. A little cilantro, and then the broth, infused with lime juice and chile, is poured at the table. The broth is viscous from the tendon, almost sticky on the tongue, and needs no thickener.

What do you call a dish like this? Beats me. But I think it tastes pretty good.

Simmer the tendons in lightly salted water for 4 to 5 hours, until they're tender. Cool and thinly slice. Strain and save the resulting liquid.

Cook and clean the crab as on page 176. Season the crab meat with salt if necessary.

To make the soup, smash the shells and sear in a large pan in pure olive oil. Add the onion and fennel, and cook for 5 minutes, until softened. Add the white wine, reduce by half, and then add the tendon stock, vegetable stock and chile. Simmer for 1½ to 2 hours, until flavorful. Strain and season with lime juice and salt. It should be more rich than acidic.

To serve, combine the crab meat, sliced tendon, diced Asian pear, finger lime and snipped cilantro stem in a mixing bowl. Season with salt. Divide the mixture between 6 warm bowls, and heat the bowls in a salamander for a minute to warm the crab. Garnish with several small pieces of cilantro on top, and sprinkle with a little piment d'Espelette. Pour the soup around and stir to combine.

2012

BEETS
bergamot, mints, wildflowers

The first time I thought about using flowers in cooking I was twenty-two, and working in a restaurant called Zola's in San Francisco. Zola's offered good, solid food, and its dishes would fit in just fine in today's market. The chefs were not terribly creative, but they did bring in some interesting ingredients from time to time. One day it was flowering cilantro. This was in 1991, when there was not exactly a thriving market for edible flowers. I was surprised and enthralled. The flavor was incredible, the simple cilantro flavor transformed into something brighter and more ethereal, the greenness of the leaf combined with coriander notes. When I moved to Sonoma I remembered that flavor, and asked a farmer to let a row of his cilantro bolt. I harvested the flowers, and then the green seeds, and then the roots.

I was fortunate at Babette's to develop close relationships with the local growers. I picked my own squash blossoms and fennel flowers. Figs came to the restaurant straight off the tree. Corn never saw the inside of a refrigerator. I gathered flowers from friends' gardens. And I thought that was normal.

When I opened Elisabeth Daniel in San Francisco, we ordered everything in little plastic containers. I was new to the city, and that also seemed normal.

Coi was a return to the kind of sourcing I did at Babette's. I started working in an ever-widening radius around my house, gathering wild herbs and flowers: oxalis, ice plant, wild radish. Cultivated flowers, on the other hand, were not always plentiful, and the farmers that came to the markets were not so keen on my special requests to let their plants go to seed.

Around Christmas 2007, a farm from which I was buying a lot of things went on vacation. While we were open. This posed a significant problem—I couldn't exactly go to the supermarket to replace the ingredients, as I had dishes built specifically around the flavor and texture of what they were growing. So I asked if I could go pick what I needed myself. No problem, they said, intrigued I'm sure about the concept of making money without doing any harvesting or delivering.

When I got to the farm, it took a little while to traverse the five or so acres that were planted in odd patches, finding my ingredients here and there amongst the mud and weeds. And then, in a corner of the farm, I found some broccoli rabé that had thrown beautiful yellow flowers. I gathered some of the flowers, and incorporated them into one of the dishes. When the farmers returned, I placed an order for the flowers along with the other vegetables. After a while they put the flowers on their price list, and then they started bringing them to the farmers' markets. The other farmers must have noticed, because soon after they too started bringing their winter flowers. Chefs bought them, and now they have become a common ingredient here, one last harvest at the end of the growing cycle.

Flowers have always appealed to me for their delicacy, their fragility. To put a perfect flower on a plate shows caring, attention to freshness and how they're harvested, how they're handled. More than that, flowers represent a moment in time. There are rosemary flowers in the spring and fall; radish flowers in late spring and early summer; fennel flowers in late summer and fall. They bloom briefly and then are lost forever. There is magic in capturing that moment and fixing it on the plate.

This is a dish of spring, when the bergamot, a special citrus that is the flavor of Earl Grey tea, is harvested, and when there are wildflowers everywhere. At that moment, the fresh shoots of new mint are intense and lively—I use up to eight kinds, from spearmint to chocolate peppermint, yerba buena (a native mint), roman mint, Persian mint, and, of course, bergamot mint. The roasted beets provide an earthy base to capture these lively flavors.

For the bergamot vinaigrette, I can't tell you ratios because bergamot juice varies wildly in sweetness and acidity. Combine the bergamot juice and bergamot oil and season with salt. Add a little vinegar if needed, but the bergamot should have plenty of acidity. Don't add too much oil (start with 4 parts bergamot juice to 1 part oil)—keep it very bright.

Toss all of the beets except 1 with pure olive oil, salt and pepper, and roast with a little water in a covered container at 350°F (180°C) until tender. Shake the pan occasionally, and make sure that the beets stay moist—not drowning in water, but moist. Cool and peel. Cut 8 of the smallest beets into different shapes—the 2 smallest ones in half, 4 of the next size in thick slices, the last 2 in quarters. Toss with the vinaigrette, salt, and sugar if necessary. Reserve the rest for the purée and gel.

Reduce the beet juice by half, cool and blend with the roasted beets until smooth. Season with rice wine vinegar, a small amount of the bergamot oil, salt, and sugar if necessary. Put half in a small squeeze bottle. Weigh the other half, and warm in a pot. Soften the gelatin (2.5% of the weight of the beet purée) in cold water and then stir into the purée to melt. Spread on a small tray lined with plastic wrap. Refrigerate for at least 2 hours. Dice the beet gel on a cold cutting board into ¼-inch (7-mm) cubes and refrigerate on a small tray lined with plastic.

Thinly slice the remaining raw beet and cut rounds the size of a dime. Vacuum seal them with salt, sugar and rice wine vinegar. You will need 3 per guest.

At this point in the recipe, you've probably noticed a theme. Everything is treated as variations on the same flavor profile, so they all need to be attuned to each other, sweet and sour, but not drivingly acidic. There should be gentleness and harmony in the seasoning.

To serve, put 3 cubes of beet gel on the plate interspersed with 3 dots of beet purée. Arrange 4 pieces of roasted, seasoned beet around them. Dot the beets with several drops of beet purée. Garnish with a few pieces of compressed beet. Drizzle with a spoonful of vinaigrette, and cover with pieces of mint and wildflowers.

ASPARAGUS/OYSTER
wheatgrass

"Minimal" in today's culture is not a compliment. It implies a style shorn of context or soul. When people call our food minimal, I'm pretty sure that means they may respect it, perhaps find it beautiful or engaging, but that they didn't enjoy it very much.

Minimalism has meant different things over the years. There were Frank Stella's black paintings, the dense color separated by thin lines of white canvas, or Donald Judd's box-like sculptures that defined clean, non-representational form. In architecture, movements like De Stijl and people like Mies van der Rohe created designs based on the idea that a space derives meaning not only from what is there, but what is not. The Japanese call it *ma*, the empty space in between tangible things.

The architect John Pawson once said, "The minimum could be defined as the perfection that an artefact achieves when it is no longer possible to improve it by subtraction." Michelangelo said something similar about *David*. The harmony that can be found in the relationship between essential forms, of reducing something down to its barest, most exposed essence, is a way of finding, or at least seeking, deeper truths.

I'm not sure what minimalism means in the context of food, but this dish is definitely focused. It's also exuberant: Minimalism need not lack emotion. The basic premise was a different kind of asparagus dish. Normally we make asparagus the star, but this time I wanted to do something new, to create more of a balance, a partnership between two ingredients: Oyster and asparagus.

It needed a sauce to connect the two related but disparate flavors. Oysters, I knew, had an affinity for wheatgrass. I had made an oyster stew flavored with wheatgrass when I first started experimenting with the stuff, and it was delicious. And asparagus ... why not? After all, it was almost a grass as well. A gel of oyster juice seasoned with lemon—a little bit firm, to have a more assertive presence—completed the dish. Only four simple elements.

Perhaps more than any other dish, this is an example of our non-demonstrative, non-technical style of cooking, which still demands absolute perfection in every way. Once, at another restaurant that was running my menu for a month, I was training a cook to make it. He cooked the asparagus while I was on the other side of the kitchen and I discovered, just before the beginning of service, that the asparagus were a fraction undercooked. There was a tiny edge of rawness at the center, a slight crunchiness that shouldn't be there, poking through the tender outside layers. My head almost exploded. The hours of painstaking work peeling the asparagus were wasted in one moment of inattention. The dish was diminished, which is to say, obliterated. Gone. *"That. Is. The. Entire. Dish,"* I spat through clenched teeth, trying very hard to be calm. *"And. You. Just. Ruined. It. Do. You. Understand?"*

To his credit, he did. Especially when I showed him the difference. I grabbed one stalk, peeled it and cooked it so that it was firm but yielding when cooled, at the exact moment when raw turns to cooked, its sweetness heightened. We tried them side by side. I could see a lightbulb go off in the cook's head, and I knew that he would not make the same mistake again.

When the oyster is perfectly fresh and carefully handled, the asparagus well-grown and properly cooked, the gel and the sauce correctly seasoned, the dish is a revelation. The briny/sweet oyster a blast of ocean, rounded by the driving licorice aromatics of the wheatgrass and the green, sweet taste of the asparagus. Minimal in form, but very expressive.

Make the wheatgrass sauce as on page 190. Season with salt.

Shuck the oysters, rinse them in ice water and strain the liquor through cheesecloth. Pour 25% of the liquor back on to the oysters and refrigerate. Season the remaining oyster liquor with lemon juice and zest, and salt if necessary. If the liquor is really briny, it may be necessary to dilute with a touch of water. Weigh the liquid and set with 3% gelatin. Stir in an ice bath as the gel is cooling, to make sure that the zest is evenly dispersed. When half set, transfer to a container and refrigerate.

Peel the asparagus as on page 168, and simmer them in asparagus juice seasoned with salt, until just tender. They shouldn't be mushy, but they shouldn't be raw in the middle either. Transfer both asparagus and juice to a lipped sheet pan set into another, deeper, sheet pan filled with ice water, and refrigerate. When cold, drain and trim to 4½ inch (11.5 cm). Taste the small pieces you cut off to check for seasoning, and add salt if necessary.

To serve, spoon some wheatgrass sauce onto the plate. Place a piece of asparagus in the center of the plate, at an angle, the bottom at 7 o'clock and the top at 1 o'clock. Place an oyster, drained of juice and gently blotted, below the asparagus, and a spoonful of gel above.

EARTH AND SEA

tofu coagulated with seawater, cherry tomato, fresh seaweeds, sylverleaf olive oil

I've never tried to be different. In spite of my best efforts to fit in, I seem to have a knack for restaurants, dishes and ideas that are either out of place or ahead of their time. Once my first wife, in a fit of frustration born of constantly being broke and working too much, told me, "You're like a doctor who's a specialist in a disease that no one has." It stayed with me.

You'd think I would have learned by now, but all these years later I still feel like I keep taking normal things and making them weird. I can't help it. It's one reason that I always look for moments of familiarity, of comfort, to push dishes back towards forms and flavors that diners will understand.

For this iteration of Earth and Sea, we took a lot of normal things and made them weird. For the underlying technique, I have Matt to thank. Hawaiian hippies apparently have a lot in common with their Californian brethren, like their love of tofu and making things at home. One day he dug out a copy of a mimeograph (remember those?) from the '70s, a recipe for a Hawaiian dish that his mother used to make. It was tofu coagulated with seawater.

Industrial tofu is usually made by curdling soy milk with the concentrated minerals that result from boiling down seawater, and maybe adding a few other coagulants along the way. This recipe uses a small amount of actual seawater instead, a common practice along the coastal areas of China, Korea and Japan. Water is so important in tofu making that the source of the spring or the site of the seawater means as much as a great vineyard does in winemaking. Like winemaking, however, the process is as important as the ingredients.

This tofu is very delicate. Without being pressed, it has the texture of fresh cheese, like ricotta. It is a completely unexpected sensation. It demands subtle, sweet accompaniments, so we combine tomato water, tofu whey and sea lettuce in a gel that shimmers with sunshine and the echo of ocean. A few cherry tomatoes and some fresh seaweeds, and a local olive oil, which is fresh and pungent without being overwhelming.

One night last summer I delivered the dish to a table of tourists, and before I could tell them what it was, one of them cried out, "This looks great, we've been eating it all week!" I was a little startled. Was there suddenly a preponderance of other dishes with seawater-coagulated tofu, tomato and fresh seaweeds floating around? Had I finally stumbled into the mainstream?

"Really?" I asked.

"Yes!" He beamed. "Tomato-mozzarella-olive oil!"

Soak the soy beans with 300 g water overnight, but for no more than 12 hours. The next morning, drain the soy beans and rinse them well. Blend the soaked soy beans with 400 g water until extremely smooth. Bring 750 g water to a boil in a large pot, and add the soy paste. Stir to combine. Bring to a light simmer for 5 minutes, and then strain through cheesecloth. Bring 150 g water to a boil and add the strained soy bean solids to the pot. Bring to a simmer for 1 minute, and then strain through the same cheesecloth into the same container, pushing the solids to extract as much liquid as possible.

Put the soy milk back on the stove in a large pot and bring to a boil. Keep at a rolling boil for 10 minutes. Remove from the heat and add 75 g seawater. Put the wooden spoon into the pot and stir 3 times, allowing the water to stop moving before removing the spoon. Pour another 75 g seawater into the pot. Cover and let stand for 3 minutes.

Uncover and put the spoon halfway into the liquid. Add the last third of the seawater and stir until the curds separate from the whey. Ladle out the curds into a serrated pan lined with a single layer of cheesecloth. Gently smooth the top with an offset spatula, and allow the whey to fully drain. Reserve the whey for other uses, and refrigerate the tofu, allowing it to set for at least 3 hours before cutting.

If anything goes wrong—and there's plenty that can—it could be a few things. The temperature of the pan and the milk is crucial. This is all about protein coagulation. Too low a temperature and the curds will be too soft, too high and they will be too firm. When you're ladling out the curds, they need to drain quickly or the proteins will set with water trapped inside, making the end product watery and possibly bland. These are just a few of the mistakes we made. I'm sure you'll discover others.

While the tofu is draining, make the tomato water as on page 58.

Combine the tomato water and whey, and season with salt. Warm about a cup of the mixture and then stir in the gelatin. When the gelatin is melted, add to the rest of the liquid and stir in the chopped sea lettuce (if it's tough then blanch in unsalted water until tender, and run under cold water to cool). Cool in an ice bath, stirring occasionally until the liquid is half-set and the sea lettuce is suspended throughout the liquid. Transfer to a container. Refrigerate for at least 2 hours.

Make the tofu-whey glaze by boiling the whey and agar and then cooling in an ice bath. When solid, blend and season with shiro dashi, shichimi togarashi and salt.

Punch out rounds of tofu in 2 sizes, 6 of about 1½ inch (4 cm) and 12 of about ¾ inch (2 cm). Soak the rounds in cold seawater for 10 minutes to season them and then refrigerate again until dry, about 30 minutes.

To serve, spread some of the tofu-whey glaze on top of each piece of tofu and transfer to a plate. Spoon some of the tomato-whey gel around, and then add 3 halves of cherry tomato on top of the gel, keeping the tops perfectly perpendicular to the surface of the plate. Season the tomatoes and tofu with flakes of crunchy salt (you can dehydrate the seawater to make the salt if you want). Garnish with fresh seaweeds, and drizzle 10 to 12 drops of fruity olive oil around.

This dish opened up many lines of exploration. We have tried pressing the tofu, and then soaking it in seawater for 10 to 30 minutes, and then back into the whey overnight, where the texture swells and becomes delightfully juicy. Making tofu is a craft, and there are endless variations on this basic technique.

BUDDHA
HSBC
中国工商银行
Canon
MINOLTA
DIGITAL
LUGGAGE

ONE WAY
RIGHT LANE
MUST
TURN RIGHT
COCKTAILS
SONY JVC

PRESERVED LEMON 6:10
chrysanthemum milk

It has often been said of California that we don't have weather, we have natural disasters. Save for the earthquakes, wildfires, floods and droughts, Northern California is a pretty tame place. There are basically two seasons—wet and dry—and a lot of sub-seasons within them. Here there is no need to preserve food in order to survive long, cold winters. There are no root cellars here, because we can pull vegetables out of the ground throughout the year. The only reason to preserve food in California is for pleasure.

Preserved citrus is a product we always have on hand. It is an old technique, common in Morocco (at least that's where I got the idea when I was in my early twenties), for curing citrus with salt (and sometimes sugar) for months, until the skin softens and the entire fruit becomes edible, a salty/sweet/sour condiment. The citrus season technically runs from late fall through late spring, but clusters of fruit show up here and there almost year-round. During the winter, as each variety hits peak flavor, we buy a few cases and preserve them for our pantry.

This dish is built around preserved Meyer lemons, a sweet, fragrant variety widely grown in California. 6:10 refers to the date that we cured the lemons, "like a Bible verse," as Matt says. June is quite late for Meyers. These were left on the tree all winter and through spring to ripen completely, coming to us soft, juicy and aromatic. Almost too soft in fact—about a quarter of them dissolved into a pulpy mush during the months that they cured. But the remaining lemons were incredible, filling the room with their floral perfume every time we worked with them. The winter lemons are great, especially in savory dishes, but these were more adaptable to pastry.

The simple form and interesting flavor combination works well in a tasting menu format, where dishes can be more focused and portions small. It's a custard made with candied preserved lemons, the saltiness and subtle fermentation giving the dessert an entirely different dimension. On top of the custard is a layer of tart Meyer lemon gel and above that a sweet, foamy blend of milk and dried chrysanthemum flowers. It's one of the few dishes that can be served at any time of year.

There are different theories of preserved lemon-making. We use half salt and half sugar. Cut the fruit in half and squeeze out the juice. Rub each with the salt/sugar mix, pack in an earthenware container and pour more salt/sugar over each layer. Pour the juice over everything. Cover the top with plastic wrap and weight the lemons with a few plates. Cover the container, let sit for a few days, until the juice is over the top of the lemons. Bag the lemons with their liquid and age in a cool, dark place for at least a few months.

Make the 30° baumé syrup by bringing the water and sugar to a boil. Stir to fully dissolve the sugar and cool.

Clean the preserved lemons by removing the pith with the back of a knife–be careful not to remove the membrane. Blanch them in boiling water for 30 seconds and then transfer to the baumé syrup and allow to cool. Once they're cool, drain them and set aside the resulting lemon syrup. Cut the candied lemon into ⅓-inch (1-cm) squares or diamonds and put 5 pieces in the bottom of each serving cup.

For the custard, whip the egg yolks with sugar until pale and homogeneous. Warm the milk and cream to 120°F (50°C) and whisk into the egg yolk and sugar mixture. Place back on the heat and bring to 162°F (72°C). Pass though a chinois and pour into prepared custard cups, two-thirds of the way up the cup. Remove any air bubbles by passing over them with a blowtorch, and bake in a water bath at 300°F (150°C) for 55 to 60 minutes, until lightly set. Remove, cover them with plastic wrap and allow to chill in the refrigerator.

To make the gel, start with the preserved lemon syrup and season with fresh juice until it tastes brightly sweet and sour. Set with 2% gelatin, pour a spoonful over the custards and cool in the refrigerator for at least 2 hours, until the gel is set.

For the chrysanthemum milk, mix the sugar and egg yolks until pale. Set aside. Warm the milk to 120°F (50°C), add the chrysanthemum flowers and allow to steep for 4 min. Strain through a chinois. Dissolve the gelatin in the warm milk and add to the sugar-yolk mixture. Return to the heat and cook to 176°F (80°C). Strain again through a chinois into an ice bath. When chilled pour into a siphon and charge twice. Allow to set in the refrigerator for at least 4 hours.

To serve, remove the custards from the refrigerator. Dispense some of the chrysanthemum milk into a container, give it a stir, and then spoon it into the top of the serving cups.

"ROCK AND MOMAGRANATE"
kohlrabi, tobacco, pomegranate, shavings/leaves/flowers

That's not really what we called this dish, except for the first night that we served it. But I'm getting ahead of myself.

It was late summer, shading into fall, and I was thinking about kohlrabi, a root in the cabbage family. I was specifically thinking about cooking them slowly and completely, so that they were utterly tender and bursting with juice. In earth. And rocks. And hay. And whatever else I could find. The idea was that they would take on something of the medium they cooked in. And after peeling and cleaning I would cover them completely in late-season leaves, herbs and flowers.

Cooking in earth is not new. A hole in the ground was humanity's first pot. Coating a bit of something in clay to keep it moist had to have been the next development. We've been doing it for at least a few thousand years, as far as I can tell. In recent years, I particularly liked a dish of potatoes cooked in the soil they grew in made by Australian chef Ben Shewry.

I was more interested in what the earth was mixed with. I didn't have a firm grasp on the whole thing until I found something at the Happy Quail Farms stand at the farmers' market that I'd never seen before: Tobacco hay.

The farm, owned by David Winsberg, is mostly known for growing fantastic peppers in the unlikely urban landscape of East Palo Alto. A few years ago David started cultivating tobacco for his own use. Native tobacco. Tobacco is a traditional plant in the Americas, and it's been grown here for thousands of years. It was a part of some Native American cultures, used for trade, ceremonial purposes, medicine and pest control.

Those traditional strains have mostly been lost, and the seeds are hard to come by. The tobacco industry has not helped; it's hardly in their best interests for people to figure out that they can grow far superior quality tobacco in their own gardens.

What David called "tobacco hay" are the wood-like remains of the entire plant, allowed to dry after the leaves have been harvested. David shreds the plants, and the result looks a little like loose bark. It smells somewhat like tobacco, but more gentle and earthy. I bought a bag of the hay, and one of cured leaves. I had some ideas.

I made a salt crust, more or less traditional. Egg whites and salt. The earth was the medium, with a small amount of the tobacco hay mixed in. I covered a whole kohlrabi completely and baked it for four hours, until a cake tester slid through easily. While it cooked, the entire kitchen filled with a smoky, intoxicating smell. We let it cool and cut away the crust and the outside of the vegetable. The flesh underneath was sweet and surprisingly delicately flavored.

To amplify the tobacco flavor, we made a fluid gel of vegetable stock seasoned heavily with Rosa's vinegar, and smoked it with the tobacco leaves. We smeared it all over the peeled kohlrabi, and that became the glue to hold all of the leaves, shavings and flowers, everything that I could find in my garden at the end of the summer that needed to be cut back anyway. A sauce of pomegranate, sharpened with salt and lime, so it tasted a little like cranberry.

The first time we put it on a menu was for a dinner I cooked at Coi with Magnus Nilsson, the chef of Fäviken in Sweden. Magnus was staying with us, and he heard my son Julian asking for "Momagranate" at breakfast. This tickled him, and that night, when we went to the table to describe the dish, armed with an unbroken kohlrabi in its shell so that we could explain the process, he started calling it "Rock and Momagranate." Maybe it was his sweet smile, or his Swedish accent, but no one questioned his pronunciation. We never actually wrote that on the menu, but it's always how I've thought of the dish.

Mix the soil, tobacco hay, egg whites and salt, and add as much water as needed to make it adhere (soil contains varying levels of water). Cover the whole kohlrabi with the soil mixture and bake at 350°F (180°C) until done, about 3 hours. Test the kohlrabi with a cake tester before removing them from the oven—they should be extremely tender, as they will harden a bit as they cool. Remove from the soil shell, trim away the skin and the outside ¾-inch (2-cm) layer of flesh, and taste. Season lightly with salt on both sides if needed. (Hey: tobacco is toxic to eat! Please don't eat what has been in direct contact with the tobacco. Thanks.)

For the pomegranate sauce, boil half of the pomegranate juice with the agar. Cool in an ice bath until hardened. Blend with the remaining juice, and season with lime juice and salt.

For the glaze, boil the vegetable stock with the agar. Cool in an ice bath and blend. Season with Rosa's vinegar and salt. Smoke with the tobacco leaf by igniting the leaf and placing it on one side of a metal pan, and the sauce on the other. Cover. It will take 5 to 10 minutes to get the flavor right—it should be reasonably strong but it should not smell like an ashtray. It wants the first, fresh notes of smoke, not the lingering, stale smell of old tobacco.

To serve, gather whatever herbs, sprouts and flowers you can find. Early in the season, we used basils and other summery herbs. Later, after the rains came, the greens became more wintry. On this version is spearmint, roman mint, lemon balm, lemon verbena, parsley, red celery leaf and stem, tarragon, nasturtium leaf and flower, young mustard green, radish sprouts, red watercress, arugula sprouts, sheep sorrel, young thistle, chickweed, miner's lettuce, bronze fennel, salvia flowers, nepitella flowers and rosemary flowers. Cover the kohlrabi with a thin layer of the glaze, and cover with the herbs and flowers and shavings of raw radish and turnip. Sprinkle with coarse salt. Dress the plate with pomegranate sauce and transfer the kohlrabi to the plate.

SILKEN WHITE CHOCOLATE
kiwi, coffee

The first meal that Alexandra ever made for me was tofu, seaweed and brown rice. It remains, along with spaghetti and meat sauce, my favorite comfort food. At times I've dusted the brown rice crackers (see page 56) with seaweed powder and served them with a tofu-ginger dipping sauce, kind of a re-imagined taste memory.

For me, tofu is a relatively recent discovery—"tofu eater" was not a compliment where I came from. When I first moved out here, I was suspicious. One reason is that the quality of the tofu sold in supermarkets is absolutely horrid. Comparing well-made tofu to the commercial stuff is like tasting a perfectly ripe heirloom tomato next to its canned brethren. By the time I visited Japan I had already grown fond of tofu, but the quality I found there was eye-opening. After one especially memorable dinner at Kappo Sakamoto, which included a dish of fresh yuba fished out of bubbling soy milk and dipped into a light soy sauce, I was inspired to find better tofu in San Francisco.

Ryuta Sakamoto, the son of Kappo Sakamoto's owner, introduced me to the Hodo Soy Beanery, currently based in Oakland. We started using their soy milk, yuba and tofu soon after we opened. We always have a soy product on the menu, and sometimes more than one. Hodo has since moved on to national-supermarket-size production, so now we make our own.

Soy milk has a bad rap as a bland dairy substitute, but eating it doesn't have to hurt. With a little imagination, it can be exciting, in fact. Like this dish, which combines soy milk and white chocolate in a sweet, nutty, earthy, not-too-sweet custard. Silken White Chocolate, Matt calls it, because it echoes the texture of silken tofu, if not the taste. A little bit of kiwi (hello, California!) tossed with lemon juice, simple syrup, olive oil, and—surprise—coffee-flavored crumbs, hidden under the custard. There's a lacy crisp of white chocolate perched on top, smartly separated from the custard by pieces of kiwi, which provide an elegant crunch. But it's the soy milk that makes the dish special, even though it doesn't take a starring role.

For the custard, melt the white chocolate to 113°F (45°C) in a bowl set over simmering water. Set aside. Place the soy milk, glucose, trimoline, and gelatin in a pan and bring to 131°F (55°C). Allow to cool to 104°F (40°C). Transfer the chocolate to a food processor, add a little bit of the soy mixture, and blend until the mixture breaks. Then continue to add more soy, a little at a time, until it becomes a tight shiny emulsion. Add the remainder of the warm soy milk and blend until it's homogeneous. Transfer the mixture to a large bowl and add the cold addition of soy milk and cream. Season with salt to taste and pour into prepared molds. Refrigerate for at least 4 hours.

For the white chocolate tuile, melt the white chocolate and set aside. Place all of the sugars in a pan and bring to 325°F (160°C). Allow to cool to 275°F (140°C) and add to the melted chocolate. Mix well and pour out over a Silpat. Allow the mixture to harden, and break into pieces. Grind the caramel in a spice grinder or a blender until it's a smooth powder. Sift evenly on a sheet pan lined with parchment paper. Use a #5 ring cutter to demarcate circles in the powder. Bake in a 400°F (200°C) oven with no fan for 2 minutes, rotating at 1 minute, until the disks are shiny, but don't let them color. Quickly move the parchment to a flat table and allow to cool. Store them in a tightly covered container.

To make the coffee panade, cream the butter, salt and sugar. Add the rest of the ingredients and mix to combine. Pass through a tamis and then refrigerate.

To serve, place a small amount of coffee panade in the center of a bowl. Unmold a disk of silken white chocolate in the center of the plate. Season the kiwi with salt, lemon juice, olive oil and 30° Baumé syrup, making a little extra syrup for the sauce. It should be bright, but not too acidic. Place 1 piece of the kiwi next to the white chocolate, and 2 pieces on top, spooning a little sauce around. Balance a white chocolate tuile on top of the kiwi on the custard.

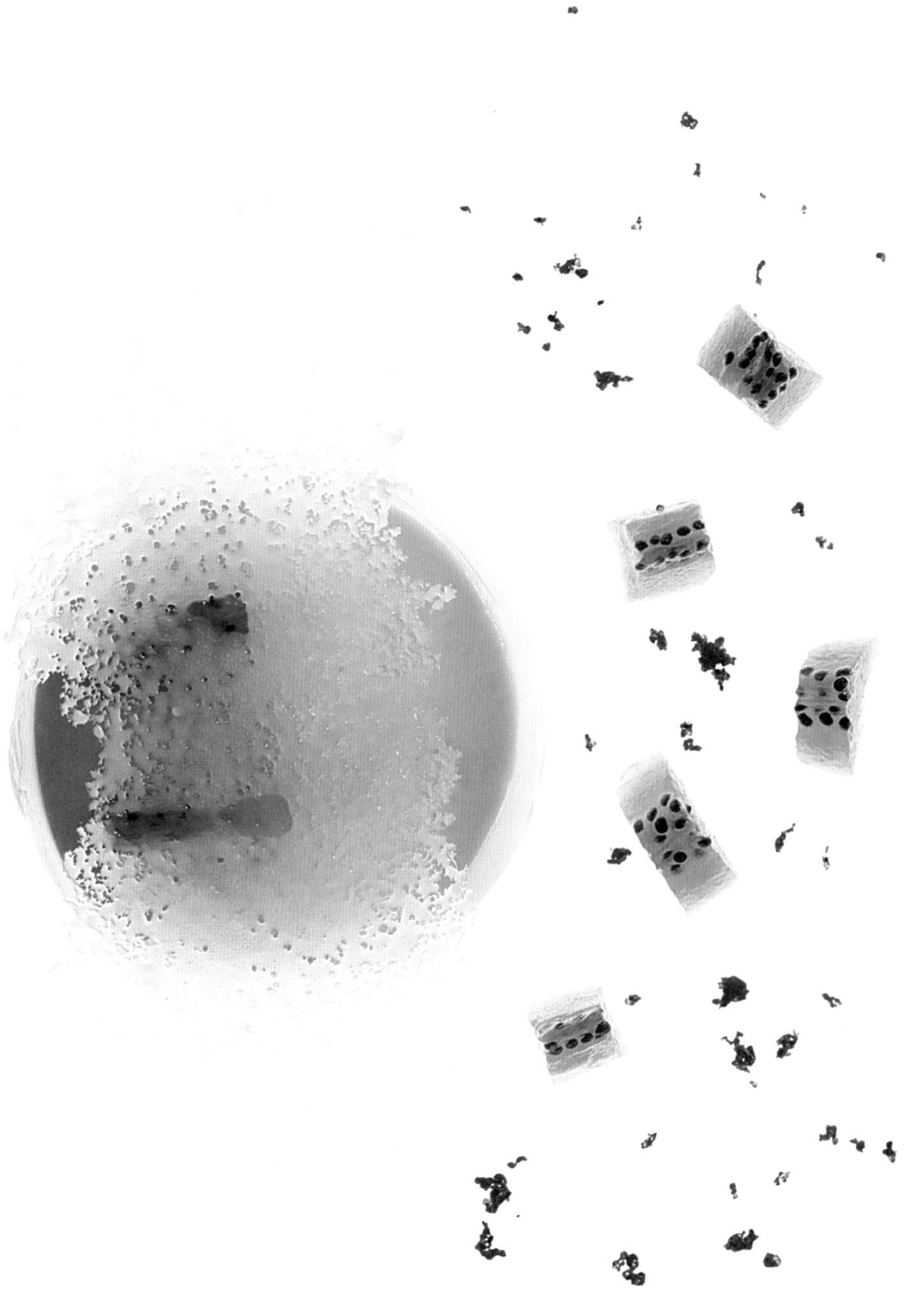

SUNCHOKE SOUP
sunflower, chanterelle

The summer sun flattens the inland countryside with its relentless stare. The grasses turn crisp and dry, crackling and scraping underfoot. Kicked-up dust lingers in the air, and by midday the light has the washed out quality of a camera lens left on full exposure. Even in San Francisco the dry months drag on, although the western edge is moistened by the fog that settles down over the coast like a cool, nubbly blanket.

The farms, mellow and weedy during the winter, kick into high gear. The land around them might be parched, but their fields are packed with neat rows of every kind of vegetable that the climate will support. On most of those farms you will find sunflowers.

People are crazy about sunflowers here. They are emblematic of Northern California culture, with their optimistic, uncomplicated countenance. Sunflowers beam at passersby from everywhere during the summer, in markets and fields and backyards. It's hard not to smile in their presence.

This is a sunflower dish, without any actual sunflowers (that would be too easy, right?). We put it on the menu in the fall, after the first rains, when the sunflowers have faded. We use their roots, also called sunchokes; their seeds, a staple California snack food; and sprouts. This dish finds moodiness, seriousness, in one of our most easygoing plants.

The soup itself is incredibly easy to make, a simple blend of sunchoke, brown butter and vegetable stock. The complexity comes from the sunflower seed pesto-like condiment that we put in the bottom of the bowl. It's a mixture of half-crushed sunflower seeds, sunflower oil, sunchoke powder and chanterelle powder, with a little lemon zest for brightness. The sunchoke powder is a powerful, haunting flavor, bitter and earthy like chicory root. Combined with a purée of chanterelles, the condiment gives the soup a remarkable depth of flavor.

Using multiple parts of a plant allows us to amplify the profile of an ingredient, to cook simple, focused dishes that still carry complexity and visceral impact. The soup looks a little bit like the late summer countryside, with layers of earth tones interrupted by a few green leaves. It's a quiet, meditative dish. But not a sad one.

Before making the soup, peel the sunchokes and deeply roast the skins. Dehydrate the skins at 140°F (60°C) and grind them into a powder. Make the chanterelle powder by dehydrating and grinding the chanterelles.

Make the soup by simmering the sunchokes with the brown butter, vegetable stock and salt until they're baby-food tender. Blend and pass through a chinois, then season with salt.

Pick through the chanterelles. Save the tiniest, most beautiful ones to shave raw. Use the rest to make the purée. First make a chanterelle stock by cooking the mushroom stock (see page 156), dried chanterelles and chanterelle scraps for about an hour, until the stock is flavorful and tastes intensely of chanterelle. Make sure the chanterelles are very fresh and sweet—sometimes they carry bitter, woody notes, which will carry over into the stock and the purée. Then sauté the remaining chanterelles with butter and salt, and simmer with chanterelle stock. When tender add the agar, boil and cool. Purée until smooth, adjust for salt and cool.

Crush the sunflower seeds—untoasted—in a mortar and pestle. Combine with the thyme, sunchoke powder, chanterelle powder, sunflower oil and lemon zest and season with salt.

To serve, spread the sunflower seed pesto at the bottom of the bowl. Put 5 dots of chanterelle purée spread around. Cut out circles of raw sunchoke, thinly slice them, then gently season with rice wine vinegar and salt, and lean 3 slices against 3 dots of purée. Shave some of the nicest chanterelles, and lean 3 slices against the other 2 dots of purée, and 1 somewhere else. Add 4 or 5 pieces of sunflower sprouts. Pour 60 g of the hot soup into each bowl.

MILK CHOCOLATE/SOY
blueberry, baguette, cocoa praline

The star of this dish is not the milk chocolate, the blueberries or the baguette. It's the cocoa praline.

There are a few traditional ways to make praline, and they all involve nuts. Matt replaced the nuts with cocoa nibs, and cooked them with sugar until the nibs browned, the sugar caramelized and the whole became something new. When it cooled, it hardened into clumps that looked like moon rocks. Grated with a microplane, the clumps released a shocking intensity of aroma, the quality of which is hard to describe. It smelled like bitter chocolate and dark caramel, coffee and roasted nuts, wet soil and flint and crushed flowers.

The process is trickier than it sounds, and far less pleasant. Cocoa nibs contain a lot of cocoa butter, which has a very low burning point. That means that the heat needs to be lower, the cooking time longer and the stirring constant. Vigorously moving a hot, stubborn, sticky mass around a pot set over a burner is not anyone's idea of a good time. But it's the only way to develop the proper depth and complexity.

This dish came after the Silken White Chocolate (see page 256), and Matt wanted to explore the chocolate-soy connection further. That's the way a lot of our dishes evolve, little pieces connecting one to the other, even when the end result is very different. Since milk chocolate is also sweet, Matt figured that it would also work well, which it did. The soy lends nutty, earthy notes, giving the milk chocolate (with a little dark chocolate mixed in for depth), unusual gravitas. It's rich without being cloying or decadent.

We ran this dish in the late spring, when blueberries are at their best. For blueberries, as for all berries, there are many cultivars, each one yielding a slightly different flavor and ripening at a slightly different time. From week to week they change, even with the same grower. We look for blueberries with intensity of flavor, which isn't just about sugar/acid balance, it's also the energy of the fruit, how exciting it is to eat. I'm not sure how else to put it, except that sometimes a well-grown, very fresh berry pops; it has an extra level of flavor. Those are the ones that we use.

There are fresh blueberries and blueberry sauce in the dish. The milk chocolate-soy custard. A bit of sweetened, frothed soy milk. And a brilliant touch—a slice of untoasted baguette. The first time I tried it I was immediately brought back to France when I was six years old, eating sandwiches of butter and chocolate on baguette. We make the baguette ourselves at Coi, and it is what ties the dish to tradition and gives the intense flavors a neutral base. Over everything goes a thick blanket of grated praline, which transforms everything it touches.

The cocoa praline is the hardest part of the dish, but it has many uses. It can be grated over all kinds of chocolate desserts for added dimension, or it can transform a simple bowl of strawberries and cream. Start by boiling the water and sugar until they begin to crystallize, then add the nibs and stir well. Pour out onto a baking pan lined with a Silpat. In a clean heavy-bottomed pan, over medium heat, cook the cocoa nibs and sugar. Stir them constantly to avoid burning, until the sugar has reached a deep caramel state. At this point the aroma will have transformed into an exhilarating combination of chocolate and caramel, and the nibs will flow loosely off of a spoon. Also, you will be hot and sweaty and your arm will be tired. Stir in the salt and spoon the praline onto another baking pan lined with a Silpat to cool.

To make the milk chocolate pudding, warm the soy milk, glucose and inverted sugar together. Set aside. Melt the chocolates in a bowl set over simmering water until they reach 120°F (50°C), then allow to cool to 113°F (45°C). Blend with the milk mixture to create an emulsion. Whip the cream to soft peaks and fold into the ganache. Place in containers and allow to cool overnight.

For the blueberry sauce, place the fruit, sugar, lemon peel and water into a pan over medium heat. Once it comes to a simmer, pull off the heat, and pass through a chinois. Weigh the liquid and whisk in the agar. Bring back to a hard boil, and pour into a bowl set over ice water and allow to cool. Once it's set, blend until smooth. Season to taste with fresh lemon juice, zest and salt.

Combine the soy milk and sugar and then stir to combine.

To serve, put a slice of shaved baguette on one side of the plate. Scoop a large spoonful of the milk chocolate-soy next to and slightly on top of it. Mix the fresh blueberries with the blueberry sauce, and spoon next to and around the chocolate. Grate enough of the praline to completely cover everything. Froth the soy milk with a hand blender and spoon some over everything.

Note: Try blending the praline until smooth and melted in a food processor fitted with a metal bowl. Pour into a container lined with plastic wrap, and then remove when cool. Wrap and store in a cool, dark place. After a few months it will soften and mellow. Cut into small pieces, it's perfect for folding into vanilla ice cream.

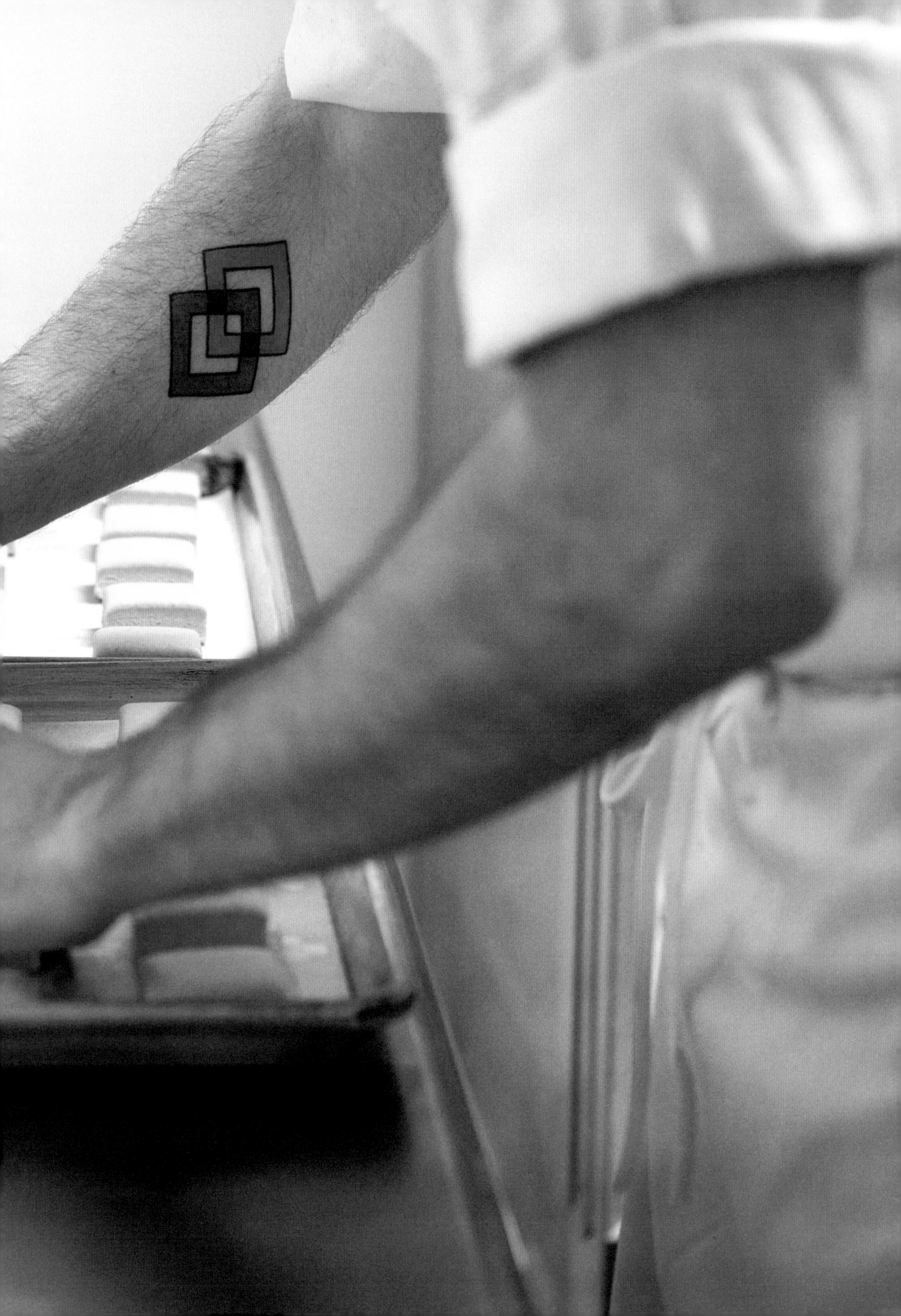

BEEHIVE

It's easy to underestimate the role of the pastry chef. They make very few courses, and, in truth, they're almost never the main draw. Their contributions come late in the meal when everyone's appetite has already been sated, making their job even harder.

But dessert, especially at a nice restaurant, is important. The modern idea of serving desserts at the end of a meal is a fairly new phenomenon—as recently as a few hundred years ago the sweet dishes were spread throughout. That idea has come back a bit, popularized by Albert Adrià's influence on the entirety of the El Bulli menu, and that restaurant's knack for interspersing sweet and savory elements during the long, winding menus that they produced. For the rest of us and for our guests, the expectation of a few true desserts at the end of the menu remains.

Matt is, to my mind, one of the best pastry chefs in the world right now, and a hell of a baker as well. He has changed the Coi kitchen for the better: his refusal to compromise, his insistence on always doing something different and better have helped me push our cuisine forward. There are some great desserts in this book, but those were not his only contribution. Ours is a constant dialog in the kitchen, and we will often help finish each other's dishes, providing the one element that makes a dish complete. At one point, when the savory part of the kitchen was struggling to keep up, he took the cheese course. We've been trading turns with it ever since.

This is a cheese course that Matt developed while he was the pastry chef at Meadowood in Napa in 2010. It was the fall, when the beekeepers were taking honey from the hives. Matt had gotten to know the beekeepers quite well, and they had taught him about the bees, what they eat and how they live. The idea for the dish was sparked by a process that comes naturally to a chef—when you need to innovate, you look at what's around that you can work with. He saw the beehive and thought that he could make a brioche that mimicked its shape, with molten cheese inside. He glazed the outside of the hive with honey, and decorated it with the same flowers on which the bees fed. When he moved to a restaurant in San Francisco, he made the same dish but with vanilla foam that swirled around the hive like fog.

In the winter, the cold weather causes honey to crystallize. So recently he made different textures of crystallized sugar, then finished with a few flowers that were in season, like rosemary from my house and the wild alyssum that was just starting to appear, with its honeyed scent. It's a dish that can morph endlessly. I can't wait to see what the next iteration brings.

To make the brioche, mix all the ingredients except the butter until well incorporated and the gluten is strengthened. Add the butter and proof the dough at room temperature for 1 hour. Roll out the dough, fold it once, and place in the freezer for 30 minutes, or until it's cold. Once it's cold, make 2 book folds in the dough (fold in half and then again). Chill the dough again, and cut it into circles with a #3 ring cutter. Stack 3 rounds on each other and place on a baking sheet covered with plastic wrap. Allow them to proof for 2½ hours at room temperature. Brush with egg wash and bake at 400°F (200°C) for 15 minutes. Cool.

For the honey glaze, boil all of the ingredients and cool at room temperature.

Place the cheese in a blender. Place the gellan F in a pan with the cream and salt and warm slowly to hydrate it, then bring to a hard boil. Pour the hot cream into the blender, and blend with the cheese until the mixture thickens and becomes smooth. Place in a piping bag with a small tip and set aside.

To serve, using tweezers, cut a hole in the bottom of the brioche. Fill with the cheese mousse. Brush the brioche with honey glaze and place back in the oven at 400°F (200°C) for 3 minutes until warm. Garnish with seasoned honeycomb, and whatever else makes sense.

YOUNG DUCK IN TWO SERVINGS
poached and chilled breast, jasmine tea, orange, endive
leg grilled over charcoal, cilantro-fermented tofu puree

I'm lucky to live in a place where the products are of such a high quality and so varied that I'm always discovering something terrific. For me, new products push creativity more than new techniques.

This dish practically fell into my lap. It was Sunday, and Alexandra had bought a duck for dinner. It was a small duck. A young duck, from Marin Sun Farms in western Marin County. I roasted it simply and was amazed: It had a sweeter, softer flavor than any duck I'd tried out here, especially in the fat, which was so good that I wanted to eat it raw. OK, I did eat it raw. Whatever.

Normally with duck, the thinking is that you need to age it to develop the flavor. In fact, I love aged duck, and we have a recipe for it on page 188. But this little duckling wanted to be as fresh as possible. There was something about the taste that would be lost in the aging process. At the restaurant, I had tried duck in three servings the year before, and it was fine, but I didn't feel like I'd really nailed it. I wanted to try again with these ducks, in two servings.

I like a dynamic shape to the menu, always unexpectedly changing temperatures, textures and looks, so I thought about serving the first dish cold. Going from a warm abalone dish to a cold duck dish felt right. My first attempt, however, was some sort of tartare. Definitely *not* right.

I settled on a chilled, poached duck breast, which triggered memories of an old-school recipe, maybe something out of Escoffier. Those dishes always had some sort of jelly, and perhaps an endive salad on the side. It was spring, when the jasmine is in bloom, so I made jasmine tea gel, but a weird one on the face of it, especially for me—completely unseasoned, just the pure flavor of the tea (solid sauce!). For the salad, red endive cooked with orange and vinegar and julienned, crunchy and bright. And, to ground the dish and give it more richness and texture, crisp pieces of skin sprinkled on top. The gel was cold and refreshing, and the breast itself was poached in seasoned consommé at a high enough temperature to make it juicy and tender when cooled and sliced. "It reminds me of a first course at a Chinese buffet," a friend told me, which I loved.

For the second serving I wanted something savory and gutsy, to contrast with the delicate floral notes of the cold breast. I liked using the thigh in the glamour spot, where typically you would find the breast—the legs are so much more flavorful anyway. We cooked them at a low temperature for a long time, kind of a new-style confit, and then finished them over charcoal. In fact I bought a grill just for the dish, and it became a fixture in the kitchen. That's how things evolve sometimes. It made a huge difference—the smell of the grilled duck jumped off the plate, announcing its presence before it hit the table.

For the sauce we made a Ducasse-style duck jus, aromatic with giblets and garlic, lots of fat emulsified in, and plenty of vinegar to cut the richness. But my favorite part of the dish was the cilantro-fermented tofu purée. Bright, sweet, and herbaceous, it has a million uses and it's easy to make—even if you don't have fermented tofu, the regular stuff will do just fine. It's a dish that delivers surprisingly powerful flavors while still feeling light.

Both dishes ended up having an Asian feel to them, which I didn't plan. But then, I didn't plan for the duck to show up at all. It just sort of happened that way.

Season the thigh with salt and let it stand for 30 minutes. Vacuum seal it in a bag with a few spoonfuls of rendered fat, and cook it at 136°F (58°C) for 10 to 12 hours. Cool by plunging the bag into ice water until cold. Remove the bone and cut into portions that look nice. Refrigerate.

The next day, take some of the bones and make a consommé: an onion, half of it charred, a few carrots, the bones, and that's it. Water just to cover, not too much. Cook it 3 to 4 hours, until it tastes clearly of duck. Save the rest of the bones and the innards for the sauce.

For the sauce, brown the rest of the duck bones, chopped up if possible, in lots of duck fat. Add the onion and carrot, and brown. At this point there should be a nice fond on the bottom of the pan. Deglaze with white wine, scraping up all the browned bits, and reduce by half. Add the AP stock and simmer for about 2 hours, not skimming. Chop the innards (to be clear, we're talking about heart, kidney and liver, which should come with the duck), and brown them in duck fat in a different pan. Add the shallot and garlic, cook for 5 minutes, and strain the jus into the innards. Reduce to sauce consistency. It should be thick with fat, about 25-30% by volume. Strain through cheesecloth, and season with champagne vinegar. Lots of it. It should be gamy and savory and acidic and irresistible.

For the breast, poach it in the consommé at 154°F (68°C) in a pot, moving it around often. Cook to medium, juicy and pink in the center. Remove from the stock and cool in a refrigerator.

Begin the jasmine tea gel by pouring hot water over the leaves, and letting them stand for 3.5 minutes. Strain the tea, and boil half of it with the agar. Off the heat, whisk in the hydrated gelatin, and then the rest of the tea. Don't season. Pour into a container and refrigerate.

Vacuum seal the endive with the orange zest, orange juice and salt. Steam at 170°F (75°C) for 20 minutes, until crisp-tender. Cool and remove from the bag, reserving the juices. Remove the stem and julienne the endive lengthwise. Toss with the reserved juices, champagne vinegar, more orange juice and salt. Refrigerate if not being used immediately. It will need to be re-seasoned if it sits any length of time.

Scrape the reserved skin with the back of a knife until smooth. Spread the skins on a baking sheet in between sheets of parchment paper. Bake at 300°F (150°C) until the skin is crisp. Chop into pieces, season and hold warm on a sheet tray lined with paper towels. Change the paper towels a few times as they become saturated with fat.

Blend all of the ingredients for the cilantro-tofu purée until it turns lime green, and season with salt.

To serve the first dish, slice the breast, season with salt if necessary, and pile into a bowl. Add a few spoons of gel, and some julienne endive. Sprinkle crisped skin on top.

To serve the second dish, hold the thigh in 150°F (65°C) fat until warmed through, and then grill over charcoal. Cook a piece of baby bok choy in water and salt, drain the liquid when cooked, and season with rice wine vinegar. Place it on top of the thigh. Put some of the cilantro-fermented tofu purée on the plate, and spoon the sauce around. Place the thigh on top of the sauce.

FARM STAND:
OPEN
FARM STAND:
OPEN FRIDAYS
FARMSTAND

LIVE SPOT PRAWN
cucumber, watermelon, lemon flavors

"I don't like vinegar," a food writer once announced to me after eating at Coi, "and I never use it myself." I was a bit taken aback. This is a little like a music critic saying that she doesn't care for minor chords. Vinegar is central to almost every important food culture around the world. It's the heartbeat of our cooking, a thin line of acidity running through the menu like an electrified wire, making everything dance. But it needs to be used carefully, because it can diminish as easily as it can improve.

This is a dish of acidity used with restraint and care. It features raw Santa Barbara spot prawns, killed just when they're ordered, and brined for a few minutes in sea water. We serve them so fresh as to be almost crunchy, with an intense, heavy sweetness. Sweetness that requires acidity—in measure.

During the summer, many of the herbs with lemon flavors that I grow at my house are at their best. We use lemon balm, lemon verbena and lemon basil for garnish. To play against the prawns, we add ripe cucumber and watermelon, both full of sugar. To balance the cucumber we dress it with rice wine vinegar just before serving; for the watermelon, we compress it ahead of time with lemon juice and salt. The sauce is a clear prawn broth, infused with lemongrass and lemon leaf, seasoned with lemon juice and rice wine vinegar, and drizzled with a few drops of olive oil. Every component has acidity.

The challenge is to keep the dish in perfect balance. The prawns are surprisingly flavorful in their raw state, but they can only take so much acidity, so much sweetness, before they become overwhelmed. Every day, we season each component carefully, tasting one with the other to make sure that there is harmony. The vinegar is crucial—it cleans up the sweetness of the lemon flavors and gives them shape and dimension. Without it, the dish is sweet and flabby. With just a little bit, it sings.

The writer never came back. I didn't say anything, even though our paths have crossed over the years, but I've often thought about that exchange. Like almost every time I pick up a bottle of vinegar.

For the spot prawns, buy them live. Set some aside to serve and some for the sauce.

For the broth, you probably have to kill a few very expensive prawns at least a couple hours before serving the dish. Think of it as a ritual sacrifice. Kill the prawns by slicing quickly through the head, and then cutting the body in half lengthwise. Wash the guts out of the heads and bodies with a spray of cold water, and then coarsely chop—shell and all. Sear the prawn pieces in pure olive oil briefly, just until they turn red, and then add the water and vegetables to the pan. Simmer for about 2 hours, until flavorful, and then take off the heat and immediately add the crushed lemongrass and the sliced lemon leaves. When the flavor seems right, strain and cool. The lemon flavors should be a little high, because they'll diminish with time and the addition of the other ingredients. Season with lemon juice, rice wine vinegar, fruity olive oil and salt. A little bit of olive oil is important to balance the acidity, and also for mouthfeel. Refrigerate.

To serve, season the watermelon cylinders with the lemon juice and salt, and vacuum seal them in a Cryovac bag to compress. Slice them into ⅛-inch (2-mm) thick rounds and season if necessary with more lemon juice and salt. They should be sweet, but bright.

Plunge the garnish spot prawns into boiling water for 5 seconds and then into ice water. Discard the head, and peel and devein the tail carefully to avoid tearing up the flesh. Keep a brine of water and 4% salt (or seawater plus an additional 0.5% salt) in a bowl over ice water so it's very cold. Soak the prawn tails in the brine for 1 minute. Drain on a paper towel in the refrigerator for a few minutes, but no more than 10 minutes. Cut each prawn tail crosswise into ¾-inch (2-cm) thick pieces, 4 per tail, and season with a little more salt if necessary. Place in the center of a shallow bowl. Thinly slice a small Japanese cucumber, and dress with a little rice wine vinegar and salt, just enough to enliven them. Place 2 pieces of cucumber on the prawns, and 2 rounds of watermelon, 1 of each color. Garnish with the lemony herbs, and spoon some broth into the bowl.

YOUNG ARTICHOKE GRILLED UNDER A WEIGHT
spicy crayfish vinaigrette, fava leaf, sesame

I always wanted a mentor. Instead I had my imagination, which was largely fueled by what I read. There are two books that crystallized how I understood my profession. One was Patricia Wells's *Simple French Food*, about the cuisine of Joël Robuchon. I was mesmerized by the precision, the absoluteness of the perfection of every ingredient in every dish. The other was a book called *Great Chefs of France*, by Anthony Blake, a late '70s classic now sadly out of print. It documented all of the three-Michelin-star chefs in France, their kitchens, their cuisine and their philosophy. At twenty-one years old, already seven years into cooking, it struck a deep chord. That, I knew instantly, was the life I wanted: A life of sacrifice and hard work, guided by the never-ending desire to create something extraordinary (which, of course, isn't much of a life at all).

They didn't seem very exuberant, those chefs. Their happiness appeared to be largely found in their work, in discrete moments, meted out frugally amongst a constancy of hardship and intense pressure. I memorized that book, and all of the quotes: "You can either ask about the quality, or you can ask about the price." It's clear to me now that I wildly over-romanticized the life of a cook, yet I still can't shake the idea.

This dish has absolutely no bearing on that book, and I would be instantly kicked out of any of those kitchens for making it. In fact, this is the only time I've ever used sriracha in a dish, a deal-killer if ever I saw one. Yet the feeling of the dish reminds me a little bit of Louis Outhier, the flamboyant chef on the Riviera who introduced a young Jean-Georges Vongerichten to Asian ingredients. I can't tell you why, but something about the sesame with the warm artichoke and cold crayfish, the stylized look of the dish, just kind of puts me in that frame of mind.

Nowadays, it's hard to get a bearing on what haute cuisine really means. For a while, including when we opened, it was out of favor. Now modern tasting-menu restaurants, serving creative food in a casual environment, are opening up everywhere. Whatever it is that we're doing, it's in constant evolution, and I may never figure it out. It's not the Michelin cuisine of old, but that cuisine is contained within it. We reference those benchmarks constantly.

Happiness for any cook can be hard to come by, but especially for those who work at the highest level. The long hours, stress, low pay and strain on marriages and friendships all lend themselves to a kind of life lived more in shadows than in light. But if you caught me in a moment of absolute honesty, I would say that the tedium of daily existence wears on me. I could never live a normal life. My job is to create an illusion based on truth, to open a passage to a world in which everything is brighter, prettier and more enduring than real life, in all its glorious fragility, could ever be. And that's not nothing.

Steam 12 large crayfish at 212°F (100°C) for 3 minutes. Cool by placing them on a sheet tray in a refrigerator. When cool, shell the meat and remove the intestinal tract with tweezers. Season with a little salt and refrigerate.

Clean the rest of the crayfish as on page 172. Make the crayfish oil as in that recipe. Remove from the heat and strain through a chinois. Cool.

Sweat the lemongrass (smashed and sliced) and fennel, coarsely chopped, in pure olive oil until the fennel is softened. Add the sriracha, white wine and tomato juice, and reduce by a third. Add a pinch of xanthan, boil for a minute, strain through cheesecloth and cool. Combine with the crayfish oil, champagne vinegar and fruity olive oil to make the spicy crayfish vinaigrette.

For the garnish artichokes, combine the peeled and trimmed young artichokes with lemon juice, vegetable stock, pure olive oil and salt, and vacuum seal. Steam at 185°F (85°C) for 30 to 40 minutes, until they are cooked but still have texture.

The artichoke mayo: This is actually the best part of the dish. One of the first things I ate in California was large, steamed artichokes with mayonnaise. They love that here. Alexandra makes it all the time at home—it's like Californians' default comfort food.

Now what if your mayonnaise had the same texture, but tasted like artichokes? Well, here it is. Take the peeled artichokes trimmed to just the heart and tender stem (small or large, they both work fine) and vacuum seal them in a bag with the measured lemon juice, olive oil and salt. Cook the bag in a pot of boiling water until the chokes are very, very soft. Cool and drain them, discarding the cooking liquid. Blend with more pure olive oil and a little lemon juice. Season with salt. Uncannily like mayonnaise texture, no?

For the fava bean leaves, cook briefly in salted water until soft but not falling apart, and then rinse under cold water to cool. Squeeze out the excess water and season with sesame oil (be careful with that stuff, it's strong!) and salt.

To serve, cut the garnish artichoke in half lengthwise, season with a little salt, and grill on the plancha, under a weight, until nicely browned. Meanwhile, place 2 small spoons of artichoke mayonnaise in a shallow bowl, and sprinkle shichimi togarashi across 1 of them. Spoon the spicy crayfish vinaigrette around the mayonnaise. Put 1 half of artichoke on each spoonful of mayonnaise, and top each with a whole, chilled crayfish tail. Sprinkle toasted black and white sesame seeds on each. Drape 3 seasoned fava leaves on and around the artichokes, and garnish with a few fava flowers.

GRASS-FED VEAL
chicories, seville orange

Turn back the clock a few decades, to the 1950s. Here in North Beach, City Lights bookstore had just opened. *Howl* was published, then *On the Road* and *A Coney Island of the Mind*. All the beat poets were running around, drinking and raising hell. A young Woody Allen played the hungry i just across the street, and so did Lenny Bruce, who used to crash in a house behind Coi. A block away was the Jazz Workshop, where Thelonious Monk recorded one of his most famous albums. Enrico Banducci held court at Enrico's, Carol Doda ushered in a new era of burlesque, and the streets pulsed with abandon and life.

It's all gone now. The jazz shops have closed down, replaced by seedy clubs and strip joints. Buses of kids from the suburbs roll in every weekend, spilling out young animals looking to get drunk, fight and worse. Enrico's is long shuttered. The old-timers have mostly moved on or died, and the rivers of restless creativity that used to flow through the streets have dried up. There's still plenty of money around, the way there has been since the Gold Rush, but not much remains of the old days, just the ghosts who haunt the back alleys and dive bars. If you look closely enough you'll find them.

San Francisco, like any big city, has its share of great old taxi drivers who remember what the city was like, although their number is dwindling. I caught a ride to work once with a guy who told me about the time in '68, when he saw Monk on the street after he played a show. I learned how to play piano as a kid, and he was my hero, with his jerky syncopation, idiosyncratic voice, and harmonic dissonance that would resolve, when you couldn't stand it any more, into the sweetest melody you'd ever heard. His sense of musical balance was perfect: complexly wrought, deeply human. Three notes and you knew who was playing, and there aren't many piano players you can say that about. Monk played in a way that came across as primitive, almost naïve at times. He faced criticisms that he didn't really have the chops, that he wasn't technically proficient, which was ridiculous—the guy could really play.

Anyway, the cabbie told me that he was walking down Broadway at 2:00 a.m. and there he was, standing unmoving in the middle of the sidewalk, porkpie hat at an angle, staring up at the sky. "Are you all right, Mr. Monk?" the cabbie asked. Monk slowly dropped his eyes and gave him a long, unblinking look. After a minute he lifted his head towards the horizon and ambled off into the North Beach night.

Deep down in our bones, I think that the pre-historic part of us still equates bitterness with death. In nature, bitterness is often a plant's self-defense mechanism. It indicates non-deliciousness at best, and danger at worst. Now, of course, we know intellectually that there are many bitter plants that are safe to eat, but I think something of their appeal is their inherent riskiness, illusory though that might be.

This is a dish of bitter and sour flavors, held together with sweet, smoky veal, and an almost classical sauce with a twist. We start by deeply browning a lot of veal bones and scraps. Add the onion and carrot, and then deglaze with white wine, scraping the fond on the bottom of the pan, and reduce until dry. Add just enough AP stock to cover the meat, and slowly reduce to a glaze. Don't skim. Scrape the bottom of the pan, and add just enough stock to cover again. Reduce, scrape, cover, and repeat. By this time there should be a beautiful, thick, shiny glaze over everything. The last time you add the stock, add enough to cover the bones, and simmer for about 45 minutes, until the flavor is intense, and the texture like fatty velvet. Strain and add the zest and juice of a Seville orange, an intensely puckery sour orange that traditionally was the base of *duck à l'orange*, before Americans decided that the dish should become treacly and disgusting. Season with salt and rice wine vinegar, to clean up the sweetness. The power and texture of the sauce will hold everything in balance.

Find some mature puntarelle, a bitter green that grows light green asparagus-like pods inside of what look like jagged dandelion greens. Cut the pods at the base and slice them thinly. Sweat them with the pure olive oil and a splash of water over medium heat, so they cook quickly (slow = oxidization), and then purée in a blender with the caper berries, pure olive oil (for texture and to mute acidity) and lemon juice (to balance bitterness and give life).

The Italian influence in Northern California is strong. We now have many of the same kinds of chicories that you find all over Italy, except they are a little sweeter here. The best ones come from Annabelle Lenderink, who grows amazing, hard-to-find things, speaks about ten languages, and makes me happy every time I see her at the market. There are many, like radicchio di Verona, radicchio di Treviso, radicchio di Castelfranco, pan di zucchero, all wild Italian plants that were domesticated and then named after the town that they came from. In Italy, they use one at a time. I use several to blend different textures and flavors. We cut them in pretty shapes, and dress them with fruity olive oil and lemon juice, just enough to balance the bitterness.

For this dish we use veal that is mid-way towards adulthood, when it's developed a bit of fat and flavor. We take the ribeye, clean up the silver skin and connective tissue, and cut into smaller pieces. We poach it in pure olive oil at 144°F (62°C) until it's pink and the proteins have coagulated softly, and then grill it over charcoal, putting a piece of fig wood on the coals to give it a bit of smoke.

To serve, spoon some punterelle purée and Seville orange sauce on a plate. The sauce is thick and beautiful, but don't be decorative, it's there for flavor. Use plenty. Slice the veal, place a piece in the center of the plate and scatter with chicories. Add a few thinly sliced caper berries here and there.

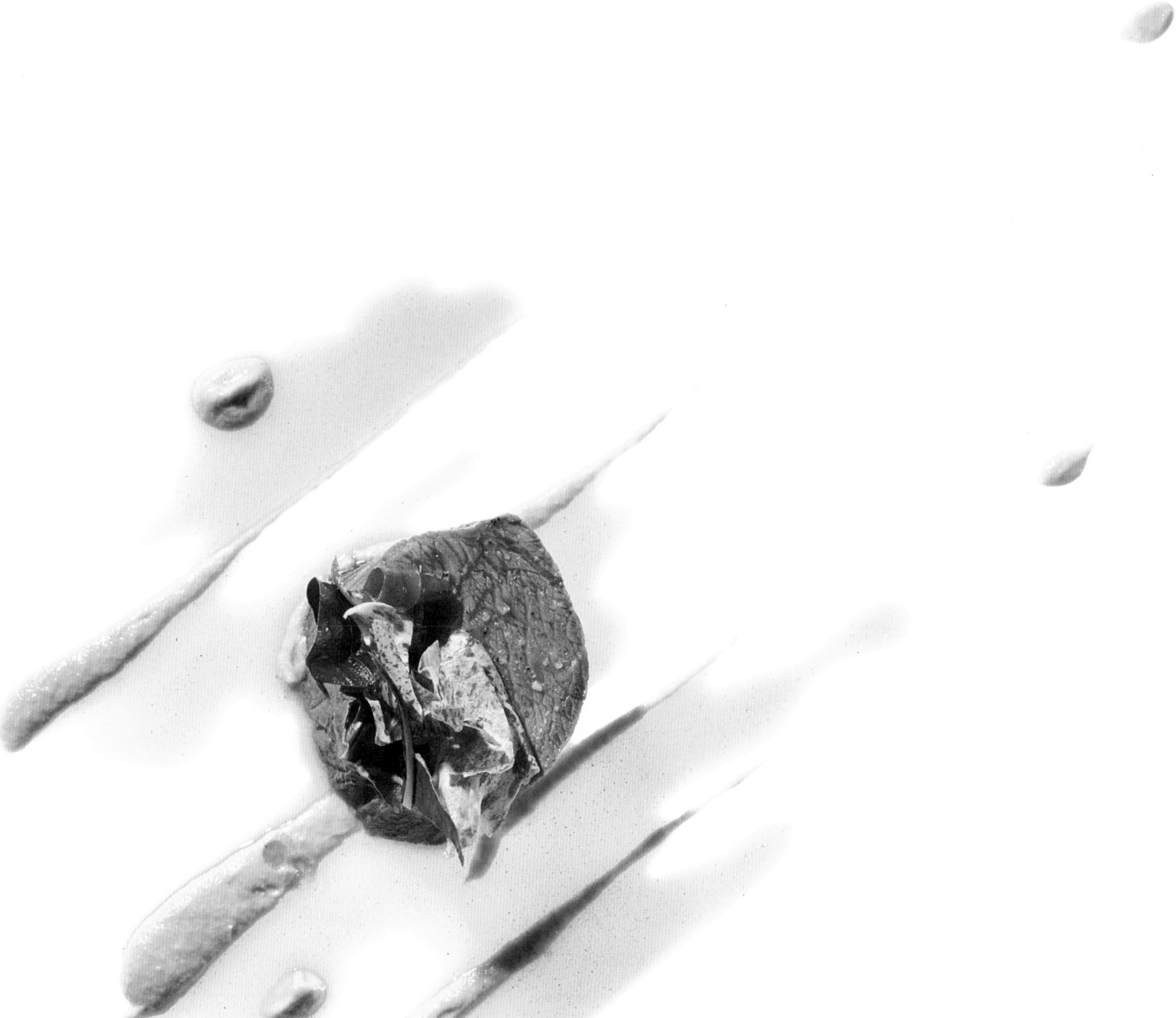

05

WEIGHTS

AND MEASURES

WEIGHTS AND MEASURES

p. 48-49

STOCKS

AP (ALL-PURPOSE) STOCK
- 4.5 kg duck carcasses
- 4.5 kg veal neck bones
- 1 pig's foot, split
- 900 g diced carrots
- 1 kg diced onions
- 15 liters water

VEGETABLE STOCK
- 500 g onion, charred
- 500 g onion dice
- 375 g carrot dice
- 375 g fennel dice
- 300 g celery root dice
- 200 g leek dice
- 7 g thyme
- 12 kg water

STANDARD MUSHROOM STOCK
- 750 g fresh baby shiitakes
- 20 g dried porcini and other wild mushrooms
- 2 kg water

p. 56

CALIFORNIA BOWL

Puffed brown rice crackers
- 240 g brown rice
- 500 g water
- soy oil
- piment d'Espelette
- 0.5 g salt

Avocado dip
- 2 avocados
- pure olive oil
- lime juice
- salt

To serve
- sprouts, like sunflower, borage, mung bean, radish

(Yields a lot)

p. 58

TOMATO
olive oil, basil

Tomato water
- 300 g Early Girl tomatoes
- 3 g sel gris

Olive oil sorbet
- 50 g Tomato water
- 25 g pain de mie
- 100 g fruity olive oil (we use McEvoy Ranch)
- 100 g pure olive oil
- 1 pinch xanthan
- salt

Tomato gel
- 150 g Tomato water
- 3.75 g gelatin
- seed sacs from 4 tomatoes
- salt

Pesto
- 500 g pine nuts
- 1 bunch basil leaves
- pure olive oil
- lemon juice
- salt

To serve
- 4 Early Girl tomatoes
- 12 tiny basil leaves
- 12 tiny basil flowers
- salt and black pepper

(Yields 4, with extra pine nut purée and possibly extra tomato water)

p. 60

MUSK MELON
nasturtium, buttermilk

Melon-buttermilk cordial
- 100 g melon
- 300 g homemade buttermilk
- lime juice
- salt

To serve
- 1 Ha'Ogen melon
- 1 Charentais melon
- 8 nasturtium leaves
- lime juice
- Murray River salt

(Yields 4, with extra Melon-buttermilk cordial and melon)

p. 62

SPOT PRAWN
new onion, sorrel

Prawn butter
- 200 g prawn shells
- 200 g butter

New onions
- 1 spoonful Prawn butter
- 4 small cipollini or other fresh onions
- salt

To serve
- 4 large, live spot prawns
- seawater or 3.5% salt brine
- 2 bunches garden sorrel
- salt

(Yields 4, with extra Prawn butter)

p. 64

CHILLED SPICED RATATOUILLE SOUP
nepitella, cilantro

Squash soup
- 450 g squash
- 115 g Vegetable stock (see page 49)
- 65 g water
- pinch of saffron
- pinch of turmeric
- pinch of red Padrón chile flakes
- 50 g pure olive oil
- lime juice
- salt

Eggplant soup
- 250 g eggplant
- 250 g Vegetable stock
- 25 g fruity olive oil
- ½ teaspoon ground cumin, toasted
- ½ teaspoon ground coriander, toasted
- ⅛ teaspoon ground red Padrón chile
- 10 g lemon juice
- 2 g Rosa's vinegar (or sherry vinegar)
- salt

Tomato-pepper soup
- 200 g Early Girl tomatoes
- 200 g red piquillo peppers
- 50 g Vegetable stock
- 25 g tomato juice
- 100 g red pepper juice
- lime juice
- salt

Ratatouille
- 50 g red onion
- 100 g summer squash
- 100 g eggplant
- 100 g red pepper
- 100 g tomato
- pure olive oil
- 10 g cilantro stems, minced
- 10 g nepitella, minced
- salt and black pepper

To serve
- fruity olive oil
- cilantro sprouts or leaves
- nepitella flowers

(Yields a lot)

p. 66

POPCORN GRITS

- 500 g vegetable or corn oil
- 1 kg popcorn
- 750 g water
- 100 g butter
- salt

To serve
- buttered popcorn

(Yields 4)

p.68

PIG HEAD
fresh pole and shelling beans, charred okra, wild sage

Pig's head stock
- 1 pig's head, without a face
- 1 large onion, charred
- 1 large carrot, chopped
- salt

Shelling bean purée
- 150 g fresh cranberry beans
- 300 g Pig head stock
- fruity olive oil
- lemon juice
- salt

Padrón pepper vinaigrette
- 100 g Padrón peppers, cooked and minced
- pure olive oil
- 50 g smoked oil
- 50 g fruity olive oil
- 35 g champagne vinegar
- salt

To serve
- 20 each different kinds shelling beans, cooked
- 8 yellow wax beans
- 8 haricots verts
- 3 okra
- 10 g pure olive oil
- 40 tiny wild sage leaves
- 450 g vegetable oil
- 2 pieces romano beans, julienned
- red wine vinegar
- fruity olive oil
- coarse salt
- salt and black pepper

(Yields 4, with extra pig head, Shelling bean purée and Padrón pepper vinaigrette)

p.70

CARROTS ROASTED IN COFFEE BEANS
mandarin, roman mint

Carrots
- 4–12 carrots, depending on size
- 15 g pure olive oil
- 250 g whole coffee beans (we use Blue Bottle decaf.)
- salt

To serve
- young carrots
- rice wine vinegar
- 80 g carrot juice
- 80 g mandarin juice
- 2 tablespoons fruity olive oil
- 20 roman mint leaves
- 12 roman mint flowers
- salt

(Yields 4)

p.72

MONTEREY BAY ABALONE
nettle-dandelion salsa verde, spicy breadcrumbs, wild fennel flowers

Salsa verde
- 15 g shallot, minced
- 25 g champagne vinegar
- 100 g dandelion greens, green stemmed
- 100 g nettles
- lemon juice
- 55 g fruity olive oil
- 15 g caper berries, minced
- salt

Breadcrumbs
- 70 g crustless levain bread
- 75 g almonds
- red Padrón chile powder
- fruity olive oil
- salt

To serve
- 160 g abalone, cleaned and sliced ⅛-inch (2-mm) thick
- pure olive oil
- zest and juice of 1 lemon
- fresh wild fennel flowers
- salt and black pepper

(Yields 4 with extra Salsa verde and Breadcrumbs)

p.74

POACHED AND GRILLED LAMB
chard leaves and stems, garum, rosemary

Lamb jus
- 375 g lamb scraps
- 75 g onion, sliced
- 50 g carrot, sliced
- 250 g white wine
- 1 kg AP stock (see page 48)

Chard stems
- bunch of golden chard with large, broad stems
- 175 g Vegetable stock (see page 49)
- 40 g pure olive oil
- 4 g garum
- salt

To serve
- 1 rack of lamb
- bunch of rosemary
- 1 kg pure olive oil for poaching
- water
- fruity olive oil
- champagne vinegar
- garum
- salt

(Yields 6–7, with extra Lamb jus, poaching oil and chard)

p.76

FRESH MIXED MILK CHEESE
fig steeped in beet juice, burnt fig leaf oil

Fresh mixed milk cheese
- 500 g whole milk
- 125 g heavy cream
- distilled vinegar
- 250 g sheep's milk fromage blanc
- 250 g fresh goat's milk cheese
- salt

Poached figs
- 4 large, ripe figs
- 300 g beet juice
- sugar, if necessary
- rice wine vinegar
- lemon juice
- salt

Burnt fig leaf oil
- 100 g fig leaves
- 200 g pure olive oil

To serve
- flaky salt, like Maldon

(Yields 8, with extra cheese. You'll want it for breakfast the next day.)

p.78

LIME MARSHMALLOW
coal-toasted meringue

Ginger marshmallow
Ginger syrup
- 250 g sugar
- 500 g water
- 2 drops ginger essential oil

Warm syrup
- 35 g trimoline
- 50 g water
- 250 g sugar

Marshmallow
- 250 g Ginger syrup
- 25 g gelatin
- Warm syrup

Frozen lime marshmallow
- 250 g Ginger marshmallow
- 50 g sugar
- 500 g lime juice
- salt

Lime oil meringue
- 125 g egg whites
- 0.5 g citric acid
- 190 g sugar

To serve
- zest of 1 lime

(Yields 20)

p.80

STRAWBERRIES AND CREAM
tiny herbs

Fresh cream ice cream
- 250 g milk
- 50 g sugar
- 15 g glucose powder
- 10 g trimoline
- 12 g milk powder
- 1 g guar gum
- 75 g heavy cream

Strawberry liquid
- 1 kg strawberries
- 100 g sugar

Compression liquid and sauce
- 150 g Strawberry liquid
- 100 g Meyer lemon juice
- fruity olive oil
- salt

Glazed strawberries
- 12 perfect strawberries, stemmed
- 50 g sugar
- 15 g pectin NH (thermo-reversible)
- 100 g water
- 400 g strawberry liquid

To serve
- tiny herbs, like anise hyssop, fennel, mint, lemon balm

(Yields 4, with extra strawberry glaze and ice cream)

p.82

PASSION FRUIT BABA
white chocolate, honeycomb, shiso

Baba cake
- 42 g water
- 21 g dry yeast
- 415 g flour
- 25 g sugar
- 9 g salt
- 333 g whole eggs
- 125 g butter, softened

Baba syrup
- 333 g water
- 83 g sugar
- 83 g dextrose
- 33 g fresh passion fruit juice

White chocolate frosting
- 73 g cream
- 67 g milk
- 53 g egg yolks
- 116 g white chocolate

Toast
- 12 thin slices pain de mie
- 1 small piece beeswax

Shiso sauce
- 50 g water
- 25 g dextrose
- 30 shiso leaves
- 50 g ice cubes
- 5 g vegetable oil
- 0.5% xanthan
- salt

Passion fruit sauce
- 200 g fresh passion fruit juice
- 0.5% xanthan
- salt

To serve
- honeycomb

(Yields 12)

p.84

CANDIED RASPBERRIES

- 60 g egg whites
- 6 g gelatin
- raspberries
- cane sugar

(Yields as much as you make)

p.90

PINK GRAPEFRUIT
ginger, tarragon, cognac, black pepper

Grapefruit sorbet
- 300 g grapefruit juice
- 10 g milk powder
- 50 g water
- 50 g dextrose
- 25 g sugar
- lemon juice
- salt

Grapefruit foam
- 415 g grapefruit juice
- 50 g sugar
- 15 g honey
- 14 g gelatin, softened in cold water
- 30 g lemon juice, plus more if needed
- 15 drops pink grapefruit essential oil
- 4 drops ginger essential oil
- 2 drops black pepper essential oil
- salt

Grapefruit salad
- 180 g grapefruit
- tarragon
- cognac
- simple syrup
- salt and black pepper

Coi perfume
- 15 drops ginger essential oil
- 15 drops black pepper essential oil
- 4 drops cognac essential oil
- 8 drops tarragon absolute
- 10 ml fractionated coconut oil

(Yields at least 12)

p.94

CHILLED ENGLISH PEA SOUP
our buttermilk, meyer lemon, nasturtium

Buttermilk mousse
- 80 g crème fraîche
- 2.4 g gelatin
- 320 g buttermilk
- salt

Fresh Meyer lemon preserve
- 1 Meyer lemon
- sugar
- Meyer lemon juice
- salt

Pea shell infusion
- 500 g peas
- 500 g water

English pea soup
- peas
- Vegetable stock (see page 49)
- Pea shell infusion
- salt

To serve
- 4 tablespoons small, shelled peas reserved from soup-making
- nasturtium petals and leaves

(Yields 8)

p.98

OUR BUTTER

- 100 g active culture
- 2 liters cream
- sel gris

(Yields about 400 g butter)

p.102

PAN-GRILLED MATSUTAKE
potato-pine needle puree, wood sorrel

Pine needle powder
- 100 g young, fragrant pine needles
- 1 drop pine needle absolute
- pinch citric acid
- salt

Potato-pine needle purée
- 325 g boiled waxy potatoes
- 25 g water from cooking potatoes
- 30 g pure olive oil
- 60 g cream
- pine needle absolute

To serve
- 5 small matsutake
- 20 g pure olive oil
- 20 pieces wood sorrel
- salt

(Yields 4, with extra Potato-pine needle purée and Pine needle powder)

p.106

PARSLEY ROOT SOUP
snails, green garlic, pickled watermelon radish

Snails
- 350 g snails
- 40 g butter
- 15 g shallots, minced
- 5 g green garlic, minced
- 40 g white wine
- 200 g Mushroom dashi (see page 112)
- salt

Pickled watermelon radish
- 50 g water
- 30 g rice vinegar
- 10 g champagne vinegar
- 2 g salt
- 7 g sugar
- 20 pieces watermelon radish, cut into ½-inch (1-cm) batons

Green garlic purée
- 200 g green garlic
- 20 g butter
- salt

Soup
- 300 g parsley root, peeled
- 300 g Vegetable stock (see page 49)
- 15 g butter
- salt

To serve
- 4 leaves parsley

(Yields 4, with extra soup and Green garlic purée)

p.110

EARTH AND SEA
new harvest potatoes, cucumber, coastal plants

Squid ink fluid gel
- 250 g Vegetable stock (see page 49)
- 4 g squid ink
- 2.5 g agar
- 0.5 g piment d'Espelette
- rice wine vinegar
- champagne vinegar
- lemon juice
- salt

To serve
- 20-25 tiny just-dug potatoes
- 4 teaspoons fruity olive oil
- 2 small Japanese or Mediterranean cucumbers
- coastal plants, like ice plant flowers, agretti, borage, sprouting greens, wild radish leaves and flowers)
- champagne vinegar
- 4 pinches piment d'Espelette
- salt

(Yields 4, with extra Squid ink fluid gel)

p.112

EARTH AND SEA
steamed tofu mousseline, yuba, mushroom dashi

Mushroom dashi
- 600 g Mushroom stock (see page 49)
- 200 g Vegetable stock (see page 49)
- 20 g kombu
- 16 g katsuobushi, shaved or grated
- shiro dashi
- 4 g agar
- salt

Pickled turnips
- 20 pieces small Tokyo turnips
- 30 g water
- 30 g rice wine vinegar
- 5 g sugar
- 1.5 g salt

Seaweeds
- seaweeds, like bull kelp, alaria, sea lettuce, eel grass, purple laver, Turkish towel, sea grapes and giant kelp

Steamed tofu mousseline
- 300 g medium tofu
- 90 g silken tofu
- 50 g egg white
- ⅛ teaspoon finely grated fresh ginger
- 10 g white soy
- salt

To serve
- shichimi togarashi
- 24 pieces yuba, cut into ¾- x 3-inch (1.5- x 8-cm) strips
- zest of 1 lime

(Yields 4, with extra Mushroom dashi and Steamed tofu mousseline)

p.116

OYSTERS UNDER GLASS
yuzu, rau ram

Oyster gel
- oyster liquor
- yuzu juice
- gelatin
- salt, if necessary

Yuzu gel sheet
- 250 g Vegetable stock (see page 49)
- 2.7 g agar
- 9.3 g gelatin
- 70 g yuzu juice
- 8 g yuzu zest
- champagne vinegar
- salt

Vegetable mignonette
- 5 g champagne vinegar
- 5 g pure olive oil
- 30 g breakfast radish
- 20 g celery
- 30 g green apple
- salt and black pepper

To serve
- 8 oysters
- 3 leaves rau răm

(Yields 4 with extra Yuzu gel sheet)

p.120

SAUTEED MONTEREY BAY ABALONE
escarole, sea lettuce-caper berry vinaigrette

Sea lettuce-caper berry vinaigrette
- 10 g shallot
- 10 g champagne vinegar
- 15 g capers
- 100 g pure olive oil
- 40 g lemon
- 100 g sea lettuce
- xanthan
- salt

To serve
- 80 g cut escarole
- 40 g butter
- rice wine vinegar
- 4 small abalone, cleaned
- flour
- 1 tablespoon lemon juice
- 4 wild mustard flowers
- salt

(Yields 4, with extra sauce)

p.124

GOAT
wheatgrass raw-almond puree, sprouted seeds, beans and nuts

Braised Goat
- 250 g goat shoulder, shanks or miscellaneous tough bits
- 25 g carrot, peeled and sliced
- 25 g onion, peeled and sliced
- 50 g white wine
- 300 g AP stock (see page 48)
- 10 g thyme
- salt and black pepper

Wheatgrass-raw almond purée
- 200 g almonds, soaked in water and peeled
- 90 g wheatgrass juice
- 30 g pure olive oil
- 10 g or more water

To serve
- 250 g goat leg, bone out
- 15 g pure olive oil, plus extra to submerge the goat loin
- 25 g onion
- 25 g carrot
- 150 g goat loin, tenderloin or ribeye trimmed of silver skin
- jus from braise
- champagne vinegar
- fruity olive oil
- 100 g sprouted seeds, beans and nuts, like almond, sunflower and garbanzo
- 1 handful of top sprouts, like buckwheat, pea shoots and radish
- salt

(Yields 6, with extra jus)

p.130

INVERTED CHERRY TOMATO TART
black olive, basil

Tomato mousse
- 500 g tomatoes
- 15 g pure olive oil
- 10 g gelatin
- salt

Black olive tuile
- 210 g isomalt
- 100 g all-purpose flour
- 165 g puréed sun-dried black olives
- 100 g egg whites
- 30 g butter, melted
- salt

To serve
- Pesto (see page 58)
- 60 cherry tomatoes
- sel gris
- black olives, dried
- basil sprouts

(Yields 6-8, with extra Black olive tuile batter and Tomato mousse)

p.132

BEET AND GOAT CHEESE TART (BROKEN, INVERTED)
rye, dill

Goat cheese
- 250 g goat cheese
- goat's milk
- salt

Beet fluid gel
- 75 g Vegetable stock (see page 49)
- 0.5 g agar
- 100 g roasted beets
- champagne vinegar
- lemon juice
- salt

Seasoned beets
- 800 g red beets, roasted
- beet fluid gel
- lemon juice
- champagne vinegar
- sugar, if necessary
- pure olive oil
- salt

Rye crisps
- 100 g dehydrated rye bread
- 50 g isomalt
- 3 g salt

Dill pesto
- 500 g walnuts
- 1 bunch dill
- pure olive oil
- lemon juice
- salt

(Yields 6-8)

p.136

CHICKEN AND EGG
poached scrambled egg, chicken jus infused with katsuobushi, radish, seaweed powder

Seaweed powder
- 200 g dried kombu
- 1 kg Vegetable stock (see page 49)
- 125 g garum*
- 25 g brown rice vinegar
- 2.5 g shiro dashi
- 2.5 g white soy

Chicken jus
- 600 g chicken parts (backs and necks)
- pure olive oil
- 75 g onion, sliced
- 50 g carrot, sliced
- 300 g white wine
- 2 kg AP stock (see page 48)
- 20 g kombu
- 15 g katsuobushi, shaved
- champagne vinegar

To serve
- 4 eggs
- breakfast, black Spanish, watermelon and/or wild radishes
- rice wine vinegar
- wild radish flowers, pods and sprouts
- salt

(Yields 4, with extra jus)

p.138

YOUNG CARROTS ROASTED IN HAY
aged sheep's milk cheese, radish powder

Hay stock
- 50 g hay
- 1 kg water

Hay gel
- 500 g Hay stock
- 2.5 g agar 0.5%
- salt

Radish powder
- 1 bunch radishes

Carrots
- 8 young carrots
- pure olive oil
- 100 g Hay stock
- 50 g charred hay
- salt

To serve
- alfafa, clover and radish bottom sprouts
- champagne vinegar
- aged sheep's milk cheese
- radish top sprouts
- salt

(Yields 4, with extra Hay stock and gel)

p.142

MELON AND CUCUMBER
aroma of mint

Melon consommé
- 150 g cucumber juice
- 200 g Ha'ogen melon juice
- lime juice
- salt

Mint spray
- mint absolute
- mint essential oil
- pure alcohol

To serve
- ¼ yellow watermelon
- ¼ red watermelon
- 2 small Japanese or Mediterranean cucumbers
- rice wine vinegar
- 8 borage leaves
- 4 borage flowers
- sel gris
- salt

(Yields 4)

p.146

SUMMER, FROZEN IN TIME
plum, frozen meringues, yogurt

Plum ice
- 8 ripe plums
- water
- lime juice
- sugar, if necessary
- salt

Yogurt
- 150 g yogurt
- salt

Frozen meringues
- 180 g egg whites, gently beaten
- 18 g sugar
- rose, ginger, citrus (lime, lemon, mandarin, blood orange), and pink pepper essential oils
- salt

To serve
- 1 ripe but not mushy plum

- rice wine vinegar
- Murray river salt
- alyssum flowers

(Yields 10-15)

p.152

CLAM
bull kelp, wild fennel, meyer lemon

Geoduck
- 1 live geoduck
- shiro dashi
- salt

Meyer lemon vinaigrette
- 10 g shiro dashi
- 15 g Mission Trail olive oil
- 40 g Sevillano olive oil
- 65 g Meyer lemon juice
- sugar, if necessary
- salt

Clam juice
- 20 g shallot
- 1 clove garlic
- 0.25 g piment d'Espelette
- 20 g pure olive oil
- 10 g squid ink
- 150 g white wine
- 500 g Manila clams
- Meyer lemon juice

Clam gel
- 240 g clam juice
- 2 g agar
- 9 g gelatin

To serve
- 500 g bull kelp
- wild fennel shoots
- zest of 1 Meyer lemon
- salt and black pepper

(Yields 4, with extra Clam gel)

p.156

SAVORY CHANTERELLE PORRIDGE
pig's foot, wood sorrel

Pig's foot
- 1 pig's foot
- 1 carrot, sliced
- 1 onion, half charred and half sliced
- ½ bunch thyme
- water
- salt

Chanterelle stock
- 175 g fresh chanterelle scraps
- 15 g dry chanterelles
- 625 g water
- 125 g Mushroom stock (see page 49)
- 125 g Vegetable stock (see page 49)

Garlic
- 100 g peeled garlic cloves
- 20 g pure olive oil

Shallots
- 100 g peeled, whole shallots
- 50 g Vegetable stock
- 5 g butter
- 5 g champagne vinegar
- salt, if necessary

Brown butter
- 113 g butter

Root vegetables
- parsnip, salsify, carrot, and whatever else you can find that will fry well
- 500 g vegetable oil
- salt

To serve
- ½ cup broken rice, preferably Anson Mills Carolina Gold or similar
- 2 cups Chanterelle stock
- wood sorrel
- wild flowers, like oxalis or radish

(Yields 6-8 with extra pig's foot)

p.160

EARLY SPRING
buttermilk panna cotta, cherry blossom, first fronds of wild fennel

Buttermilk infusion
- 150 g buttermilk
- 5 g cured cherry blossoms
- 2 g cured cherry leaves

Buttermilk panna cotta
- Buttermilk infusion
- cured cherry blossoms and leaves from Buttermilk infusion
- 90 g heavy cream
- 7 g sugar
- 3 g gelatin
- 2 g salt

Cherry blossom fluid gel
- 150 g water
- 22 g cured cherry blossoms
- 3 g cured cherry leaves
- 13 g sugar, plus extra to season
- 0.45% agar
- lemon juice
- salt

Pickled fennel
- 30 pieces sliced fennel
- 40 g rice vinegar
- 125 g water
- 10 g sugar
- 5 g salt

To serve
- tiny wild fennel fronds
- branches of flowering cherry blossoms

(Yields 6)

p.164

MOREL/FAVA
angelica root, tarragon

Morel stock
- 250 g Mushroom stock (see page 49)
- 50 g Vegetable stock (see page 49)
- 50 g morel scraps

Fava bean purée
- 125 g fava beans
- water
- salt

Morel sauce
- 30 g morel trim
- 30 g tablespoons butter
- 100 g Morel stock
- pinch of angelica root powder
- champagne vinegar
- salt

To serve
- 15 g tablespoons butter
- 28 small morels
- 40 small fava beans
- 3-4 tablespoons morel stock
- 20 tarragon leaves
- a pinch of angelica powder
- salt

(Yields 4, with extra purée)

p.168

ASPARAGUS COOKED IN ITS JUICE
seaweed powder, meyer lemon sabayon

Seaweed Powder
(see page 136)

Citrus oil
- lemon, blood orange, lime, red mandarin essential oils
- 30 g pure olive oil

Meyer lemon sabayon
- 125 g Vegetable stock (see page 49)
- 50 g whole eggs
- 30 g Meyer lemon juice
- salt

Asparagus juice
- 2 bunches asparagus

Asparagus vinaigrette
- 200 g Vegetable stock
- 6 g agar
- 200 g Asparagus juice

To serve
- 8 large asparagus
- 20 g pure olive oil
- salt

(Yields 4, with extra sabayon base)

p. 172

CRAYFISH AND SPRING VEGETABLE STEW
spicy crayfish jelly

Seared Crayfish
- 1530 g live crayfish
- pure olive oil

Crayfish oil
- 200 g Seared crayfish (330 g live weight)
- 200 g pure olive oil

Crayfish broth
- 720 g Seared crayfish (1200 g live weight)
- 100 g white wine
- 75 g fennel, sliced
- 75 g onion, sliced
- 1.5 kg water
- 5 g dried piquillo pepper
- ½ hot chile
- 5 g dried tomato
- ½ stalk lemongrass, smashed and chopped
- ½ medium knob ginger, sliced
- lime juice
- rice wine vinegar
- salt

Spicy crayfish jelly
- 250 g reserved Crayfish broth
- dried red chile, ground
- 0.67 g gellan LT
- 0.33 g gellan F
- salt

To serve
- 12 live crayfish
- 4 spring onions
- 2 heads baby fennel
- 2 young artichokes
- 2 tablespoons young peas
- 2 tablespoons fava beans
- pea shoots
- fava bean flowers
- 2 baby turnips
- salt

(Yields 4)

p. 176

DUNGENESS CRAB ENCASED IN ITS CONSOMME
buttered crab broth, wild winter herbs

Crab broth
- 1 kg crab shells
- pure olive oil
- 200 g white wine
- 1 kg water
- 800 g Vegetable stock (see page 49)
- salt

Crab squares
- 700 g crab meat
- 450 g Crab broth
- 4.5 g agar
- 27 g gelatin

Consommé gel
- 500 g Crab broth
- 3 g gellan LT
- 1.5 g gellan F

To serve
- 120 g butter, lightly browned
- 360 g reserved Crab broth
- sheep sorrel, chickweed, miner's lettuce, oxalis flowers and alyssum flowers
- salt

(Yields 24 small portions–it can be scaled down, but it won't work as well)

p. 180

FRIED EGG (NOT FRIED)
brassica, smoked oil, herbs

Egg white sauce
- 75 g egg whites
- 4 g chives
- 4 g chervil
- 4 g parsley
- 3 g tarragon
- 5 g champagne vinegar
- 100 g water
- 75 g pure olive oil
- 75 g smoked oil
- salt

Smoked breadcrumbs
- 200 g levain loaf, crusts removed
- smoked oil
- salt

Brassica
- broccoli, cauliflower, cabbages, flowering rabes, romanesco and whatever else you can find
- pure olive oil

To serve
- 1 live crab
- 6 egg yolks
- pure olive oil (enough to fill a small metal container big enough to hold the egg yolks half full)
- salt

(Yields 6, with extra Egg white sauce)

p. 184

BEET ROSE
yogurt, rose petal ice

Rose petal ice
- 10 g dried rose petals
- 400 g water
- 15 g honey
- lemon juice
- 20 g sugar
- salt

Beet rose
- beets
- water
- olive oil
- beet juice
- rice wine vinegar
- sugar, if necessary
- salt and black pepper

Yogurt
- 150 g yogurt
- lime juice
- salt

(Yields 4, with extra Rose petal ice and Yogurt)

p. 188

AGED DUCK BREAST COOKED ON THE BONE
sprouted wheatberries, radish, redwood tips

Redwood oil
- 100 g redwood tips and needles
- 500 g pure olive oil

Duck jus
- 750 g duck bones
- 1 onion, sliced
- 1 carrot, sliced
- 200 g white wine
- 1 kg AP stock (see page 48)
- champagne vinegar
- salt

Radish vinaigrette
- 30 g finely diced red radish
- 15 g Redwood oil
- 20 g champagne vinegar
- salt

To serve
- 1 double duck breast, aged
- 100 g sprouted wheatberries
- 10 g radish bottom sprouts
- 2 breakfast radishes
- 16 pieces redwood shoots
- salt and black pepper

(Yields 4, with extra Duck jus, Redwood oil and Radish vinaigrette)

p. 190

INVERTED FROMAGE BLANC TART
fennel, wheatgrass

Burnt fennel oil
- fennel scraps
- pure olive oil

Fennel stock
- 225 g fennel scraps
- 375 g water

Fennel fluid gel
- 250 g Fennel stock, strained
- 2 g agar
- 50 g cooked fennel
- dried fennel pollen

- champagne vinegar
- salt

Buckwheat crisp
- 100 g dried, finely ground pain de mie
- 100 g finely ground buckwheat
- 100 g finely ground isomalt
- 3 g finely ground salt

Wheatgrass sauce
- 150 g wheatgrass juice
- 30 g pure olive oil
- xanthan

To serve
- 48 pieces diced raw fennel
- 48 pieces diced cooked fennel
- 200 g cow or sheep's milk fromage blanc
- champagne vinegar
- 10 nice pieces chervil
- salt

(Yields 8)

p.194

CARROTS ROASTED IN COFFEE BEANS
creme fraiche, oats, cilantro

Oats
- 50 g rolled oats
- 36 g light brown sugar
- 28 g unsalted butter
- 20 g honey
- 1.5 g finely ground chicory root
- 3 g salt

Carrots
- several carrots, of any size or color you like
- pure olive oil
- 250 g whole coffee beans
- salt

To serve
- 1 tablespoon finely ground coffee
- 100 g thick crème fraîche
- 1 large spoonful fruity olive oil
- ½ bunch cilantro
- cilantro flowers
- Maldon salt

(Yields 4)

p.198

QUINOA
almond, cauliflower, popped sorghum

Cauliflower purée
- 1 x 250-g cauliflower
- 25 g pure olive oil
- 100 g water
- milk, as necessary
- salt

Popped sorghum
- 50 g vegetable oil
- 100 g sorghum
- salt

To serve
- 20 g white quinoa
- 20 g red quinoa
- 25 g toasted almonds
- 1 small spoonful snipped chive
- rice wine vinegar
- fruity olive oil
- Popped sorghum
- salt

(Yields 4, with extra Cauliflower purée)

p.204

PRATHER RANCH BEEF ENCRUSTED IN LICHEN
wild spinach, chanterelles, bordelaise infused with native spices

Lichen powder
- 500 g raw parmotrema lichen

Marrow stock
- 2 kg marrow bones, cut into 2-inch (5-cm) pieces
- 2 kg water

Beef jus
- 500 g beef scraps
- pure olive oil
- 100 g carrot
- 150 g yellow onion
- 500 g red wine
- 1 kg Marrow stock
- 250 g AP stock (see page 48)
- 250 g Vegetable stock (see page 49)
- 1-4 wild California bay leaves
- 1 slice dried angelica root
- 25 g wild fennel stem, sliced
- 15 g Monterey cypress leaves, tips only, snipped
- lime juice
- rice wine vinegar
- xantham, if necessary
- salt

To serve
- 250 g beef tenderloin
- 15 small chanterelles
- 15 g pure olive oil
- 12 New Zealand spinach leaves
- rice wine vinegar
- a few pieces of shaved raw chanterelle
- salt

(Yields 4, with extra sauce and Lichen powder)

p.208

SALSIFY
black trumpet, wood sorrel, salsify-milk curd

Lichen vinaigrette
- 3 g Lichen powder (see page 204)
- 12 g water
- 15 g pure olive oil
- 9 g champagne vinegar
- salt

Salsify
- 4 nice pieces of salsify
- milk
- salt

Black trumpet purée
- 50 g black trumpet stems
- 30 g butter
- 150 cooked salsify scraps
- 250 g salsify milk
- salt

To serve
- thinly sliced black trumpet tops
- butter
- wood sorrel
- salt

(Yields 4)

p.214

ABALONE/DUCK TONGUE
little gem, sprouts, mint

Duck tongues
- 100 g cooked and cleaned duck tongues (about 20-24 tongues)
- 1 tablespoon duck fat

To serve
- 100 g abalone, cleaned (see page 40) and sliced
- 10 g pure olive oil
- 60 g julienne gem lettuce
- 12 radishes, shaved
- 6 mint leaves, thinly snipped
- lemon juice
- rice wine vinegar
- sprouts and flowers
- salt and black pepper

(Yields 4)

p.218

CELTUCE
brown butter, burnt hay, tarragon, comte

Burnt hay butter
- 3 g burnt hay powder
- 30 g brown butter

Celtuce leaf purée
- 300 g celtuce leaves
- 30 g tarragon leaves
- 50 g pure olive oil

- 15 g ice
- salt

To serve
- 3 large stalks celtuce
- 6 new potatoes, yellow flesh, about ⅛-inch (4-mm) diameter
- butter
- champagne vinegar
- Comté cheese, shaved
- 12 nice tarragon leaves
- salt

(Yields 4-6)

p.222

MORELS ROASTED IN BUTTER
just-harvested potatoes, popcorn, basil

Morel stock (see page 164)

Popcorn grits
(see page 66)

To serve
- 12 tiny new potatoes
- butter
- 20 pieces morel
- 20 pieces basil sprouts
- salt

(Yields 4)

p.224

NEW OLIVE OIL
brassica, charred onion broth

Charred onion broth
- 500 g yellow onions
- 500 g water
- 2 lemon leaves, roughly sliced
- champagne vinegar
- Rosa's vinegar
- salt

Dandelion-potato purée
- 100 g potatoes
- 200 g dandelion greens
- 30 g pure olive oil
- lemon juice
- salt

Pickled red cabbage
- 50 g red cabbage, charred on a plancha and julienned
- 40 g rice wine vinegar
- 100 g water
- 8 g salt
- 8 g sugar

To serve
- brassica
- rosemary flowers
- 4 tablespoons new olive oil
- salt

(Yields 4, with extra Charred onion broth)

p.228

MONTEREY BAY ABALONE
grains, fresh seaweeds, raw turnip

Seaweed sauce
- 18 g kombu
- 8 g fresh seaweed
- 500 g Vegetable stock (see page 48)
- 250 g water
- 18 g garum
- 10 g pure olive oil
- 5 g white soy
- 5 g squid ink
- champagne vinegar
- salt

To serve
- 50 g each farro, wheatberries and barley
- 200 g fresh seaweeds, like bull kelp, alaria, sea lettuce, eel grass, purple laver, Turkish towel, sea grape and giant kelp
- 4 small abalone, cleaned (see page 40)
- flour, for dusting
- butter
- lemon juice
- 4 Tokyo turnips, shaved
- salt and pepper

(Yields 4, with extra Seaweed Sauce)

p.232

DUNGENESS CRAB AND BEEF TENDON SOUP
asian pear, finger lime

Tendon stock
- 1 kg beef tendons
- 2 kg water
- salt

Crab soup
- 600 g crab shell
- pure olive oil
- 1 onion
- 1 fennel
- 150 g white wine
- 1 kg Tendon stock
- 250 g Vegetable stock (see page 49)
- 1 dried chile
- lime juice
- salt

To serve
- 150 g crab meat
- 60 g beef tendon, sliced
- 30 g Asian pear, diced
- 18 g finger lime
- 6 g cilantro stem, snipped
- 36 small pieces of cilantro leaf
- piment d'Espelette
- 300 g Crab soup
- salt

(Yields 6, with extra crab, tendon and broths)

p.238

BEETS
bergamot, mints, wildflowers

Bergamot oil
- 150 g pure olive oil
- 6 drops bergamot essential oil

Bergamot vinaigrette
- bergamot juice
- Bergamot oil
- champagne vinegar, if necessary
- salt

Beet purée and gel
- 200 g roasted beets
- 125 g beet juice
- rice wine vinegar
- Bergamot oil
- sugar, if necessary
- gelatin
- salt

To serve
- 8 young beets
- pure olive oil
- sugar
- rice wine vinegar
- mint
- wildflowers
- salt

(Yields 4)

p.242

ASPARAGUS/OYSTER
wheatgrass

Wheatgrass sauce
- 150 g wheatgrass juice
- 30 g pure olive oil
- xanthan
- salt

To serve
- 8 crisp, briny oysters
- zest and juice of 1 lemon
- gelatin
- 8 large stalks asparagus
- 200 g asparagus juice
- salt

(Yields 8)

p.244

EARTH AND SEA
tofu coagulated with seawater, cherry tomato, fresh seaweeds, sylverleaf olive oil

Tofu
- 150 g soy beans
- 1.6 kg water
- 225 g seawater

Tomato-whey gel
- 100 g Tomato water (see page 58)

- 100 g tofu whey
- 4.6 g gelatin
- sea lettuce, chopped
- salt

Tofu-whey glaze
- 150 g tofu whey
- 1.5 g agar
- shiro dashi
- shichimi togarashi
- salt

To serve
- 9 cherry tomatoes, peeled
- 36 pieces fresh seaweeds (see page 228)
- 10-12 drops of fruity olive oil, like Sylverleaf
- crunchy salt

(Yields 6)

p. 248

PRESERVED LEMON 6:10
chrysanthemum milk

30° Baumé syrup
- 370 g water
- 277 g sugar

Candied preserved lemon
- 1 preserved lemon
- 150 g 30° Baumé syrup

Lemon custard
- 4 egg yolks
- 50 g sugar
- 83 g milk
- 250 g cream

Lemon gel
- preserved lemon syrup
- Meyer lemon juice
- 2% gelatin

Chrysanthemum milk
- 50 g sugar
- 52 g egg yolk
- 300 g milk
- 4.6 g dried chrysanthemum flowers
- 2.2 g gelatin

(Yields 12, with extra Chrysanthemum milk and 30° Baumé syrup)

p. 252

"ROCK AND MOMAGRANATE"
kohlrabi, tobacco, pomegranate, shavings/ leaves/flowers

Kohlrabi cooking medium
- 700 g soil
- 50 g tobacco hay
- 70 g egg white
- 300 g salt
- water

Pomegranate sauce
- 150 g pomegranate juice
- 1.2 g agar
- lime juice
- salt

Tobacco glaze
- 150 g Vegetable stock (see page 49)
- 1.5 g agar
- Rosa's vinegar
- tobacco leaf for smoking
- salt

To serve
- 4 kohlrabi
- various sprouts, herbs and flowers
- 2 breakfast or red radishes
- 2 baby turnips
- sel gris

(Yields 4)

p. 256

SILKEN WHITE CHOCOLATE
kiwi, coffee

Soy-white chocolate custard

Warm addition
- 305 g white chocolate
- 225 g plain soy milk
- 25 g glucose
- 25 g trimoline
- 8 g gelatin

Cold addition
- 208 g soy milk
- 333 g cream
- salt

White chocolate tuile
- 80 g white chocolate
- 200 g fondant
- 100 g glucose
- 100 g isomalt

Coffee panade
- 60 g butter
- 6 g salt
- 38 g sugar
- 75 g almond meal
- 45 g flour
- 30 g fine ground coffee

To serve
- 2 kiwi, peeled and cut into twelfths
- lemon juice
- fruity olive oil
- 30° Baumé syrup (see page 248)
- salt

(Yields 12)

p. 258

SUNCHOKE SOUP
sunflower, chanterelle

Sunchoke soup
- 500 g sunchokes
- 50 g brown butter
- 333 g Vegetable stock (see page 49)
- salt

Chanterelle purée
- 200 g chanterelles
- 200 g chanterelle stock (see page 156)
- 50 g butter
- 0.8 g agar
- salt

Sunflower seed pesto
- 50 g sunflower seed
- 5 g thyme
- 1 g sunchoke powder
- 1 g chanterelle powder
- 50 g sunflower oil
- zest of 1½ lemons
- salt

To serve
- rice wine vinegar
- 4 nice chanterelles
- 32-40 pieces sunflower sprouts

(Yields 8, with extra soup)

p. 262

MILK CHOCOLATE/SOY
blueberry, baguette, cocoa praline

Cocoa praline
- 250 g water
- 300 g sugar
- 500 g cocoa nibs
- 2.5 g salt

Milk chocolate pudding
- 110 g soy milk
- 60 g glucose
- 10 g inverted sugar
- 90 g 66% chocolate
- 150 g 45% chocolate
- 150 g cream, whipped

Blueberry sauce
- 250 g blueberries
- 25 g sugar
- peel of ¼ lemon
- 12 g water
- 0.5% agar
- zest and juice of 1 lemon
- salt

Soy milk
- 200 g soy milk
- 2 g sugar

To serve
- 6 thin slices of baguette
- 60-70 blueberries

(Yields 6, with extra Cocoa praline and Milk chocolate pudding)

p. 266

BEEHIVE

Brioche
- 500 g bread flour
- 50 g sugar
- 11 g salt
- 8 g dry yeast
- 50 g whole egg
- 150 g egg yolk
- 212 g milk
- 325 g butter

Honey glaze
• 250 g water
• 50 g sugar
• 150 g sugar
• 11 g pectin

Warm cheese mousse
• 150 g soft sheep's milk cheese
• 1.5 g gellan F
• 250 g cream
• 2.5 g salt

To serve
• honeycomb

(Yields 8)

p. 271

YOUNG DUCK IN TWO SERVINGS
poached and chilled breast, jasmine tea, orange, endive
leg grilled over charcoal, cilantro-fermented tofu puree

Duck consommé
• 1 kg duck bones
• 150 g onion, half charred
• 150 g carrot
• 1 kg water
• salt

Duck jus
• 1 kg duck bones
• 50 g duck fat
• 100 g onion, sliced
• 100 g carrot, sliced
• 250 g white wine
• 2 kg AP stock (see page 48)
• 150 g giblets
• 50 g shallot, peeled and sliced
• 20 g garlic, peeled and sliced
• champagne vinegar
• salt

Jasmine tea gel
• 350 g water
• 5.5 g jasmine tea leaves
• 0.7 g agar
• 6.5 g gelatin

Red endive
• 3 red endives
• zest of 1 orange
• 100 g orange juice
• champagne vinegar
• salt

Cilantro-fermented tofu purée
• 300 g medium tofu
• 20 g cilantro
• 20 g fermented tofu
• 10 g white soy
• 8 g rau răm
• 50 g soy milk
• 50 g pure olive oil
• salt

To serve
• 2 young ducks
• 4 pieces baby bok choy
• rice wine vinegar
• salt

(Yields 4, with extra Duck jus and consommé)

p. 276

LIVE SPOT PRAWN
cucumber, watermelon, lemon flavors

Prawn broth
• 250 g live spot prawns, cleaned and coarsely chopped
• pure olive oil
• 1200 g water
• 100 g onion, sliced
• 100 g carrot, sliced
• 100 g fennel, sliced
• 200 g leeks, sliced
• ½ stick lemongrass, smashed and sliced
• 3 lemon leaves, sliced
• lemon juice
• rice wine vinegar
• fruity olive oil
• salt

To serve
• 6 live spot prawns
• 1 red watermelon cylinder, about ¾-inch (2-cm) wide by 2½-inch (6-cm) long
• 1 yellow watermelon cylinder, about ¾-inch (2-cm) wide by 2½-inch (6-cm) long
• lemon juice
• 4% brine
• 1 small Japanese or Mediterranean cucumber
• rice wine vinegar
• lemony herbs, like lemon verbena, lemon balm and lemon basil
• salt

(Yields 6, with extra Prawn broth)

p. 278

YOUNG ARTICHOKE GRILLED UNDER A WEIGHT
spicy crayfish vinaigrette, fava leaf, sesame

Spicy crayfish vinaigrette
• 10 g Crayfish oil (see page 172)
• 13 g lemongrass, smashed and sliced
• 38 g fennel, coarsely chopped
• 5 g pure vegetable oil
• 5 g sriracha
• 50 g white wine
• 30 g tomato purée
• 1 pinch xantham
• 5 g champagne vinegar
• 2 g fruity olive oil
• salt

Artichokes
• 300 g artichokes, peeled and trimmed
• 10 g lemon juice
• 100 g Vegetable stock (see page 49)
• 20 g pure olive oil
• 2 g salt

Artichoke mayonnaise
• 90 g artichokes, peeled
• 8 g lemon juice
• 25 g pure olive oil
• 1 g salt
• more lemon juice, pure olive oil and salt

Fava bean leaves
• 18 fava bean leaves
• sesame oil
• salt

To serve
• 12 large crayfish
• shichimi togarashi
• black and white sesame seeds, toasted
• 12 fava bean flowers

(Yields 6, with extra Artichoke mayonnaise and Spicy crayfish vinaigrette)

p. 282

GRASS-FED VEAL
chicories, seville orange

Seville orange-veal sauce
• 3 veal rib bones
• 800 g veal scraps, peeled and sliced
• 1 onion
• 1 carrot
• 500 g white wine
• 3 kg AP stock (see page 48)
• zest and juice of 1 Seville orange
• rice wine vinegar
• salt

Puntarelle purée
• 300 g puntarelle stem
• 60 g pure olive oil
• 150 g Vegetable stock (see page 49)
• 10 caper berries, thinly sliced
• 15 g fruity olive oil
• lemon juice
• salt

To serve
• various chicories, cleaned and cut
• fruity olive oil
• lemon juice
• 250 g veal loin, trimmed
• pure olive oil, for poaching
• 2 caper berries, thinly sliced
• salt and black pepper

(Yields 4, with extra sauce and Puntarelle purée)

numbers in *bold* refer to illustrations
numbers underlined refer to recipes

THE BOOK

To Emilia Terragni, I am incredibly grateful for your trust and support. Thanks to the rest of the Phaidon team for their hard work, talent and good cheer: Emma Robertson, Sophie Hodgkin, Liz Thompson. It was a pleasure working with all of you.

The look of the book in some ways started a few years ago with Maren Caruso, who thought it would be fun to do some light-box pictures together. Thank you for your hard work and positive approach. Most of all, thank you for your discerning eye and brilliant images. It was inspiring watching you work.

I am infinitely grateful to Tienlon Ho for her close reading of the manuscript. Thank you to Chris Ying for his help with the intro. Harold McGee, thank you so much for the foreword, for your insightful suggestions about the text and especially for your friendship. A huge thank you to Peter Meehan for the nice words and moral support, I can't tell you how much it's meant to me.

Thank you to my agent, Kim Witherspoon.

I was very fortunate to have learned from some wonderful editors, especially Amanda Hesser, who patiently taught me so much when I knew nothing, and who once sent a story back to me with a note that I think of often: "Needs a little more time in the oven." Thanks to so many colleagues and friends for their inspiration, advice and support, especially Christine Muhlke, Jill Santopietro, Jan Newberry, Francis Lam, Jennifer Steinhauer and Gabrielle Hamilton, who told me to treat my readers with the same generosity as I would guests in my restaurant. I tried.

COI

Coi is the result of many years of hard work by many people. Many of you are in the text of the book. Some I name here. I know that I missed many of you. Please accept my apologies, and also my gratitude.

My partner Ron Boyd is not in this book, but the book would not have been possible without him. We worked together at Elisabeth Daniel in the kitchen, and he came back to help me run our restaurant group. I am endlessly inspired by his palate and creativity, his work ethic and drive for excellence, his kindness.

Many people lent their talents to help build Coi. Scott Kester for the design. Catherine Wagner for her amazing artwork. Debbie Glass for the graphic design and so many other ways she made the restaurant better. Mark Stech-Novak for helping to make our tiny kitchen not only functional, but a pleasure to work in. Dick Jacobson for his intelligence, hard work and great eye as construction manager. Andrew Garay, whose company has built every restaurant I've opened since 1999, for his integrity and friendship.

Thank you to my cooks—this book is for you. To my chefs and sous chefs—Jake Godby, John Marquez, Brett Cooper, Nico Borzee, Katy Jane Millard, Gavin Schmidt, Carlos Salgado, Deanie Hickox, Bill Corbett, Evan Rich, Brandon Rice and Chris Johnson—thanks for your hard work and talents.

Thank you to our wonderful purveyors, it's a joy to work with you.

To Andrew Miller, thank you for thoughtfulness, even temper and sensitive palate. You're a great cook, and have made the kitchen better than I could have ever imagined.

To Matt Tinder: I think I pretty much said it all in the text, but I'll say it again. Thank you. You and Andrew are a great team.

Thank you to my friends and colleagues in the Bay Area and around the world who have supported the restaurant (in no particular order): Mandy Aftel, Laurence and Allyson Jossel, Mourad Lahlou and Farnoush Deylamian, David Kinch and Pim Techamuanvivit, Rajat Parr, Soyoung Scanlan, Andrea Petrini, Thomas Keller, Shelley and Greg Lindgren, Susan Xu, Erin Zhu and Blixa Bargeld, Maryellen and Frank Herringer, Charlie Hallowell, Sean Brock, Daniel Humm, Carlo Mirarchi, Johnny Iuzzini, Wylie Dufresne, Omer Horvitz, Laura Chenel, Michael Bauer, Patricia Unterman, Sean Thackrey, Paula Wolfert and Bill Bayer, Stuart Brioza and Nicole Krasinski, Staffan Terje, Josh Sens, Sid Nappi and Sherry Flammer, Paul and Robin Kirby, John Clark and Gayle Pirie, Paolo Lucchesi, Anya von Bremzen, James and Caitlin Freeman, Rose Levy Beranbaum, Corey Lee, Joel Peterson and family, Bob Sessions and family, Christie Dufault and Jordan MacKay, Joel Muchmore, Dana Cowin, Kate Krader, George Mendes, Christopher Kostow, Enrique Olvera, Joe and Emily Wetzel, Loretta Gargan.

To my far-flung band of brothers: René, Dave, Massimo, Claude, Inaki, Alex, Magnus, Albert, Pascal, Davide, Ben—I love you guys!

Thanks to all of my incredibly supportive partners at Coi, especially John and Chris and Ken and Barbara. The restaurant also would not have opened without the support of my family. Julia, Norman, Myrna, Michele and especially my father, John Patterson, thank you.

Finally, to my wife, Alexandra: You have supported me in so many ways. There would be no restaurant, no book, and not much of a life without you. I have no words to adequately express how much I love you and our babies.

For our families

NOTES ON THE RECIPES

Some of the recipes require advanced techniques, specialist equipment and professional experience to achieve good results.

Exercise a high level of caution when following recipes involving any potentially hazardous activity, including the use of high temperatures, tobacco, hot charcoal, open flames, and when deep-frying. In particular, when deep-frying, add food carefully to avoid splashing, wear long sleeves and never leave the pan unattended.

Cooking times are for guidance only. If using a convection oven, follow the manufacturer's instructions concerning the oven temperatures.

Some recipes include lightly cooked eggs, meat and fish, and fermented products. These should be avoided by the elderly, infants, pregnant women, convalescents and anyone with an impaired immune system.

Exercise caution when making fermented products, ensuring all equipment is spotlessly clean, and seek expert advice if in any doubt.

All herbs, shoots, flowers, berries, seeds and vegetables should be picked fresh from a clean source. Exercise caution when foraging for ingredients. Any foraged ingredients should only be eaten if an expert has deemed them safe to eat.

When no quantity is specified, for example of oils, salts and herbs used for finishing dishes, quantities are discretionary and flexible.

Phaidon Press Limited
Regent's Wharf
All Saints Street
London N1 9PA

Phaidon Press Inc.
180 Varick Street
New York, NY 10014

First published 2013

ISBN: 978 0 7148 6590 4

A CIP catalogue record for this book is available from the British Library.

Commissioning Editor: Emilia Terragni
Project Editor: Sophie Hodgkin
Production Controller: Laurence Poos

Photographs by Maren Caruso

Printed in China